MORMON ANSWER TO SKEPTICISM,
Why Joseph Smith Wrote the Book of Mormon

JOSEPH SMITH
Courtesy of Utah State Historical Society

MORMON ANSWER TO SKEPTICISM,

Why Joseph Smith Wrote the Book of Mormon

By
Robert N. Hullinger

Robert N. Hullinger

CLAYTON PUBLISHING HOUSE, INC.
PO Box 9258
St. Louis, Missouri 63117

MORMON ANSWER TO SKEPTICISM, Why Joseph Smith Wrote the Book of Mormon

Robert N. Hullinger

Copyright © 1980 Clayton Publishing House, Inc.
Library of Congress Catalog Card No.: 79-54055
International Standard Book No. 0-915644-18-5

ACKNOWLEDGEMENTS

Acknowledgement is gratefully made to the following for permission to quote from the sources indicated or to reproduce the items cited.

BRIGHAM YOUNG UNIVERSITY STUDIES
From "View of the Hebrews: Subsitute for Inspiration?," *BRIGHAM YOUNG UNIVERSITY STUDIES,* V, 2 (Winter, 1962).

THE CHURCH OF JESUS CHRIST OF LATTER-DAY SAINTS, CHURCH ARCHIVES, Salt Lake City, Utah
From Joseph Smith's Letter Book, Joseph Smith's "Manuscript History of the Church," and the Martha Jane Coray 2nd manuscript of Lucy Mack Smith's *Biographical Sketches.*

CINCINNATI HISTORICAL SOCIETY
Photograph of Methodist camp meeting at night in the 1830s and the 1774 Map of the Six Nations.

CONCORDIA PUBLISHING HOUSE
From "Joseph Smith, Defender of the Faith," *CONCORDIA THEOLOGICAL MONTHLY,* XLII, 2 (February, 1971). By Robert N. Hullinger. Portions of the Introduction, chapters 1, 3, 9, 10, and 11 appeared briefly here.
From *Religious Bodies of America,* by F. E. Mayer. Copyright 1961.
From *Church, State, and the American Indians,* by R. Pearce Beaver. Copyright 1966.

CORNELL UNIVERSITY PRESS
From *The Burned-over District: The Social and Intellectual History of Enthusiastic Religion in Western New York, 1800-1850,* by Whitney R. Cross. Copyright, 1961.

DESERET BOOK COMPANY
History of the Church of Jesus Christ of Latter-day Saints, by Joseph Smith, Jr.

HARPER AND ROW, INC.
From *The Lively Experiment: The Shaping of Christianity in America,* by Sidney E. Mead. Copyright 1963.
From *The Story of Religions in America,* by Warren W. Sweet. Copyright 1930.

HARVARD UNIVERSITY PRESS
From *Nature's Nation,* by Perry Miller. Copyright 1967 by The Belknap Press of Harvard University Press.

HERALD PUBLISHING HOUSE
From *Restoration Scriptures: A Study of Their Textual Development,* by Richard P. Howard. Copyright 1969.

ALFRED A. KNOPF, INC.
From *Among the Mormons: Historic Accounts by Contemporary Observers,* by William Mulder and A. Russell Motensen. Copyright 1958.

THE LUTHERAN QUARTERLY
From "The Lost Tribes of Israel and the Book of Mormon," *THE LUTHERAN QUARTERLY,* XXII, 3 (August, 1970). By Robert N. Hullinger. Portions of chapter 6 appeared briefly here.

MICHIGAN STATE UNIVERSITY PRESS

From *Quest for Empire: The Political Kingdom of God and the Council of Fifty in Mormon History*, by Klaus J. Hansen. Copyright 1967.

MORMON HISTORY ASSOCIATION

From "The Prophet Puzzle: Suggestions Leading Toward a More Comparative Interpretation of Joseph Smith," *JOURNAL OF MORMON HISTORY*, I (1974). By Jan Shipps.

REORGANIZED CHURCH OF JESUS CHRIST OF LATTER DAY SAINTS RESEARCH LIBRARY AND ARCHIVES, Independence, Missouri, The Auditorium

Prints of the E MS 2 Nephi excerpt; and the Anthon Transcript.

CHARLES SCRIBNER'S SONS

From *Religion in America: An Historical Account of the Developments of American Religious Life*, by Winthrop E. Hudson. Copyright 1966.

UTAH STATE HISTORICAL SOCIETY

Print of Joseph Smith, Jr.

WESLEY P. WALTERS

For the following photographs: Albert Neely's Bill for Holding Joseph Smith, Jr. on the Misdemeanor Charge of "Glass-Looking"; Manchester Rental Library Record Book; Manchester Accession Numbers 119 and 208.

To Charlotte,
        my inspiration,

and

to Lisa,
   Jennie,
   and Robby,

      our on-going revelations

      . . . well, most of the time.

Abbreviations

An Address	*An Address to All Believers in Christ*, by David Whitmer
BYUS	*Brigham Young University Studies*
CH	*Church History*
Dialogue	*Dialogue: A Journal of Mormon Thought*
DAB	*Dictionary of American Biography*
DC	Doctrine and Covenants
DHC	*History of the Church of Jesus Christ of Latter-day Saints*
D MS	Dictated manuscript of the Book of Mormon (April-June, 1829)
DN	*Deseret News*
E MS	Emended manuscript of the Book of Mormon, prepared for the printer (July-December, 1829)
EMS	*Evening and Morning Star*
IA	*The Improvement Era*
MA	*Latter Day Saints' Messenger and Advocate*
MM	*Methodist Magazine*
MS	*Millenial Star*
PF	*Palmyra Freeman*
PH	*Palmyra Herald*
PR	*Palmyra Register*
PT	*Painesville Telegraph*
SH	*Saints' Herald*
TS	*Times and Seasons*
WF	*Western Farmer*
WS	*Wayne Sentinel*
WTJ	*Westminster Theological Journal*

BOOK OF MORMON

1 Ne	1 Nephi
2 Ne	2 Nephi
Jac	Jacob
Enos	Enos
Jar	Jarom
Om	Omni
W. Morm	The Words of Mormon
Mos	Mosiah
Al	Alma
Hel	Helaman
3 Ne	3 Nephi
4 Ne	4 Nephi
Morm	Mormon
Eth	Ether
Moro	Moroni

CONTENTS

LIST OF TABLES

ILLUSTRATIONS

FOREWORD

Any attempt to describe Joseph Smith as a defender of God will strike many as strange, especially when they remember some of his activities. They may think it strange, indeed, that Smith could be motivated by the noble desire to defend revealed religion.

From both a biblical and psychological viewpoint, however, no one is perfectly motivated, and everyone is more or less inconsistent. It is quite conceivable, therefore, that Joseph Smith could engage in questionable activities and try to defend revealed religion during the same time period.

Mr. Hullinger provides a strong and considered case for Smith as a defender of revealed religion against the attacks of the infidel. His study of Thomas Paine's deistic propositions and Smith's answer to them in the Book of Mormon is very important. Deistic objections to the Bible do provide the rationale for much of the specific material in the Book of Mormon, and Smith's answers to them explain why the work was so readily accepted by a number of church people of that period.

Smith does seem to have had some idea of removing criticism from biblical materials when he turned to revising the Bible soon after completing the Book of Mormon. He rendered "lead us not into temptation" from the Lord's Prayer as "suffer us not to be led into temptation." That relieved God from appearing responsible for our falling into sin. Again, he changed the statement about Rebekah's virginity from "neither had any man known her" to "neither had any man known the like unto her." That made more sense to a reader who was unaware that the Hebrew term "know" often refers to sexual relations.

Deistic objections to language as an unfit medium for revelation (there is no universal language; copyist and translator often err) explain why Smith, elsewhere and in his book, stressed the purely mechanical means of translating by "interpreters" — thus assuring absolute correctness—while in his revelations he claimed to have translated by his inner feelings rather than by anything mechanical.

Deists found the Bible unreliable because the authors of some biblical books are unknown. That explains why Smith has every author in the Book of Mormon named and precisely dated—a phenomenon that appears nowhere else in all the records of ancient history.

Smith's revisions and corrections of what he perceived to be problems in the biblical text and materials created more problems than they solved, however well-intentioned he may have been. Nevertheless, even if one remains unsympathetic to him, one must appreciate what Smith was trying to do.

Even if one does not accept Mr. Hullinger's main argument, he will still find this work of great value. Hullinger extracted the major religious thought patterns from the Book of Mormon, steeped himself in the ideas and literature of Smith's time, correlated his findings into a readable account, and demonstrated how Joseph Smith took the leading ideas of his day and incorporated them into his gold-plated story of the early inhabitants of this continent. The real strength of this work lies in the great amount of material it makes available to the reader, much of it for the first time, in bringing to our generation the flavor and overtones of those days in western New York.

The result provides still further evidence that the Book of Mormon is a wholely modern production, not a translation of some ancient, long-buried record. Mr. Hullinger has done the field of early Mormon studies a great service in making his research available to us.

Wesley P. Walters
Marissa, Illinois

PREFACE

As a child in Grand Island, Nebraska, I treasured the legend told me by a worldly-wise fifth grader, that every time I crossed Koenig and Locust streets I was traveling the Mormon Trail. Since that was my way to school, I walked daily with those pioneers, struggling westward in the face of Indian harassment. It has been a long time since I walked my legendary trail alongside those pioneers, but their real story I still find fascinating, even though my path to Zion leads in a different direction.

The reader should note that Thomas Paine's *Age of Reason* is used in this study to indicate what kind of climate popular deism fostered in the world of Joseph Smith. I do not necessarily imply that the Mormon prophet had read Paine's book, although I believe that he did.

Even if one holds that Smith was the worst scoundrel of his day, one still must account for the content of the Book of Mormon. If Smith was trying to sway the world for his own purposes, one still must deal with the way he chose to do it, and that means looking at the appeal of the Book of Mormon. I prefer to put the best construction on Smith, let his expressed motives speak for themselves, and then draw conclusions from the evidence. That approach does not rule out a negative opinion of Joseph Smith, but it allows for a more charitable estimate of his intentions.

Many have helped bring this book to life in the fifteen years since I began work on it. Dr. George B. Arbaugh provide the initial impetus by encouraging me in my brash suggestion that I help him update his 1932 study of Mormonism. Neither of us could have foreseen that my conclusions would call into question his central thesis about the Book of Mormon. The sainted Pastor Walter E. Kraemer of Oakland, California lent moral support during my research days in Berkeley. Dr. Arthur Carl Piepkorn of Concordia Seminary, St. Louis, and Dr. Jan Shipps of Indiana-Purdue University at Indianapolis shared some of their research with me. Mr. H. Michael Marquardt of Sandy, Utah provided some of his research for my use as well as critiqued portions of the manuscript. Dr. Richard L. Bushman, noted Mormon historian, critiqued the manuscript with the exception of chapter 8. Several other Saints of both the LDS and RLDS bodies have read portions of the manuscript. They do not, of course, necessarily accept my conclusions. A word of appreciation is due the archivists of the Church of Jesus Christ of Latter-day Saints in Salt Lake City and those of the Reorganized Church of Jesus Christ of Latter Day Saints in Independence, Missouri for their helpfulness during my research. Misses Gertrude and Clara Moellering of Cincinnati, members of Prince of Peace Lutheran Church which I serve, provided a working translation of Rev. Diedrich Willers's 1830 letter.

A special word of gratitude is due Pastor Wesley P. Walters, who has shared a great deal of source material from his files, the conclusions of his pioneering work in Mormon origins, and much time and effort in reading critically and helpfully several drafts of this work. His standard of scholarship and painstaking detail set a goal toward which I strained in completing this study.

Further thanks are due Charles Wooton, Ed Gallenstein, Jim Greenhalgh and Bob Harper of the *Cincinnati Enquirer* composing and computer rooms for their help in typesetting the manuscript. To Dr. Fred Danker and his wife, Lois, who is president of Clayton Publishing House, I owe not only thanks for their publishing this book, but also for friendship, encouragement, and bonds that will endure.

Finally, the reader will notice that the variations of nineteenth century English usage are reproduced exactly as they occur in the sources. No "sic" calls attention to mistakes. No italics or capitalizations are there except those that occur in the sources. Only an occasional editorial bracket is used to clarify.

Cincinnati, Ohio
Pentecost, 1979

Introduction

The man who established a religion in the age of free debate, who was and is to-day accepted by hundreds of thousands as a direct emissary from the Most High—such a rare human being is not to be disposed of by pelting his memory with unsavory epithets. Fanatic, impostor, charlatan, he may have been; but these hard names furnish no solution to the problems he presents to us. . . the wonderful influence which this founder of a religion exerted and still exerts throws him into relief before us, not as a rogue to be criminated, but as a phenomenon to be explained . . ."

Josiah Quincy[1]

When the Book of Mormon[2] appeared in March, 1830 and a new church organized the following month, America saw the beginning of still one more effort to defend Jesus Christ against all adversaries. To lead the way out of perplexity generated by religious strife, denominational polemics, and rationalistic views of Jesus Christ, Joseph Smith, Jr. forged his own theology of revelation.

Those whom he came to lead responded by attacking his character and person. To discredit him, they recited his money-digging activities and court trials. They dismissed his new scripture because of its style and language, its use of concerns then current, and because they saw it as a religious imposition.

As early as 1831 the personal influence of Sidney Rigdon was cited to explain the origin of the new scripture.[3] Rigdon was supposed to have purloined Solomon Spaulding's manuscript that dealt with the origin of the American Indians. Eber D. Howe, newspaper publisher in Painesville, Ohio, publicized the theory in 1834 in a book that still has influence.[4] A hundred years later the Spaulding Manuscript Theory found its best presentation by George B. Arbaugh.[5]

At the turn of the century psychology was used as a tool to explain Smith. Once again he was considered capable of producing the Book of Mormon. He was an epileptic, a dissociated personality, and paranoid; but, nevertheless, the author. This explanation is still advanced.[6]

Fawn Brodie buried the dying Spaulding Manuscript Theory[7] in her monumental biography (1945) of Joseph Smith. Her greatest service was to document the thought currents of the 1820's as they related to the personal life of the Mormon prophet. This greatly strengthened the case for an environmentally based understanding of Smith. Her portrait of Smith has, however, some blurred edges.

Marvin Hill called Brodie to task for explaining Smith by his charisma, dismissing his religious motivations, and neglecting the religious force of his message.[8] Jan Shipps pointed out the need to go beyond seeing Smith as either a saint or fraud to reveal a "larger than life *whole* man." To that end she challenged scholars to determine to what extent the scriptures Smith authored can be used as "primary source material" in better understanding this historic figure.[9] My study is a partial acceptance of her challenge. It probes the reasons Smith had for bringing forth the Book of Mormon and uses the Mormon scriptures as "primary source material" to do it.

Mario De Pillis emphasized the religious impulses that guided Smith: like that of others, his was a quest for religious authority.[10] De Pillis looked to Smith's explanation of his First Vision as the springboard for his quest.[11] Smith found that no church was right and determined not to join any until the full gospel came clear to him. De Pillis was the first non-Mormon to take Smith as a serious respondent to the issues of early 19th century society.[12]

While De Pillis is fully aware of the importance of the Book of Mormon as a base for Smith's authority, he looked primarily to developments that followed completion of the manuscript of the Book of Mormon. To overcome skepticism about his book,[13] Smith created a dual priesthood, settled doctrinal questions, and mediated God's revelations to reestablish divine control. My study complements De Pillis's findings by concentrating on the Mormon scriptures as primary source material to determine Smith's basic objective in writing the Book of Mormon.

There has been a growing awareness that deism was as much a factor in the cultural milieu of Joseph Smith as the revivalism and sectarian strife of New York's "burned-over district." I. W. Riley first saw deism as an influence in the story of Korihor in the book of Alma, but he did not see how the deistic factor inter-related with Freemasonry and Roman Catholicism.[14] David B. Davis saw Mormonism as a link in the Puritan tradition in opposition to deism, revivalism, Methodism and Unitarianism, but he did not develop this insight.[15] Milton Backman and Ivan Barrett saw deism as an important background influence, but did not see Smith responding to it.[16] Richard Bushman suggested ways in which Smith met skepticism from his own constituency, but he did not delve into the Book of Mormon. He found that the First Vision story was designed to meet rationalistic demands for evidence by following the arguments of William Paley.[17]

Religious authority in the 1820s was based on the assumption that the Bible was a special revelation, as opposed to a natural revelation deducible from the works of nature. Behind this assumption lay the question of the nature of God. Was He personal and in reach of man, or was He an absentee landlord?

The argument of this study is that Joseph Smith tried to defend faith in the personal God of Christian belief in face of current denominational strife and popular skepticism. He staked out the principle of revelation as the ground for battle and regarded himself as the defender of God. He intended the Book of Mormon to be an apologetic for Jesus Christ.[18]

FOOTNOTES

1. *Figures of the Past* (Boston, 1883), cited in William Mulder and A. Russell Mortensen, *Among the*

Mormons: Historic Accounts by Contemporary Observers (New York: A. A. Knopf, c. 1958), p. 132.

2. Joseph Smith, Jr., *The Book of Mormon* (Palmyra, N. Y.: E. B. Grandin, 1830). Herald House Reprint, 1970. Unless otherwise noted, the edition used is *The Book of Mormon* (Salt Lake City: The Church of Jesus Christ of Latter-day Saints, 1952).

3. James Gordon Bennett cited a Henry Rangdon, Ringdon or Rigdon as the person. After a few years of successful journalism, Bennett interviewed people who knew the first Mormons and wrote a two-part article in the *New York Courier and Enquirer.* Leonard J. Arrington published the article in "James Gordon Bennett's 1831 Report on 'The Mormonites,'" BYUS, X, 3 (Spring, 1970), 355-64.

4. *Mormonism Unvailed* (Painesville, Ohio: By the author, 1834).

5. *Revelation in Mormonism: Its Character and Changing Forms* (Chicago: University of Chicago Press), c. 1932).

6. Isaac Woodbridge Riley, *The Founder of Mormonism: A Psychological Study of Joseph Smith, Jr.* (New York: Dodd, Mead & Co., c. 1903); Eduard Meyer, *Ursprung und Geschichte der Mormonen mit Exkursen über die Angange des Islams und des Christentums* (Halle: Max Niemeyer, 1912); Walter F. Prince, "Psychological Tests for the Authorship of the Book of Mormon," *American Journal of Psychology,* XXVIII (July, 1917), 373-89; contra, Theodore Schroeder, "Authorship of the Book of Mormon,) *ibid.,* XXX (January, 1919), 66-72; Bernard DeVoto, "The Centennial of Mormonism," *American Mercury,* XIX (January, 1930), 1-13; Arbaugh, Appendix II, pp. 227-29, rejects Prince and DeVoto; Fawn M. Brodie, *No Man Knows My History: The Life of Joseph Smith* (New York: A. A. Knopf, c. 1945; 2nd rev., c. 1971): pp. 418-21.

7. *Ibid.,* Appendix B.

8. Marvin S. Hill, "Secular or Sectarian History? A Critique of No Man Knows My History," CH, XL, 1 (March, 1974), 78-96.

9. "The Prophet Puzzle: Suggestions Leading Toward a more Comprehensive Interpretation of Joseph Smith," JMH, I, (1974), 6, 19, 20.

10. "The Quest for Religious Authority and the Rise of Mormonism," *Dialogue,* 1 (March, 1966), 69-88.

11. This has traditionally been dated in 1820. It is found in DHC, I, 3-4; also in *Pearl of Great Price* (Salt Lake City: The Church of Jesus Christ of Latter-day Saints, 1921).

12. Milton V. Backman, Jr., *American Religions and the Rise of Mormonism* (Salt Lake City: Deseret Book Company, c. 1965) does this from a Mormon perspective. Cf. also Ivan Barrett, *Joseph Smith and the Restoration: A History of the Church to 1846* (Provo, Utah: Young House; Brigham Young University Press, c. 1973), pp. 5-13.

13. *Ibid.,* p. 82.

14. Riley, pp. 151-59. Robert C. Webb, *The Real Mormonism: A Candid Analysis of an Interesting but much Misunderstood Subject in History, Life and Thought* (New York: Sturgis & Welton Company, c. 1916), pp. 429-43, objected to Riley's placing excerpts from Paine in parallel with Korihor's remarks. He charged Riley with tearing Paine out of context.

15. David Brion Davis, "The New England Origins of Mormonism," *The New England Quarterly,* XXXVII (June, 1953), p. 158.

16. Backman, *passim;* Barrett, pp. 7-9.

17. That is, Smith was a neutral observer of the vision and became committed to it in spite of persecution and personal loss. Richard L. Bushman, *Joseph Smith and Skepticism* (Brigham Young University Press, c. 1974).

18. The writer presented this argument in brief in "Joseph Smith, Defender of the Faith," *Concordia Theological Monthly,* XLII, 2 (February, 1971), 72-87.

Part I: The Defender

1

Smith's Goals for the Book of Mormon

> The Book of Mormon . . . is to shew unto the remnant of the House of Israel how great things the LORD hath done for their fathers; and that they may know the covenants of the LORD, that they are not cast off forever; and also to the convincing of the Jew and Gentile that JESUS is the CHRIST, the ETERNAL GOD, manifesting Himself unto all nations.
>
> **Book of Mormon, Title Page, 1830 edition[1]**

> He said he verily believed that an important epoch had arrived—that a great flood of light was about to burst upon the world. . . . that a GOLDEN BIBLE had recently been dug from the earth . . . and that this would . . . settle all religious controversies and speedily bring on the glorious millennium.
>
> **John A. Clark[2]**

There has been a long history of probing Smith's motives for writing the Book of Mormon. Recently, Mario De Pillis argued that Smith wanted to establish a sect to end sectarian fighting.[3] Jan Shipps concluded that Smith found, or wanted to find, Indian artifacts: "that the discovery or the desire for the discovery inspired the writing of the Book of Mormon."[4] Neither sufficiently considers, however, the many statements Smith made about the purpose of the Book of Mormon. One must go back to Joseph Smith to discover why he wrote the Book of Mormon. The *History*[5] that he began dictating in 1838 is only moderately helpful, for by that time he had greatly modified his theology. One must go back to the early period before and during the production of the Book of Mormon and the organization of the new church. Smith states his overall purpose for the new scripture on its title page and elaborates his goals through the characters in his book. He would offer proof for the Christian claims for the Bible, for Christ, and for God. He would inspire faith, encourage steadfastness in it, corroborate biblical facts, prophecies and doctrine.[6] Mormons and non-Mormons alike have not taken seriously the expressed aims of the Book of Mormon. Not only does it defend God, but Smith wrote it *intending* to defend Him. His sources, the concerns he dealt with, and the solutions he proposed all relate to his objective: to make the remaining descendants of the lost tribes of Israel (the American Indians) sensible of their relationship with God, and to convince the Jews and Gentiles that "Jesus is the CHRIST, the ETERNAL GOD, manifesting himself to all nations.

PROVIDE PROOF

The Book of Mormon is meant to validate God's eternal existence and His unchanging manner of relating to mankind (DC 20:12, 17).[7] It certifies that He created man, gave him commandments, and gave His Son to save the race when man transgressed (DC 20:18-20). It proves that God is merciful (1 Ne 1:20) and that He calls and inspires men in all generations to do His will and work (DC 20:11).

The Book of Mormon is meant to prove New Testament claims about Jesus. He was sinless, suffered crucifixion, died, rose on the third day, ascended into heaven, presently rules with God, and has secured salvation for the human race. Christ has come (2 Ne 2:6).

The American scripture is also a witness of and proof for the truth of the biblical message (DC 20:11). That message was the same in the pre-Christian era as it is now. People knew of his future mission long before Christ came as Redeemer. The prophet Nephi wrote of his foreknowledge of Christ and, to convince his posterity that this was true (2 Ne 11:2-6), added the testimony of his brother, Jacob, and that of biblical Isaiah to his own.

Similarly, the Book of Mormon itself needed three witnesses to tell the world that its existence was real and its contents true (2 Ne 27:12). After an angel deliberately delivered golden plates to Joseph Smith, he translated the characters inscribed upon them and thus brought forth the Book of Mormon. Three witnesses would see the plates and then would know that their translated contents were true. Their testimony, plus that of the Book of Mormon, would stand as proof of God's power and the truth of God's word (Eth 5:2-4). Joseph Smith would be ordained to bring to an unbelieving generation the message of the Book of Mormon, and to bring forth the Church of Christ. The testimony of the three witnesses would confirm the message of Smith and the new scripture (DC 5:6-15).

CHRISTIANIZE THE INDIANS

Smith thought that the Book of Mormon would profit the American Indians[8] by contributing to their spiritual welfare[9] and by bringing them the word of God (DC 3:16). He was certain that they would believe the Book of Mormon (Morm 7:9) after they were first convinced of the truth of the Bible (1 Ne 13:39). The former would convince them of the latter.

When the Indians accepted the new scriptures they would come to a knowledge of God (Al 37:8-9), which is knowledge of the redemption worked out by Christ (W. Mormon 8). It would inform them of God's promises (DC 3:20), show them that they were to be in covenant with Him (Title Page) and induce them to accept their part in that covenant (Morm 7:9). Then they would become a *delightsome people* (W. Mormon 8).

First the Indians needed to know who their ancestors were and how God had dealt with them (Morm 7:9). The Book of Mormon would teach them their past and convince them of the error of their fathers' traditions (Al 37:8-9) and their great iniquity (Mos 28:1-2). They needed to be shown their Israelite ancestry (DC 3:20) to be convinced that they, too, were Israelites (Morm 7:1-2).

Since Smith believed that the Indians would remain strangers to God unless they had some reason to believe in Him (Al 26:9), he intended the Book of Mormon's testimony to lead them to fruits of repentance (Al 34:30). That meant persuading them to remember their Lord, the Redeemer (1 Ne 19:18, 23), to come to Christ (Om 26), and to believe in Jesus and be saved.[10]

If the Indians could know of the ancient battles and carnage by which their Nephite-Lamanite ancestors eliminated each other, they might more fully believe the gospel that the Mormon missionaries would bring them (Morm 5:9, 14).[11] The Book of Mormon would lead the Indians to end their hatred of others, to befriend each other and stop their contentious ways, thereby bringing peace (Al 26:9). That peace would lead them to rejoice in covenant with God (Mos 28:1-2). Their faith in Christ and restored covenant with God would create that peace, and thus fulfill God's promises to Israel (DC 3:19).

CONVERT THE GENTILES

Joseph Smith wanted the Gentiles to accept Jesus as Savior (Morm 5:9, 11, 14). He meant to convince them that "Jesus is Christ, the Eternal God," who shows Himself to all who believe in Him (2 Ne 26:12-13). Like the Jews, the Gentiles must be convinced that the Bible is true (1 Ne 13:39). If they are to know of God's decree, come to repentance and be kept from following the dismal example of previous generations, then they must know how the unbelieving rebellion of the Indians' forefather led to their destruction (Eth 2:11).

Once convinced, the Gentiles would perform a two-fold mission for Christ. They would use the Nephite reports of Jesus' messages given during his post-resurrection appearances in America to convince the Jews that he is their Redeemer.[12] At the same time they would also convert the Indians.

CONVERT THE JEWS

The Book of Mormon was meant to bring Jews to accept Jesus as their Messiah,[13] the only Messiah they should look for. Acceptance of Christ, however, meant prior acceptance of the New Testament as true (1 Ne 13:39). The Book of Mormon is a witness that the one they killed was very Christ and truly God (Morm 3:21). It aims to persuade them, so that God might restore them to their own land (Morm 5:14).[15] Unbelief kept the Jews in dispersion, but they would be restored a second time to their land when they accepted Christ as their Messiah (2 Ne 15:15-18). The Book of Mormon would come into public view about the time that the Lord began that restoration, and it would hasten the day.

WIN THE WORLD

Joseph Smith had a broad vision. By means of his American scripture he hoped to induce mankind to believe in Jesus and perservere in that faith,[16] even in the face of suffering (Jac 1:8). Smith was aware that people might not accept his book (2 Ne 33:10), but he wanted to let all know that the ancestors of the American Indians, and before them the Hebrew prophets, had known of Christ's coming and had had a hope of his glory (Hel 14:12-13). He wanted it known that people in all eras, before and after Christ, are saved only by faith.

Winning the world to the gospel (Morm 3:21-22) and strengthening the faith of those who believe it (DC 10:52) was one of the goals for the Book of Mormon. Smith was certain that if all people would accept Christ's words they would also accept the Book of Mormon, for he meant it to contain the message of Christ (2 Ne 33:10).

He also intended to warn against ungodliness and to show the folly of those who neglect their spiritual status. If people could be persuaded not to rebel against God, but to believe in Christ (Jac 1:8); if they could be warned of the awful state into which transgressors are led (Mos 2:40); if they could know the judgments of God, then they might be persuaded.[17]

In the face of impending judgment (Morm 3:21-22), the Book of Mormon was intended to save people by leading them to repentance and getting them ready to meet God. Smith wanted them to look to the Messiah, obey him, be faithful to him, and choose eternal life instead of eternal death (2 Ne 2:28-30). Through faith in Christ, Smith hoped to see them reconciled to the God of Abraham, Isaac and Jacob.[18] His book is saturated with talk of Christ so that people might know "to what source they might look for a remission of their sins" (2 Ne 35:26). To forestall misunderstanding, he explained clearly how to believe in Christ (2 Ne 25:28-30).

The Book of Mormon will settle all doctrinal differences among those who accept the Christ it presents (DC 10:63). Its purpose is to make clear what is true doctrine and to dissolve doctrinal disputes by setting forth all parts of the gospel of Christ (DC 10:46-63).

Existing churches would continue their strife because they misunderstood and misinterpreted the Bible (DC 10:46-63), but the forthcoming publication of the Book of Mormon would reestablish the true Church of Christ (DC 5:14). Then people would have Christ's true word and doctrine at hand in the Book of Mormon and in the restored true Church (DC 11:16; 18:13).

RING IN THE MILLENNIUM

The view of the Book of Mormon is that when it is accepted, the thousand year reign of Christ will soon come. This is one of the backdrops against which the whole book was placed. In the millennial view all depended upon the restoration of the ten tribes of Israel and the dispersed tribe of Judah to their homeland.

The Book of Mormon describes in detail the condition to prevail at the time of the restoration. No one could mistake the signs which indicated fulfillment (2 Ne 25:15-20). When the Indians, Jews, and Gentiles are persuaded that Jesus is the Christ, the Eternal God, then the Lord will bring back from their hiding places Israel's lost tribes (Morm 5:12).

American Indians were a segment broken off from the ten tribes. Through the Book of Mormon's message the Indians would rejoin their kinsmen and be restored to their fathers. The Lord's promise to the patriarch, Joseph in Egypt, therefore, will be fulfilled: his posterity will not perish from the earth (2 Ne 25:21).

TO BE A PROPHET

An ambitious program required the right kind of man to carry it out, and all signs pointed to Joseph Smith, Jr. He was himself the "seer" promised to the biblical Joseph; the seer whose name, like that of his father, was to be Joseph. This was in memory of the biblical patriarch and in fulfillment of a promise made to him (2 Ne 3:6-7, 15). The seer would be like Moses in the eyes of God, blessed by Him to impart to the Indians the knowledge of God's covenants. He would have the power to convince the Indians of the message he would bring. He would receive the strength needed to restore the Indians by means of the Book of Mormon.

While Smith was translating the Book of Mormon he saw himself declared as the one ordained to bring God's word to his generation (DC 5:6, 10). That word would be heard only through Smith (DC 5:10). He was announced as Christ's servant (DC 6:18): "a seer, a translator, a prophet, an apostle" (DC 21:1). His position was spelled out by the Nephite prophet, Moroni:

> everything which inviteth to do good, and to persuade to believe in Christ, is sent forth by the power and gift of Christ. . . . Nothing that is good denieth the Christ, but acknowledgeth that he is. (Moro 7:16; 10:6)

Anything that "persuadeth men to do evil, and believe not in Christ, and deny him, and serve not God . . . is of the devil" (Moro 7:17). "Wherefore, a man being a servant of the devil cannot follow Christ; and if he follow Christ he cannot be a servant of the devil" (Moro 7:11). By his expressed goals and stated values, then, Smith saw himself qualified as a servant of Christ.

WHAT DOES IT PROFIT?

Many judged Joseph Smith the devil's servant because they thought he produced his scripture for profit. The memory of the Smiths' past activities as money-diggers,[19] the conduct and speculations of Martin Harris, and early Mormons speaking of their hope for a profit from sales encouraged that belief.

Smith admitted that he had thought of using the plates for personal gain. He was "tempted of the advisary and sought the Plates to obtain riches and kept not the Commandment that I would have an eye singled to the glory of God," he said in 1832.[20] Having a history of the pre-Columbian American might "be interesting to every man," and the possibility seemed to inspire further thoughts of

> gain . . . and income from such a valuable history. Surely, thought he, every man will seize with eagerness, this knowledge, and this incalculable income will be mine.[21]

The thought that he would get the plates only by the mercy of God momentarily offset the temptation, but by the time he reached the location of the plates he fully intended to use them for selfish purposes.

An angel rebuffed Smith's efforts to get the plates and told him:

> they are not deposited here for the sake of accumulating gain and wealth for the glory of this world; they were sealed by the prayer of faith, and because of the knowledge which they contain they are of no worth among the children of men, only for their knowledge.[22]

Smith's own explanation, then, is that originally he did intend to make his fortune with the plates, but that he had been purged of this motive by the time he got them four years later in 1827. The angel "truly saith that no one shall have them to get gain" (Morm 8:14). Smith never fully conquered the impulse to use his book for personal advantage, but his intention to defend God is equally, or perhaps even more, a factor at this early period.

SUMMARY

Smith's stated purposes in the Book of Mormon and early revelations show him intent upon the defense of God's name, honor and existence. Smith would reclaim for Him the Jews, Gentiles, and Indians and set the stage for the on-coming millennium. The story and theology found in the Book of Mormon reveal how he mounted his defense. The circumstances that led Smith to defend God are found in his time and place in American history.

FOOTNOTES

1. Nearly every statement in this chapter, with the exception of some conclusions or transitions and the section "What Does It Profit?," is recorded in the Book of Mormon and Smith's early revelations through April, 1830. The references cited have words, phrases and clauses expressing purpose or result. A Mormon account of the goals for the Book of Mormon is Brigham Henry Roberts's *New Witnesses for God* (3 vols.; Salt Lake City: Deseret Book Company, c. 1926), II, 61-68.

2. *Gleanings By the Way* (Philadelphia: W. J. & J. K. Simon, 1842), pp. 223-24.

3. De Pillis, "The Quest," p. 88.

4. Shipps, "Prophet Puzzle," p. 11.

5. Marvin Hill, "Secular or Sectarian History," p. 50, sees Smith writing diaries used in compiling the *History* only for 1832 and 1839. He claims that the journal of Dec. 21, 1842 to June 27, 1844 was written by George A. Smith and Willard Richards as Smith's own dictated words, although they were not. In 1973, however, the Historical Department of the LDS Church in Salt Lake City published a Register of the Joseph Smith Collection in the Church Archives. On p. 7 the following diaries are listed as Smith's: 1832-34, 1835-36, 1838, 1839, 1842-44.

6. The four main writers of the Book of Mormon are Nephi, Alma, Mormon and Moroni.

7. *Doctrine and Covenants* (Salt Lake City: The Church of Jesus Christ of Latter-day Saints, c. 1921) is a modern edition of the revelations of Joseph Smith. First published in Kirtland, Ohio in 1835, this was a revision and enlargement of the *Book of Commandments* (Zion [Independence, Mo.]: W. W. Phelps & Co., 1833). Unless otherwise noted, the citations will be from the 1921 edition.

8. The term "Indian" does not occur in the Book of Mormon, but it is synonymous with "Lamanite." Lamanites were descended from Laman, the older brother of Nephi. Laman scorned his father's reliance upon the gifts of the Spirit and was by-passed in favor of Nephi when their father, Lehi, consecrated his successor to the priesthood. The resulting enmity between the Lamanites and Nephites led to the Nephites' total destruction. The surviving Lamanites were cursed with a dark skin because of their unbelief and became the ancestors of the American Indians.

9. Jar 2; Enos 14-15; Morm 8:15; Moro 1:4.

10. Enos 14-15; Morm 7:5-7; DC 3:20. Smith felt that current missionary efforts among the Indians were ineffective. He had Enos say of Nephite attempts to evangelize the Lamanites: "at the present our strugglings were vain in restoring them to the true faith," vss. 14-15. W. W. Phelps, editor of the first Mormon newspaper, explained that neither Jews nor Indians can be converted "by ministers, though the Gentiles are," but they would be willing when the Messiah returned: EMS, I, 3 (August, 1832), p. 5.

11. 2 Nephi 3 shows that Smith began the Book of Mormon the second time, in 1829, intent upon forming a church. Smith is predicted as the one promised to biblical Joseph to bring back the patriarch's descendants to the Lord, as a prophet, a Moses. Like Moses, he would form a nation (2 Ne 3:7-11). The two books of Nephi replace the lost 116 page manuscript that Smith dictated to Martin Harris in the spring of 1828. In the beginning of the book, then, evidence indicates that Smith meant to found a church. Taken in connection with his revelations given during the translation period of March-June, 1829, that is even more certain.

12. Morm 5:9, 14-15; DC 14:10.

13. 2 Ne 26:12; Morm 3:21; 5:12; DC 19:27.

14. 2 Ne 25:15-18; DC 19:27.

15. As today, pre-millennial systems at Smith's time depended upon the conversion of the Jews to take place before the millennial events could proceed.

16. 2 Ne 33:4; Hel 14:12-13.

17. 2 Ne 25:3; Hel 14:12-13.

18. I Ne 6:4; 2 Ne 35:23.

19. David Marks, a Free-will Baptist evangelist, stayed at the home of Peter Whitmer on March 29, 1830 in Fayette, N. Y., just a week before the legal organization of the church. Joseph Smith had been staying at the Whitmer home finishing the manuscript of the Book of Mormon since June, 1829 and stayed on for a total of ten months, but Marks saw only the Eight Witnesses: the prophet's father, brothers Hyrum and Samuel, Peter Whitmer and his sons Jacob, Peter, Jr., and John. David Whitmer, one of the Three Witnesses, was also there. They told Marks about seeing the plates and spoke of the just published Book of Mormon.

> Five thousand copies were published—and they said the angel told Smith to sell the book at a price which was one dollar and eight cents per copy more than the cost, that they *might have the temporal profit*, as well as the spiritual.

The Life of David Marks to the 26th Year of His Age   (Limerick, Me.: Printed at the Office of the Morning Star, 1831), p. 341.

20. Smith dictated this in 1832 as a beginning of his history. It first came to public view in Paul Cheesman, "An Analysis of the Accounts Relating to Joseph Smith's Early Vision," (unpublished Masters thesis, Brigham Young University, 1965), Appendix D. Dean C. Jesse published an authoritative account of it in "The Early Accounts of Joseph Smith's First Vision," BYUS, IX, 3 (Spring, 1969), 275-94.

21. Oliver Cowdery, Letters to W. W. Phelps, VII, MA I, 10 (July, 1835), p. 157. This series of letters presented a brief history of the church and was written with Smith's cooperation.

22. *Ibid.*, Letter VIII, II, 1 (October, 1835), p. 198.

2

Joseph Smith:
Translator or Author?

The Mormon Bible was communicated to him direct from heaven. If there was such a thing on earth as the author of it, then he (Smith) was the author; but the idea that he wished to impress was that he had penned it as dictated by God.   **Matthew L. Davis**[1]

" . . it was not intended to tell the world all the particulars of the coming forth of the Book of Mormon."

Joseph Smith[2]

On a wintry February 5 in 1840, political correspondent Matthew L. Davis crossed Washington, D. C. to hear Joseph Smith expound his faith and speak on the Book of Mormon. The report that he wrote to his wife placed into relief the assumptions most modern investigators of Mormon origins bring to their task.

Mormon investigators suppose that God was involved somehow in the production of the book. They hold that the facts of the story yield the same results that led them to their faith, even if historical understanding progresses so that some aspects of Mormon origins must be explained differently or laid aside. They will accept the thesis that the Book of Mormon defends God, but will object that Smith could not have written it without divine aid.

SMITH'S ROLE
Early stories about the discovery of the golden plate mention the spectacles that

came with them to enable their translation. Smith spoke of them as the device by which he translated the hieroglyphics upon the golden plates. But another version was given by the earliest participants in Mormon origins; namely, that Smith used a "peep-stone" or "seerstone" to translate at least a greater part of the Book of Mormon. This was the same stone that Smith used from 1824-26 to locate buried treasure for those who hired him for that service.[3]

Martin Harris and David Whitmer reported his use of the stone in place of the spectacles.[4] They said that Smith buried his face in a hat to read the translation that was superimposed upon the stone that he had placed in his hat. The Egyptian hieroglyphics appeared on the stone with the English translation beneath each character. Smith read the translation to his scribe, who then verbally repeated it to check for accuracy. If the scribe had incorrectly transcribed Smith's dictation, the sentence image remained on the stone until the correction was made.[5]

SMITH AS READER

The Harris-Whitmer version long has been the understanding of many non-Mormons and Mormons alike. Three of the earliest converts to Mormonism carried that understanding into old age. "Translating" for them really meant "reading." Smith's wife, Emma, supported this version when she said that she saw her husband bury his face in his hat when she served as his scribe.[6]

The same understanding of the translation process was given to Father John A. Clark of Palmyra's Episcopal Church when Martin Harris visited him. Clark wrote that Smith had found the "GOLDEN BIBLE . . . and two transparent stones, through which as a sort of spectacles, he could read the Bible."[7] Smith looked "through his spectacles . . . and would then write down or repeat what he saw, which, when repeated aloud, was written down by Harris."[8] The spectacles enabled Smith "to read the golden letters on the plates in the box. . . . by means of them he could read all the book contained."[9]

Clark, however, mentioned two stones used as spectacles, not just one. The Harris-Whitmer version may have come from the story that Harris told Charles Anthon soon after he spoke with Clark. As Anthon reported Harris, the spectacles were so large that Smith could look only through *one* of the lenses.[10] There was confusion about the spectacles and stone, and Smith was its source, since he included both in the Book of Mormon.[11]

If Smith simply read the *translation*, word-for-word correspondence could be expected if ever he would have to repeat a section. That expectation paralysed Smith when Martin Harris lost 116 manuscript pages in 1828 and suggests why he chose not to retranslate those pages. Smith knew that people operated with a word-for-word inspiration theory of the Bible. In Section 10 of Doctrine and Covenants and the Foreword of the 1830 edition of the Book of Mormon,[12] he explained why he did not retranslate the lost material. God knew that evil men planned to alter the words of the lost manuscript to conflict with the forthcoming translation. God, therefore, gave Smith different plates with the same information.

Smith was thought originally to be a reader, although he did not actually read the ancient characters, but their *translation*. Who*ever* used the spectacles could translate ancient languages, Smith said in his scripture.[13] But Harris's request to take the manuscript home, and then its loss, led Smith to ascribe another power to the spectacles.

At first they assured an errorless translation by *providing* the translation for Smith to read. That was necessary to fulfill Isaiah 29:11-12, where the one "not learned" was reinterpreted by Smith to mean that he could read what the "learned" could not. It went unnoticed that Smith could not read the hieroglyphic characters on the plates, but only the translation.

In response to Harris, the spectacles became the medium also of revelation. They gave the Lord's answer to Harris's request.[14] After the loss of the manuscript, an angel removed them from Smith's possession, but returned them in July, 1828 so that he could receive DC 3 and, possibly, DC 10. Then the angel removed both the spectacles and plates until September 22, 1828, when he returned them to Smith.[15]

SMITH AS TRANSLATOR

When Oliver Cowdery took over scribal duties in April, 1829, he told Smith that he wanted to try his hand at translating the plates. He tried and faltered, thereby forcing another shift in the role of the spectacles. Cowdery had the idea that translating was merely a matter of reading the translation. Smith answered Cowdery's question about his failure with a revelation. Cowdery should have studied his proposed translation "out in his mind" (DC 8:1-3) and his bosom would "burn" within him when he felt "that it is right." But he had been told that Christ would "tell" him in his "mind" and "heart" the knowledge concerning the engravings of old records. As a result, Cowdery forced Smith to explain that the translation really took place within oneself and not in the lenses of the spectacles or in the seer stone.

It was Smith, then, who made the mind and heart of the translator the translation medium and ruled out the spectacles. Diedrich Willers strengthened this view of the translation process. He said that reports current were that Smith wore the spectacles and that "the Holy Ghost would by inspiration give him the translation in the English language."[17] Smith told E. B. Grandin that the translation was completed by inspiration. Thus the translation process lay in the realm of revelation or inspiration.[18]

Further, Smith did not need to have the plates present or the leaves open to translate. Harris told John Clark that when Smith first put on the spectacles the plates were in the box, or chest, but he could read the plates even though the chest was closed.[20] Joseph Smith, Sr. said that after the Lord removed the plates,

> Joseph put on the spectacles, and saw where the Lord had hid them, among the rocks, in the mountains. Though not allowed to get them, he could by the help of the spectacles, read them where they were, as well as if they were before him.[21]

Emma Smith supported John Clark's report with her own. In the time from September, 1828 to March, 1829 that she served as her husband's scribe, she saw him translate, face in hat, while the plates lay covered upon the table, unopened and unconsulted.[22] After completion of the first draft manuscript (referred to as the D MS) in 1829, Smith handed the plates and spectacles over to the angel.[23] From that time the revelations he received came within his "heart" and "mind." In the 3000 changes from the 1830 Palmyra edition to the 1837 Kirtland edition,[24] and in the parenthetical phrase that Smith added to 1 Nephi 20:1 in the 1840 Nauvoo edition,[25] there were no spectacles as medium—only mind and heart. Smith began to write the Book of Moses in June, 1830 and received it by means of a vision, not through the spectacles.[26] All

TABLE I

DEVELOPMENT OF THE
TRANSLATION PROCESS STORY

DATE	SMITH'S ACTIVITY	FUNCTION OF MEDIUM USED	RESULT
1827-- June, 1828	Reading & translating characters	Stone & spectacles mediums of translation	Open plates, stone & spectacles needed
July, 1828 to April, 1829	Reading & translating characters, receiving revelations	Spectacles medium of receiving translation & revelation	Stone & plates not always used, but spectacles used
April, 1829	Explains why Cowdery cannot translate	Mind & heart medium of translation	Spectacles not needed, but used
July, 1829 to June, 1830	Gives plates & spectacles to angel; still receives revelations, corrects manuscript for printer	Mind & heart medium of translation, revision & revelation	Spectacles & plates gone; not needed, not used
June, 1830 Onward	Writes Book of Moses; revises Bible; corrects, revises Book of Mormon	Mind & heart medium of translation, revision & revelation	Spectacles gone, not needed

the work of revising the Bible—his Inspired Translation, the revelations, and the making of an alphabet for Egyptian hieroglyphics—all this he did without the spectacles, solely by revelation. The final result of the shifts that Smith made to adapt to change and challenge left him a translator, not a reader. The ultimate displacement of the plates, stone and spectacles by July, 1829 shows a progression that can already be seen operating in April. Smith did not need the plates, stone, or spectacles to translate. He was doing it by revelation. The progression is charted in Table I.

SMITH AS AUTHOR

Joseph Smith has a reputation to live down if one is to see him as the author of the Book of Mormon. The fact that he was "unlearned" and yet could "read" what the "learned" could not was a sign to Martin Harris that Smith's calling was authentic. The Spaulding Manuscript Theory relied upon an illiterate country bumpkin needing the guiding hand of a trained and educated preacher like Sidney Rigdon to explain the origin of the Mormon scripture.

The record is not unanimous about that reputation. Orasmus Turner knew Smith in Palmyra, New York and opposed the faith he headed, yet said that Smith had made a "passable" Methodist "exhorter" after catching "a spark of religion."[27] He credited the Smith family with the production of the Book of Mormon and specifically dismissed the Spaulding Manuscript Theory with its claim that Smith was too ignorant to write the Book of Mormon.[28] John Greenleaf Whittier and Josiah Quincy gave him high marks as a person with ability and intelligence.[29]

Smith was literate. He lamented his inability with the written word, but knew that he had an impressive speaking style.[30] His mother told of his holding his family spellbound with Indian stories. Modern Mormon writers credit him with knowing the Bible and contemporary affairs, in contrast to an early Mormon apologist like Orson Pratt, who denied him even a rudimentary knowledge of the Bible at the beginning of his 1828 attempt to produce his scripture.

SMITH AS WRITER

It was forgotten that Smith himself did some writing during the translation process. Martin Harris told John Clark that "Smith was to prepare for the conversion of the world . . by transcribing the characters from the plates."[31] Harris told Charles Anthon that Smith "deciphered the characters in the book" and committed some of them to paper, or "communicated their contents in writing."[32]

Smith used twenty chapters of Isaiah, almost verbatim in the Book of Mormon. The "Isaiah problem" is now being explained by crediting Smith with having a Bible at hand while he translated. Where the King James Version agreed with the text on the plates, Smith simply read that. Out of 433 verses in Isaiah, 234 were altered or changed when Smith dictated the Book of Mormon. He left 199 verses identical to the KJV.[33]

SMITH'S DRY SPELLS

Diedrich Willers reported that Smith's sojourn at the Peter Whitmer home during the last weeks of the translation process was the 11th place where he had worked on the translation and the 11th place where others had also seen angels.[34] He needed people who affirmed and supported what he was doing. This gels with the fact that he chose those who had already seen angels or visions as witnesses to see the plates.

The prophet needed emotional balance to do his work, as was shown once when he was at odds with his wife, Emma. When he was unable to continue dictating, he went into the woods for an hour of prayer, returned, and asked her forgiveness. Then he could resume his task.[35] At times he could not translate and "would go out and pray, and when he became sufficiently humble before God, he could then proceed with the translation.[36] Or he would take time out to skip stones on the Susquehannah River to rejuvenate himself.[37] In terms of the creative process, Smith's dry spells were the same that any creative person has known.

THE TIME FACTOR

Many are convinced that no 24 year old man could produce the quantity of material in the brief time it took Smith to produce the Book of Mormon and argue, therefore, for divine help. Smith turned out 8800 words in eight days with Emma serving as scribe, and 266,200 words in 75 days with Oliver Cowdery as scribe. The average jumped from 1100 to 3550 words per day. Twenty-five thousand words are Old Testament quotations that Smith read from the Bible. The expression "it came to pass" accounts for over 6000 words. Allowing for at least ten per cent of the daily production as biblical materials, Smith produced a daily average of nearly 3000 words.

This was not done without preparation. For over a year before Smith began his first try at getting the Book of Mormon down on paper with Martin Harris in 1828, Smith was talking about the themes of the book. He lived with those concerns for two years— possibly more—before he began dictating to Cowdery in 1829.

SUMMARY

The role of Smith as *author* comes to the forefront. He had the ability, the motive, and the opportunity to write a brief in defense of God. He was at the scene where a defense seemed needed. When the Book of Mormon came off the press in March, 1830 and the Church of Christ was formed in April of the same year, Smith had laid a foundation upon which he could rest his defense.

The final judgment to be made about the inspiration Smith had to bring forth the Book of Mormon is a value judgment that each person will make for himself. The Mormon believer will see that inspiration as divine. The non-Mormon, more likely, will see it as flowing from within Smith himself, making him not the reader or translator, but the author.

FOOTNOTES

1. Ben E. Rich, *Scrap Book of Mormon Literature* Chicago: Henry C. Etten & Co., n. d.), Vol. II, p. 404.

2. DHC, I, 220. This was said at a conference at Orange, Ohio on October 26-28, 1831 in response to his brother Hyrum's request for Joseph to elaborate upon the details of the translation process.

3. Cf. Wesley P. Walters, "Joseph Smith's Bainbridge, N. Y. Court Trials," WTJ, XXXVI, 2 (Winter, 1974), 123-55; and Jerald and Sandra Tanner, *Joseph Smith's 1826 Trial* (Salt Lake City: Modern Microfilm Company, 1971), for discussions of this aspect of Smith's career.

4. David Whitmer, *An Address*, p. 12; Martin Harris, MS, February 6, 1882.

5. Brigham Henry Roberts conceded that the two witnesses heard this version from Smith, but that the "mere mechanical process" was incorrect. Rather, it was after Smith had worked out the interpretation in his mind that the translation "was reflected in the sacred instrument, there to remain until correctly written by the scribe." B. H. Roberts, *New Witnesses for God* (3 vols.; Salt Lake City: Deseret Book Company, c. 1926), II, 137-38. In *Restoration Scriptures: A Study of Their Textual Development* (Independence, Mo.: Herald Publishing House, c. 1969), p. 40, Richard P. Howard concludes that the Whitmer-Harris version is untenable. Unlike Roberts, Howard dismissed the idea that Smith saw the translation of the characters "as if through some kind of visually projected medium." Both agree that Smith used the stone and Roberts adds that Smith read the translation. Although both hold to Smith's working out the translation in his mind, Howard points to the text that Smith and Cowdery improved in the 1837 edition of the Book of Mormon and notes that such improvement would have been unnecessary if the Whitmer-Harris version were correct. It was with the Whitmer-Harris rationale in mind that Lamoni Call's *2000 Changes in The Book of Mormon* (Bountiful, Utah: By the Author, 1898) attempted to discredit Mormonism.

6. She stated this in a personal interview with a committee from the Reorganized Church in 1879, shortly before her death. Joseph Smith, III, "Last Testimony of Sister Emma," SH, October 1, 1879, p. 220.

7. *Gleanings*, p. 224.

8. *Ibid.*, p. 230.

9. *Ibid.*, p. 228.

10. Charles Anthon to Eber D. Howe, February 17, 1834. Howe, *Mormonism Unvailed*, pp. 270-72. Often reprinted. Hereafter cited as Anthon's 1834 letter. Charles Anthon to T. W. Coit, April 3, 1841; published in *The Church Record*, I (April 24, 1841), pp. 231-32. It appears in Clark's *Gleanings*, pp. 233-28. Cited hereafter as Anthon 1841 letter.

11. The confusion comes from the many statements of those who were with Smith during the translation period. First, there were two stones, or spectacles, used as the translation device, often called the Urim and Thummim. Second, Emma Smith and David Whitmer both said that after the spectacles were removed from Joseph's possession in June, 1828 they were never returned, but that Smith translated with only one stone. Many witnesses claim that Smith used one stone in the successful attempt of 1829. An excellent discussion of these ramifications with supporting documentation is that of James E. Lancaster, "'By the Gift and Power of God': The Method of Translation of the Book of Mormon," SH, November 15, 1962, pp. 798-806, 817. "Urim and Thummim" was used for the single stone *and* the two-stone spectacles, he concludes.

Smith wrote the spectacles into the Book of Mormon in Mos 8:13, 19; 21:27-28; 28:11-19; Om 20-22; Al 10:2; 37:21-26 Eth 3:23, 28; 4:5. Note the confusion that results from Al 37:23-24, where verse 23 reads: "And the Lord said: I will prepare unto my servant Gazelem, a stone . . . that I may discover unto my people who serve me . . . the works of their brethren"; but verse 24 speaks of the "interpreters" used for the same purpose. In Smith's 1830 Bainbridge trial he described the spectacles as "two transparent stones, resembling glass, set in silver bows." Reported in the *Evangelical Magazine and Advocate*, April 9, 1831, p. 120. In the 1830 edition of the Book of Mormon, p. 328, line 8, "directors" is used instead of "interpreters" (Al 37:31). The 1920 LDS edition was the first to change the word. Cf. Howard, *Restoration Scriptures*, p. 59.

12. That foreword was not printed in subsequent editions of the Book of Mormon.

13. Mos 8:13.

14. DHC, I, 21.

15. Lucy Mack Smith, *Biographical Sketches of Joseph Smith, the Prophet, and His Progenitors for Many Generations* (Liverpool: S. W. Richards, 1853), pp. 125-26. The prophet's mother quotes him as having said this. However, his wife, Emma, wrote in 1876 that Joseph had used the spectacles, the Urim and Thummim, during the 1828 session with Martin Harris, but after that a small stone. Emma Bidamon to Sister Pilgrim, March 27, 1876, Reorganized LDS Archives. David Whitmer also says the same thing. See Lancaster, "Gift and Power," pp. 799-800 for his discussion, presentation of statements, and documentation.

16. Richard P. Howard, *Restoration Scriptures*, p. 159, summarized the progression of thought:

Section 6
  1. The "translator" must have righteous desires for heavenly treasure.
  2. "Translation" ability is a gift from God.
Section 8
  1. Faith is the key to the use of the gift of "translation."
  2. Faith must be exercised with honesty of heart.
  3. Only then will truth be perceived. Such perception is registered in the mind and heart of the "translator" by the power of the Holy Ghost.
Section 9
  1. "Translation" is not an automatic process.
  2. "Translation" is a thoughtful, studious, faithful approach.
  3. The "translator" will know that what he is considering in his mind is either valid or invalid by the God-given impressions and intuitions and feelings born of such studious, faithful approach.

17. Willers to L. Mayer and D. Young, June 18, 1830. The John M. Olin Library, Cornell University, Ithaca, N. Y. Diedrich Willers Collection. Written in German. An English translation is given by D. Michael Quinn, "The First Months of Mormonism: A Contemporary View by Rev. Diedrich Willers," *New York History*, LIV (July, 1973), 317-31.

18. Later Mormons distinguished between inspiration and revelation, but that distinction does not appear in the Book of Mormon or in usage at this early period.

19. WS, June 26, 1829.

20. *Gleanings*, p. 228.

21. Fayette Lapham, "The Mormons," *Historical Magazine* (New Series), VII, 5 (May, 1870), 308. This

would have to have happened after the angel returned the spectacles to Smith so that he could receive DC 3, since they were taken with the plates.

22. Cf. n. 6 above.

23. DHC, I, 19.

24. Howard, *Restoration Scriptures*, states that over 2000 changes were made in the E MS (the emended manuscript that Oliver Cowdery prepared for the printer from the dictated manuscript, the D MS) in preparation for the 1837 edition, and that more than 1000 changes are found in the 2nd edition than were noted in the E MS, p. 41.

25. I Ne 20:1 and the parenthetical phrase read: "Hearken and hear this, O house of Jacob, who are called out of the waters of Judah, (or out of the waters of baptism), who swear by the name of the Lord . . ." Hugh Nibley, *Since Cumorah* (Salt Lake City: Deseret Book Company, c. 1967), p. 151, explains that the addition is needed for the modern mind, which would not get the meaning of "Waters of Judah," although the original audiences would have understood. The translator, therefore, gave his own rendition of what he perceived to be in the mind of the author, since a modern reader would be misled without the phrase.

26. Cf. the Book of Moses, ch. 1, superscript, in the *Pearl of Great Price.*

27. O[rasmus] Turner, *History of the Pioneer Settlement of Phelps and Gorham's Purchase* (Rochester Wm. Alling, 1851), p. 214.

28. *Ibid.*

29. A 20th century non-Mormon scholar agrees with Whittier and Quincy. Jan Shipps, in "Prophet Puzzle," p. 1 states that the prophet was an "extraordinarily talented individual—a genius beyond question." In her current research-in-progress, Shipps is studying Smith in the context of the structure and dynamics of the families from which prodigies emerge. Defining a prodigy as a person who produces, at an early age, a significant body of work of a mature character, she considers Smith a religious prodigy in quite the same way that Mozart and Mendelssohn were musical prodigies and Carl Friederich Gause and Norbert Weiner were mathematical prodigies. Jan Shipps to Robert Hullinger, June 10, 1975.

30. Smith referred to his "lack of fluency" in a letter to Moses C. Nickerson, November 19, 1833; DHC, I, 441-42. At a church conference on November 1, 1831, Christ consoles Smith in a revelation, showing that he was aware of his servant's weakness, DC 1:24. In a letter to W. W. Phelps, November, 1832, Smith wrote of language as a "narrow prison," DHC, I, 299.

31. *Gleanings*, p. 228.

32. Anthon's 1834 and 1841 letters.

32. B. H. Roberts used this explanation to account for the words added and changes made in the KJV translation of Isaiah found in the Book of Mormon. Smith compared the KJV with the text on the plates and kept the English version when it correctly gave the thought in the plates. *New Witnesses*, III, 438, n. i. Sidney B. Sperry says the same thing in *The Voice of Israel's Prophets* (Salt Lake City: Bookcraft, Inc., c. 1952), p. 90.

34. Letter to Mayer and Young.

35. David Whitmer, *An Address*, p. 12.

36. Quoted in William E. Berrett and Alma P. Burton, *Readings in L. D. S. History from Original Manuscripts* (3 vols.; Salt Lake City: Deseret Book Company, c. 1953), I, 51.

37. Whitmer, *An Address*, p. 12.

3

The Setting: New England and Western New York

Revelation means something communicated immediately from God to man. . . . His account of it to another is not revelation; and whoever puts faith in that account, puts it in the man from whom the account comes. . . . My disbelief of the Bible is founded on a pure and religious belief in God.

Thomas Paine[1]

TO TOM PAINE
When Life's electric spark shall quit thy frame,
Myriads of devils wait to seize their prey;
With shouts and yell they loudly call thy name,
Then bear thee to thy destin'd doom away.[2]

REASON, REVELATION, AND POLITICS
AFTER THE AMERICAN REVOLUTION

When Joseph Smith announced his intention to convince "the Jew and Gentile that JESUS is the CHRIST, the ETERNAL GOD, manifesting himself to all nations,"[3] he tried to check forces set in motion by deism, American rationalism, and sectarian wars.[4] Deism attacked revealed religion in the interest of natural religion. Its creed was one deduced from nature: (1) there is a God (2) whom one must revere (3) through moral living. (4) One should abandon sin because it works to man's disadvantage, (5) and also because there is divine recompense here and hereafter. Natural religion heeded no special revelation, such as the Bible. It had an ethic derived from reasonable principles, just as its religious concepts were arrived at by reasoning. Some deists held that the contents of the Bible might be above reason, but not contrary to it. Others denied that possibility on grounds that the Bible has nothing in it that was previously unrelated.

Deists concluded that the Bible's records were not genuine, its narratives were neither reliable nor unique, the two testaments were unrelated, the miracles and prophecies were absurd if interpreted literally—but fraudulent if not, and the mysterious elements were corruptions of later times. Since the very means that won acceptance for the Bible were now negated, Paine said, reason demands its rejection.

Christianity was deemed a corrupt variation of natural religion. The Church had obscured religion with unreasonable and immoral concepts, such as the doctrines of the Trinity, predestination, arbitrary judgments, and the innocent suffering for the guilty. Worse, it had aggrandized itself at the expense of the people it purportedly served.

Rationalism in the New World was an outgrowth of New England's Puritan heritage and was watered from the same spring as deism. Rationalists repudiated revivalism and accepted special revelation as long as it was reasonable.[5] Jesus was not co-equal with God the Father, but subordinate to Him. Jesus' death was seen as a way to alert sinners to God's authority, to the dignity of His government and law, not as a way to appease Him. Christ died for *all* people, and all will achieve salvation here or hereafter. Original sin, the imputation of sin and guilt, and Calvinistic predestination were judged contrary to reason. They made God immoral, but God is benevolent and brings happiness to man. Above all, God is a unity; He is one, not three-in-one.

Boston's Charles Chauncy and Jonathen Mayhew expounded rationalism in the mid-18th century. Gradually it infiltrated the established Congregational Church and led to the formation of the Unitarian Church. Unitarians stressed the *uni*personal nature of God.[6] A simultaneous development was the formation of the Universalists, who shared many Unitarian accents, but stressed the *benevolence* of God, who saves all.

Universalists began from the ministry of John Murray, an English emigrant who came to Vermont in the 1770s. The Universalists first convened in Oxford, Massachusetts in 1785. They were uneducated and tended to draw their themes from the Bible, whereas the Unitarians had educated clergy and often drew from non-biblical sources for inspiration. Universalists tended to locate in rural areas; Unitarians in the cities. Writers often termed the Universalists Unitarians because they thought of some teaching the two shared.

Rationalists were a bridge between the deists and pietists (conservative Christians who subordinated reason to biblical revelation, held orthodox views on the nature of Christ and God, and were disestablished). From the French and Indian War through the Revolutionary War, political concerns forged a marriage of convenience between the reationalists and pietists. Political and religious issues were submerged while they united against the established churches.[7]

Rationalists considered theological disagreements of minor importance in view of their common belief in God, immortality and a virtuous life. Pietists ignored the theological differences because their sympathies were with those unnourished by the established churches' rituals, creeds and theologies—all immaterial between those like-minded. Both agreed that religion was between God and the individual, that the churches' presence was not needed. Both opposed the churchly and clerical authoritarianism of the conservative, established churches.[8]

The marriage dissolved when the Second Great Awakening brought out into the open the division between pietistic and rationalistic Christianity.[9] The latter phase of the French Revolution, with its anti-clerical and atheistic tendencies, led pietists to see a cause and effect relationship between Jacobin infidelity and barbarity. Alarmed at the demise of the French monarchy, the Prussian and Austrian kings declared war on Revolutionary France and were supported by British diplomacy. In 1793 France went to war with Britain and overran much of Europe in the name of liberty.[10]

If political activity was an expression of anti-religious views, then America had to beware of French infidelity, for it was believed to have been a sign of an Infidel International. Who was behind the French Revolution and, seemingly, was trying to overthrow all religion and government? The International! And the person and political party of Thomas Jefferson were labeled as its American agents.

Jefferson was suspect because of his French ambassadorship from 1785-89, and his anti-Federalist political activities. The Federalists painted him as an atheist, a Jacobin, even a foe of private property and civic order. When Thomas Paine's *Age of Reason* appeared in 1793, it reinforced the anti-Jeffersonian, anti-Republican excitement because of Paine's stay in France and his friendship with Jefferson. The Federalists pushed into law the Alien and Sedition Acts of 1798 to keep their power and to attack the ideas of the French Revolution.

New England was the hub of wealth, Federalist sympathies and religious conservatism—the center of the storm. Congregational churches were established and their clergy were Federalists. They were the main opponents of the rising Jeffersonian party and often identified the established order with true religion.[11]

Ethan Allen's publication of *Reason the Only Oracles of Man* in 1784, Elihu Palmer's attempted anti-church crusade, Paine's book, the formation of deistic societies and publication of deistic papers upset the region. Deism and French barbarity were coming to the common folk, and New England Christendom was alarmed.

POPULAR DEISM

Thomas Paine's *Age of Reason*[12] distilled and simplified deistic thinking *to defend God*. Paine's belief in God required him to reject the Bible, "for in my opinion," he wrote to a friend, "the Bible is a gross libel against the justice and goodness of God, in almost every part of it."[13]

The Bible limited God, forcing Him to "act like a passionate man, that killed his son, when he could not revenge himself any other way."[14] Christian theology's use of the devil in connection with Christ's death and the doctrine of the atonement made Satan's power greater than God's.[15]

Paine scorned the Bible for attributing to God obscenity, debauchery, vindictiveness and cruel executions. The innocent were made to suffer for the guilty.[16] Genocidal wars were waged by Moses and Joshua by God's express command.[17] Rather than being the word of God, Paine said, the Bible would better be recognized as the word of a demon.[18]

Prophecy had long been used as an argument for the divine authorship of the Bible, but Paine ridiculed it. He traced its development from poetry to prediction and maintained that the meaning of "seer" was later incorporated into "prophecy" when men wanted to know what might befall their plans.[19] The seer's prophecies referred only to impending battles or immediate interests, not to far distant times and events.[20] Ultimately, the prophet was made the historian of the future, and posterity credited him with accurate prediction if he came within a thousand years of the mark.[21]

Then, Paine stormed, the Bible found a way to exonerate God when prophecy failed. If He blessed people and they kept on sinning, then God changed His mind and destroyed them. If God led a man to prophesy destruction upon an evil nation and it repented, then God spared it. "What a fool do fabulous systems make of man!"[22]

Granted, for the sake of argument, that prophecy was prediction, Paine still found it useless. No one could know if it were a lie, conceit, revelation, or the truth. If the prophesied event, or something like it, took place, no one could know if it were an accident or truly foreknown. He would not grant that God would communicate in terms "so equivocal as to fit almost any circumstances that might happen afterwards," any event important enough for people to know beforehand. [23]

The Bible damaged its own case for predictive prophecy, Paine said, by showing the prophets to have been "impostors and liars." Jeremiah lied for Zedekiah because it served his own purpose.[24] He told Zedekiah that he would be captured by the king of Babylon and die in peace in the foreign capital. Instead, Zedekiah saw his sons killed, was blinded, and spent the rest of his life in a dungeon.[25]

Neither would Paine accept miracles as an argument or evidence for special revelation. The Bible appealed to miracles to produce belief, but belief is based upon the one who reported the miracle, not upon the miracle itself. If the miracle were true, it "would have no better chance of being believed than if it were a lie."[26] One cannot truly judge something miraculous without knowing the full extent of the laws under which the supposed miracle operated. Further knowledge might reveal a miracle to have been natural, after all, and that would remove its belief-producing effect.[27] If knowledge removes the supernatural element from the miracle, then it will also take the mysterious from religion.

Paine set his own definition of revelation against the Bible's claim to be special revelation.

> Revelation is a communication of something, which person to whom that thing is revealed, did not know before. For if I have done a thing, or seen it done, it needs no revelation to tell me I have done it, or seen it, nor to enable me to tell it, or to write it.
>
> Revelation, therefore, cannot be applied to anything done upon earth of which man himself is the actor or the witness; and consequently all the historical and anecdotal part of the Bible . . . is not within the meaning and compass of the word revelation, and, therefore, is not the word of God.[28]

Revelation is "something communicated immediately from God to man."[29] Another's account of revelation is only hearsay. People believe that God spoke to Moses because the Bible says so, but will not believe that God spoke to Mohammed on the word of the Koran.

Why not? Because, you will say, you do not believe it; and so because you *do*, and because you *don't* is all the reason you can give for believing or disbelieving except that you will say that Mahomet was an impostor. And how do you know Moses was not an impostor?[30]

So if the account is believed, he concluded, one necessarily believes that person who gave the account.[31]

Revelation cannot admit either accidental or historical change. Language, therefore, is ruled out as a medium of God's word. Instruments of human communication cannot convey God's word because there is no universal language, translations are subject to error, and copyists and printers make mistakes or purposely alter words.[32]

Revelation must also disclaim any contradiction, for that shows that the story is false. On the other hand, agreement in all its parts does not make a story true, since the whole may be false. Agreement does not prove truth, but disagreement absolutely disproves it.[33]

One his terms, then, Paine denied the Old Testament any status as revelation. Books of testimony, for example, depend upon the certain identity of their authors; but even if their authorship were certain, their testimony would be only probable.[34] Mosaic authorship of the Pentateuch was most unlikely because Genesis depends upon Chronicles for a time reference. Exodus, Leviticus and Deuteronomy were written in the third person about Moses at a later time.[34] Paine held for a time lapse between the life of Joshua and the writing of the biblical book by that name because of the many instances of the phrase "unto this day," and because of a comparison dependent upon a time lapse to make its point.[36] The writer's need to explain the word "beforetimes" also showed that the books of Samuel came after Samuel's time.[37]

Then there were contradictions. Paine found two differing accounts of the numberings of the Ten Commandments, two reasons for celebrating the Sabbath,[38] two accounts of Saul's first meeting with David,[39] and two accounts of Jeremiah's imprisonment.[40] Deuteronomy describes Moses' burial place, although no man was supposed to have known it.[41] Judges 18 claims that the Danites captured and destroyed Laish and then called it Dan, although it was known as Dan in Genesis 14. That was either a contradiction or a blow to Mosaic authorship, Paine concluded.[42]

The New Testament fared no better under Paine. The anecdotal character of the four Gospels, their disagreements with each other, and their failures to substantiate each other's details were cases in point.[43] Differences in the resurrection stories showed that the writers were neither eyewitnesses nor apostles, and that they wrote independently of one another.[44] "If the story of Jesus Christ be fabulous, all reasoning founded upon it, as a supposed truth, must fall with it."[45]

If God is wise, Paine asked, how can anyone suppose that He would commit Himself and His will to precarious language and manuscripts that are edited, altered, and changed?[46] How can anyone place faith in a book not canonized until 300 years after Christ—and then by a committee vote?[47]

Paine's demolition of the Bible freed him to urge the deistic view. No one should despair of finding revelation or a word of God:

> there is a Word of God; there is a revelation. THE WORD OF GOD IS THE CREATION WE BEHOLD: And it is in *this word*, which no human invention can counterfeit or alter, that God speaketh universally to man.[48]

Nature reveals mathematical laws, and man discovers how to apply them to the earth and heavenly bodies. To study nature is to study true theology and discover the existence of God. It was incomprehensible that anyone might want to know more. "We might then say that another *canonical book* of the word of God had been discovered."[49]

Paine also allowed a testimony of the conscience. Reason falls infinitely short in discovering God's attributes, but men know judgment as a probability. "If we knew it as a fact, we should be the mere slaves of terror; our belief would have no merit, and our best actions no virtue."[50]

The sum total of revelation is the knowledge that God exists and that judgment is probable—the testimony of nature and conscience. Corruption looms ahead for those who want more, for it has "been produced by admitting of what man calls *revealed religion*."[51] The Christian Church is irreconcilable with reason and scientific inquiry. It is maintained by the clergy only because of self-interest.[52] For the honor of God, therefore, Paine repudiated all revealed religions and priests and called for a return to the God revealed by nature and reason.

Paine spurred the formation of organized deism in America. *Age of Reason* was widely read and often reprinted. The Deistical Society of New York published *The Temple of Reason* from 1800 to 1803. Revived as the *Prospect, or View of the Moral World*, it finally was discontinued in March, 1805.[53] Sixty miles north of New York on the Hudson River, the Druidical Society of Newburgh reprinted and circulated the works of Hume, Voltaire and Paine in taverns, shops and homes. But it disbanded in 1804.[54]

Jedidiah Morse, pastor in Charlestown, Massachusetts, scorned Paine's book as a product of the Infidel International and as a symbol of its power base in America. Yale's Timothy Dwight offered a reasoned defense, marshalled hatred against deism, and popularized the anti-deistic argument.[55] Nathaniel Emmons of Franklin, Massachusetts warned that Jefferson's person, party, and principles endangered patriotism and conservative piety. That typified clergy reaction.

Three factors brought efforts to spread deism to an end about 1805. First, the presidential election of 1800 caused a split between republican-political and deistical-religious sentiment. It was now possible to be one without being the other. Second, political republicanism was rapidly taken over by the revivalists and their supporters. Third, the prophets of deism died: Elihu Palmer in 1805; John Foster in 1806; and Thomas Paine in 1809. The demise of Napoleon brought the struggling, dying Federalist Party and the excesses of the French Revolution to a close.[56] Only then did the cry against French infidelity subside in the churches. In its heyday from 1784 to 1805, deistic influence was felt from the Atlantic to the Mississippi.

Paine transmitted the results of 150 years of philosophical and biblical inquiry in his book. The rhetoric about proper credentials for biblical authors, copyists' errors, contradictions, the nature of God and His communication with man, all these ultimately reflected concern about the concept of revelation. Thomas Hobbes and John Locke had left their mark on deistic studies of the Bible.

Hobbes (1588-1679) held that all knowledge comes from the senses and reason; that the Bible might be above reason, but not contrary to it. Locke (1632-1704) held that Christianity is not a product of reason, but is not contrary to it. It is a revelation. Revelation teaches matters that reason may not have discovered, but which reason can comprehend. Revelation, therefore, communicates knowledge. Long after deism died as a vital force, this concept of revelation lived on in rationalistic and pietistic churches alike.

HALF-WAY HOUSES TO DEISM

Rationalists wished to purge Christianity of the doctrines that forced thinking people to choose infidelity, but few were willing to share the extent of Paine's repudiation.[57] The time span from 1750 to 1825 brought rationalism to the simultaneous development of Universalism and Unitarianism. Both held to special revelation against deism. They had different emphases and differences within each movement, but the unipersonal nature of God and the salvation of all mankind was acceptable within both. They were divided by class, education, and style.

Unitarians were mainly a New England phenomenon, whose development centered around the cities of eastern Massachusetts. Universalism developed in the western section and in Vermont, the hill country of New England. There were Unitarians in western New York, but it was the Universalists who mixed with the people in the small towns and rural areas that formed the tinder for revivalistic fires. Anti-trinitarian tendencies in other religious movements would be called Unitarian, but their connection with the Unitarian Church was quite remote.

Universalism in its early phase was shaped by men who held different views of Christianity. John Murray was a Calvinist and a trinitarian. He held that Christ was Savior, but in contrast to Calvinism he taught that all people were the Elect of God.

Elhanan Winchester taught that all souls would be saved, but those who were not pure enough would have to suffer a purgatorial existence for as much as 50,000 years to satisfy the justice of God.

Hosea Ballou cut Universalism's ties with Calvinism and established it on the basis of reason in *A Treatise on Atonement*.[58] He rejected the Trinity. Hell was suffered in this life as a result of sin, and it was from this that Christ came to free us. Ballou rejected the picture of the Old Testament God in favor of a God who wants to make men happy. Such a God could not allow man to choose misery for himself, even if freewill had to be denied to present this image of God.[59]

COUNTERATTACK: SECTARIANISM AND REVIVALISM

Issues raised during the 1790s were to have a long life. Thousands left the western sections of Connecticut, Massachusetts and Vermont, for western New York from 1790 to 1820 and brought with them the deistic-rationalistic-pietistic debate.[60] Their leaving left foreboding in the east that they would "revert to 'barbarism' and thus subvert the moral order of society."[61]

Pioneer missionary James Hotchkin described western New York of the 1790s as a "wasteland of infidelity." Not only at Scottsville, but also at Wheatland and Rochester, deistic societies had their circulating libraries. Diverse backgrounds and poor transportation kept religious observances from advancing as rapidly as land settlement. The price of land brought from the east people who looked for economic improvement. The greater part of the population was irreligious, Hotchkin said. They used the sabbath for business, pleasure, drinking, and carousing.[62]

Eastern churches saw this as a dark cloud on the western horizon. In 1798 the Presbyterian General Assembly declared that it perceived a loss of religious observances and respect for institutional religion in the west, plus "an abounding infidelity, which in many cases tends to atheism itself."[63] In response, the churches launched the Second Great Awakening to convert the west.

Presbyterians and Congregationalists united to supply enough doctrinally sound clergy to serve the scattered settlements. Presbyterians were the stronger partner in western New York. Through them came the benevolence agencies with their tracts,[64] Bibles,[65] Sunday Schools, and the pietistic rationale. Presbyterians, Congregationalists, and Methodists held regular conferences, sessions, and revival meetings. Their religious journals informed readers of revival meetings and campaigns, provided theological comment, appealed to a wide readership, and provided a bond to populations on the move.[66]

The Great Revival of 1799-1800 paved the way for the churches to organize and settle in with the population in western New York.[67] Hotchkin saw the Revival as a means that God used to build up "Zion."

> "The tide of infidelity which was settling in with so strong a current, was rolled back, and Western New York was delivered from the moral desolation which threatened it."[68]

The Awakening made its greatest impact upon that large segment of the population that resisted "deism and irreligion during the era of the Revolutionary War."[69] In fact, from 1800 to 1835, revivalism would boost church attendance until it averaged three times the membership.[70]

After 1815 the Universalists spread their rationalistic gospel in western New York and established nearly 90 congregations in the lower Black River Valley, the Finger Lakes region, and the country of the Genesee River.[71] Their favorite tactic was to engage the pietists in public debate and apply popularized deistic and rationalistic arguments to their opponents' views.[72]

Mr. Evarts, presiding Methodist Elder of the Black River Conference, debated Mr. Morse of the Universalists in Ellisburg in May, 1821 for nearly a week. Evarts presented the traditional arguments to support "the doctrine of endless misery."

> And both the faith and morality of Universalists, were assailed, as equally destructive of individual peace and public safety. On the other hand, Mr. Morse labored with very obvious success to repel the aspersions cast upon the denomination—to remove the objections to the faith of Universalism—and successfully threw back upon his opponent, the charge of maintaining dogmas, alike dishonorable to God.[73]

Each side left the debate convinced that it had won.

Charles Finney took to task much of the preaching against Universalists. Clergy fought with arguments from out of date books. "They suppose Universalists hold the doctrine that God is all mercy." Not so, said Finney.

> They reject the idea of *mercy* in the salvation of man, for they hold that every man is punished in full according to his just deserts. . . . they hold to the justice of God alone as the ground of salvation.[74]

The result was that "people either laugh at them, or say it is all lies, for they know Universalists do not hold such sentiments."[75]

The charge that Universalists were inimical to "individual peace and safety" was

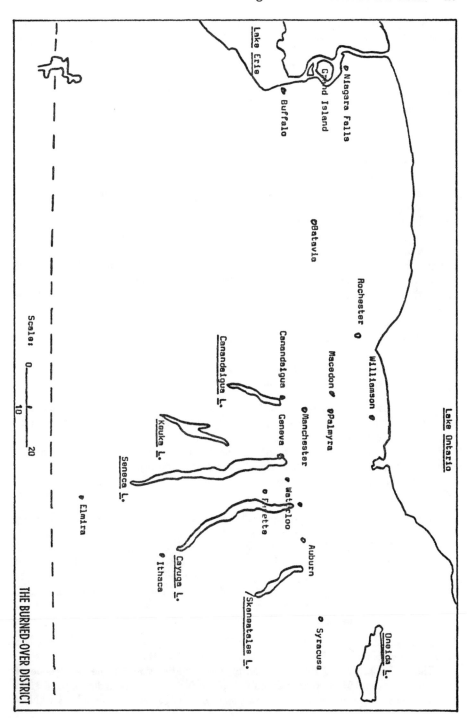

THE BURNED-OVER DISTRICT

an echo of anti-deistic, anti-French sentiment of the 1790s. But the appeal to God's justice, rather than His mercy, as the basis for man's salvation, was a deistic argument that Universalists had made their own.

During this era another important factor of Protestant motivation emerged. G. A. Koch observed that the 1790s seemed the time when American independence would sweep the globe, but the idea of a social and political millennium faded away with deism after 1800. Human salvation was seen no longer as coming through revision of social institutions, but through belief in an end-of-the-world millennium.[76]

Protestants united in their hope of inaugurating the millennium within the immediate future. A new system of education such as the Oneida Institute, missions to convert the Jews, the emergence of numerous sects—all were begun in the belief that such activity would hasten the thousand-year reign of Christ. This was a form of American optimism of which, compared to New England, "the Burned-over District certainly exhibited a disproportionate amount."[77]

Itinerant missionaries and evangelists shared that optimism. Charles Finney, dean of them all, believed that the right kind of ministers at the head of the revivals could bring in the millennium.[78] If the clergy could have risen above doctrinal pettiness and denominational competition in their joint efforts and could have agreed "as to what ought to be done for the salvation of the world," then the millennium would have "come at once."[79]

Finney blamed the clergy for the sectarian spirit that went with the joint revivals. Clerical cries of "Heresy" and "New Measures," and their "controversial *spirit and manner*" in discussing disputed doctrinal issues only confused the churches.[80] Converts who were concerned with denominational peculiarities were usually "mighty zealous for the traditions of the elders, and very little concerned for the salvation of souls."[81]

The problem of any revival was to maintain the spirit of unity. Finney pleaded with his colleagues to bear down only on the fundamentals of salvation and to exclude sectarian differences.[82] Proselyting converts for church membership proved the most divisive practice.[83] Whenever a minister neglected the revival-in-progress to indoctrinate converts, Finney warned, the revival ground to a standstill.[84]

Hostilities attendant upon revivalistic and benevolent activities, according to Whitney Cross,

> made up a sectarian hierarchy. All Protestant churches united in condemning Catholics. All evangelical sects united, too, against Universalists and Unitarians. Methodists, Baptists, and Presbyterians could share their hatred of Christians. Baptist and Presbyterians co-operated in damning Methodists and Free-will Baptists. Presbyterians all too often proved disagreeably intolerant of Baptists. To cap the climax, both Baptists and Presbyterians, particularly the latter, maintained a constant and bitter strife between the enthusiasts and the conservatives in their own ranks.[85]

Local newspapers followed the Protestant-Catholic struggle and "carried a swelling volume of notices and articles devoted to the threat of Catholicism."[86]

The active press and the formation of new societies signaled the resurgence of freethought in the 1820s. Robert Owen's utopia in New Harmony, Indiana, from 1824 to 1829, was meant to be an infidel community. In 1828 the Free Enquirers of New

York organized and regularly sponsored lectures for themselves and the public.[87] Within a few months the National Tract Society afforded the skeptics a propaganda medium and outlet in New York, Albany and Utica.[88]

The new wave of infidelity was recognized only by a few as different from the deism of Paine and others. It was treated with the same arguments as deism, and tracts written against the school of Paine were reissued against the new wave.

Conservative Christians sounded the alarm. They warned Americans in 1824 that French infidelity and the Reign of Terror were not associated by accident.[89] Paine was castigated—again—in 1826[90] and the faithful were assured that God's wrath would strike down the infidels.[91] The fitting example was William Carver, a deistic pauper, whose condition in life was living proof of freethought's consequences.[92] The popular "dying infidel" stories had their subjects contritely confess lives of shame on their deathbeds and were standard weapons in faith's arsenal.[93]

Protestant antagonism showed itself also in political action. Dissenters were refused the right of testifying in court in 1828 because they were thought to be incapable of swearing an oath. When Finney used the name of the Universalists as a synonym for "ungodliness," "infidelity" and "terror," he struck a sympathetic chord in the burned-over district.[94] The religious press applied the name to criminals.

THE FREEMASONS

The churches found another common cause when William Morgan published an expose of Freemasonry[95] and then mysteriously disappeared. Attention focused upon an institution that served many as a church and that formerly had been linked with the Infidel International. It was regarded as deism with ritual. Public awareness of the lodges' secrecy, titles and ritual centered upon an alleged connection with deism, terrorism, and anti-Americanism.

The Congregationalists in New York retained many of their Federalist sympathies, sentiments that included a bias against the Masonic Lodge. Now they were joined in outrage by large numbers of pietistically and rationalistically inclined churches and individuals. Since lodge membership carried with it the social and political privilege of the large towns— the urban versus the rural, the professionals against the laborers—the anti-masonic movement was headed more by lay direction than by clerical. Presbyterians and others tried to use the energies released as

> a means to develop universal revivalism and reform than [as] an end in itself. Antimasonry thus became another gun in the benevolent system's artillery to convert the world and introduce the millenium.[96]

Minor sect emigrants from New England shared Jeffersonian opposition to Federalist tenets, but found land agents and others of the establishment associated with Jefferson's party and with ideals that were shared with the Masons. Thus the anti-masonic movement seemed more in keeping with the egalitarian principles of Jefferson, although in its later development the movement revived the Federalist principles opposed to Jefferson.[97]

Church action was largely responsible, Finney believed, for the lodges' almost complete shutdown in western New York. They disbanded and relinquished their charters. By 1830 the greatest revival the world had then ever seen commenced in the center of the anti-masonic region, and spread over the whole field where the church action had been taken until its converts numbered 100,000 souls.[98]

NEW BEGINNINGS

Early 19th century America fostered many religious responses to cultural and social problems. Two deserve special notice. Both tried to obviate sectarian abuses: the one by abandoning denominational divisions; the other by starting anew. They shared the millennial hopes and anti-deistic concerns of Protestantism, but were scandalized by rampant sectarianism. As an alternative they offered—themselves.

The Shakers

The Shakers attributed Europe's religious wars and America's religious discord to the belief that the Bible is God's word for all future ages. Religious strife demonstrated the Bible's insufficiency. "Instead of the knowledge of the true and quickening Spirit of revelation," the orthodox position left people with only human precepts for comfort, left them ignorant of the spiritual life.[99] The dogmatic confinement of spiritual revelations to a book written for former ages is attended by dead formalism in Christendom and a rapid increase in infidelity—proof positive of apostasy. "The idea . . . that all inspired revelation ceased with the canon of Scripture, is inconsistent with both reason and *Scripture*."[100]

Shakers declared the situation desperate. There was a true Church in apostolic times, but it was displaced.[101] "The true order of the primitive Church was wholly lost, and the great apostasy established as early as 457."[102] Anti-Christ took over during the reign of Leo the Great.[103]

Joseph Meachem was a former Free-will Baptist preacher who formed the Shaker movement into a communal society in preparation for the impending millennium. Before his death, communities were set up in New York, New Hampshire, Connecticut, Massachusetts and Maine. By 1825 there were at least 20 communities scattered from New England to the western borders of Indiana and Kentucky. In 1827 a Shaker community was formed at Sodus Bay on Lake Ontario, just 30 miles from Palmyra.[104]

The Restorationists

The second movement was the restoration sought by the Christian Connection (or Christians) and the Campbellites (or Disciples), both part of what would become America's largest indigenous religious movement.[105] Multiplying church schisms led them to a pole opposite the Shakers. They tried to heal the divisions by scrapping all creeds, confessions and theological terminology post-dating the New Testament. Abandon denominational peculiarities. Bring in the millennium by restoring a faithful observance of New Testament revelation, they urged, not by seeking new revelation. Return the "Church to its original status under the perfect constitution, or body of laws and regulations prescribed by Christ, the Messiah."[106]

The Christians were formed from Methodist, Baptist and Presbyterian secessions that left their parent bodies in 1793, 1800 and 1801. They held to the divinity of Christ, but many were anti-trinitarians. Their only creed was the Bible and their only name Christian.

The Disciples regarded the laity as spiritually competent and independent, held to an Arminian theology, defined faith as an intellectual test given to Christ's moral principles[107] and saw its essence as obedience to Christ, held sympathy for antitrinitarian sentiments, taught an anthropology that gave man the rational and moral ability to understand and fulfill New Testament demands, and were repulsed by the ordinary revival because of its emotional appeal.

The sectarian struggle among the churches was a "quest for authority." Christians and Disciples located that authority "in the ability of a congregation to find truth in the scriptures."[108] Shakers found their authority in the restoration of the true Church—absent since 457 A. D.— and relied on continuing, present-day revelation to direct its life. By contrast, other Protestants relied upon a body of doctrine that was in their judgment in agreement with the Bible and correctly taught.

Like the Disciples and Christians, Joseph Smith would locate authority in a correct interpretation of the Bible by the Church. Like the Shakers, he would restore the Church and be led to the correct interpretation by new and constant revelation. Like other Protestants, he would also see correct doctrine as a mark of the true Church. But Smith added something else: a new scripture and a dual priesthood based not on apostolic succession like the Roman Catholic claim to authority, but on prophetic succession.[19]

SUMMARY

This has been an overview of a period in American history of religious, political and social ferment; of boundless optimism over the American political experiment; of peace following two wars; of the west opening to New England across the stretch of western New York. The westward push of emigration brought to western New York an economically, socially and religiously displaced population. This was the social basis for the search for religious authority and for the extensive rejection of the Baptist, Methodist and Presbyterian churches by those of a seeker mentality.

In response to the turbulence about him, Smith would seek to heal the wounds of sectarianism such upheaval brought about, which De Pillis characterized as the "classic rule of the sociology of religion."[110] He would defend God against deism, rationalism, and sectarianism, not by the revival,[111] but by the experience of personalized revelation.

FOOTNOTES

1. Thomas Paine, *Age of Reason: Being An Investigation of True and Fabulous Theology*, Moncure Daniel Conway, ed. (New York: G. P. Putnam's Sons, c. 1898), pp. 23, 183, 199.

2. *New-York Evening Post*, December 8, 1802, cited by G. Adolph Koch, *Religion of the American Enlightenment* (New York: Thomas Y. Crowell Company, c. 1968), p. 133.

3. Title Page, Book of Mormon.

4. The following works, in addition to Koch's, are invaluable in tracing American deism: Herbert N. Morais, *Deism in Eighteenth Century America* (New York: Russell & Russell, c. 1934); Albert Post, *Popular Freethought in America, 1825-1850* (New York: Columbia University Press, c. 1943); Martin E. Marty, *The Infidel: Freethought and American Religion* (Cleveland: The World Publishing Company, c. 1961.

5. Cf. comments on Charles Chauncy and Jonathan Mayhew in Robert T. Handy, Lefferts A. Loetscher, and H. Shelton Smith, *American Christianity: An Historical Interpretation with Representative Documents* (New York: Charles Scribner's Sons, c. 1960), I, 382.

6. Unitarianism shifted grounds many times since then. The older Unitarians taught what was called "modal trinitarianism," known usually as Sabellianism. That is, God appeared first in the mode of Father,

then as Son, then as Holy Spirit. It was three consecutive appearances rather than simultaneous being—as the orthodox doctrine teaches.

7. "Established" means that a Church body was supported by the state. The established Church in Massachusetts was the Congregational Church. This was the kind of support against which the constitutional amendment was directed. By 1820 the last state to comply with the amendment finally disestablished its favored Church.

8. Sidney E. Mead, *The Living Experiment: The Shaping of Christianity in America* (New York: Harper & Row, c. 1963), pp. 39-42.

9. The use of "pietist" follows Mead.

10. Charles A., Mary R., and William Beard, *New Basic History of the United States* (Garden City, N. Y.: Doubleday & Company, Inc., c. 1960), p. 162.

11. Mead, p. 57.

12. The book was written in France while Paine was imprisoned by the Jacobin regime. Paine wanted to show that belief in God did not require acceptance of doctrines and churches that drove people to infidelity—and to the excesses of the Jacobins.

13. "Letter to a Friend," May 27, 1797, *Age of Reason*, p. 199.

14. *Ibid.*, p. 65.

15. *Ibid.*, pp. 29-30.

16. *Ibid.*, p. 24.

17. *Ibid.*, p. 90.

18. *Ibid.*, p. 34.

19. *Ibid.*, p. 141.

20. *Ibid.*

21. *Ibid.*, p. 81.

22. *Ibid.*, p. 134.

23. *Ibid.*, p. 82.

24. *Ibid.*

25. *Ibid.*, pp. 138-39.

26. *Ibid.*, p. 139.

27. *Ibid.*, p. 79.

28. *Ibid.*, p. 77.

29. *Ibid.*, p. 33.

30. *Ibid.*, p. 23.

31. *Ibid.*, p. 197.

32. *Ibid.*, p. 183.

33. *Ibid.*, p. 38.

34. *Ibid.*, p. 153.

35. *Ibid.*, pp. 91-92.

36. *Ibid.*, pp. 94-95, 118-19.

37. *Ibid.*, pp. 105-09.

38. *Ibid.*, p. 111.

39. *Ibid.*, p. 96.

40. *Ibid.*, p. 137.

41. *Ibid.*, p. 136.

42. *Ibid.*, p. 96.

43. *Ibid.*, . 98-99.

44. *Ibid.*, pp. 41-42, 158-62.

45. *Ibid.*, p. 168.

46. *Ibid.*, p. 181.

47. *Ibid.*, p. 170.

48. *Ibid.*, p. 45.

49. *Ibid.*, p. 53; cf. p. 48.

50. *Ibid.*, p. 188.

51. *Ibid.*, p. 61.

52. *Ibid.*, pp. 58-60.

53. Morais, pp. 137-39.

54. Koch, pp. 114-29. An "infidel" club was formed about 1794 on the Genesee River on the site of what would later be Scottsville. It had a circulating library "composed of the works of Voltaire, Volney,

Hume, Payne, and others of a similar character. No church of the Presbyterian or Congregational order existed in this place till March, 1822." James H. Hotchkin, *A History of the Purchase and Settlement of Western New York, and of the Rise, Progress, and Present State of the Presbyterian Church in That Region* (New York: M. W. Dodd, 1848), p. 90. This was west of the Smith's home at Palmyra.

55. Koch, pp. 239-84; cf. Morais, pp. 159-78.

56. Koch, pp. 281-84.

57. For example, they still retained belief in the Bible as special revelation. Cf. Koch, chap. VIII; Marty, *The Infidel*, chap. 6.

58. Hosea Ballou, *A Treatise on Atonement* (Randolph, Vt.: Serano Wright, 1805). This was available in Palmyra bookstores.

59. Cf. Ernest Casssra (ed.), *Universalism in America: A Documentary History* (Boston: Beacon Press, c. 1971), pp. 17-24.

60. Whitney R. Cross, *The Burned-over District: The Social and Intellectual History of Enthusiastic Religion in Western New York, 1800-1850* (Ithaca, N. Y.: Cornell University Press, c. 1950), p. 6.

61. Winthrop S. Hudson, *Religion in America: An Historical Account of the Development of American Religious Life* (New York: Charles Scribner's Sons, c. 1965), p. 133.

62. Hotchkin, pp. 24-29.

63. Quoted by William Warren Sweet, *The Story of Religions in America* (New York: Harper and Brothers, c. 1930), p. 324.

64. From 1825 to 1827 the American Tract Society, in its first two years of existence, printed 44 million pages and kept 43 million east of the Allegheny Mountains. By 1835 it had printed almost 30 million tracts. Three fourths of this output stayed in New York. Cross, p. 25.

65. Elias Boudinot, first president of the American Bible Society, attended the Society's fourth anniversary meeting in Palmyra at the Palmyra City Hotel in June, 1820. He reported that 173,752 Bibles and Testaments had been given out; PR, June 7, 1820. The benevolence agencies had their local affiliates in nearly every town and village. The Palmyra Auxiliary Missionary Society routinely printed notices of their meetings in the local paper; PR, August 18, 1818. Auxiliaries like this distributed the output of the Bible and tract societies.

66. *The Methodist Magazine* (New York) regularly printed reports of the Bible societies. Cf. Vol. IV (1821), p. 312.

67. Hotchkin, pp. 79-118.

68. *Ibid* p. 74.

69. Cross, p. 7.

70. Hudson, p. 129.

71. Cross, pp. 17-18.

72. *Ibid.*, p. 44. David Marks, the young Free-will Baptist evangelist, preached twice in West Bloomfield one Sunday in 1823 "and was much opposed by a Universalist." In April, 1827, he "attended a debate, that was appointed to be held between a Calvinistic Baptist and a Universalist." Marks, pp. 161, 233.

73. Cassara, p. 128.

74. Charles G. Finney, *Lectures on Revivals of Religion* (rev.; Oberlin, Ohio: E. J. Goodrich, 1868), p. 171.

75. *Ibid.*

76. Koch, p. 292.

77. Cross, p. 79.

78. Finney, p. 211.

79. *Ibid.*, p. 312.

80. *Ibid.*, pp. 192-93.

81. *Ibid.*, p. 381.

82. *Ibid.*, p. 153.

83. *Ibid.*, p. 267.

84. *Ibid.*, p. 189.

85. Cross, p. 43.

86. *Ibid.*, p. 230.

87. Post, p. 80.

88. *Ibid.*, pp. 24, 122.

89. *Ibid.*, p. 210.

90. *Ibid.*, p. 203, n. 17.

91. *Ibid.*, p. 76.

92. *Ibid.,* pp. 221-22.
93. *Ibid.,* pp. 204-05.
94. Finney, pp. 119, 196.
95. *Freemasonry Exposed and Explained* (New York: William Brisbane, 1826).
96. Cross, p. 123.
97. *Ibid.,* p. 79. Cross recalls the social aspects of the anti-masonic movement in chap. 6, "The Martyr," pp. 113-25.
98. Finney, p. 284.
99. *Testimony of Christ's Second Appearing, Exemplified by the Principles and Practice of the True Church of Christ* (4th ed.; Albany: The United Society [Shakers], 1856), p. 592. First edition, 1808; second, 1810; third, 1823.
100. *Ibid.,* p. iii.
101. *Ibid.,* p. 462.
102. *Ibid.,* pp. 460-62.
103. *Ibid.,* p. 462. Evidence abounded that the spiritual manifestations of the time fulfilled ancient prophecy that the last days had come. A new work of God was imminent.

> The work which God purposed to do in the latter days, was not to be according to the systems of human intervention known and understood among men; but was to be *a strange work;* and the act which he intended to bring to pass, was to be *a strange act,* even A MARVELOUS WORK AND A WONDER.

Ibid., p. xi.
104. Hudson, pp. 183-85.
105. *Ibid.,* pp. 122-24; F. E. Mayer, *The Religious Bodies of America* (St. Louis: Concordia Publishing House, c. 1961), pp. 371-86.
106. Mayer, p. 383.
107. Note that the influence of John Locke is at work here.
108. De Pillis, "Quest for Authority," p. 74.
109. *Ibid.,* p. 77.
110. "The Social Sources of Mormonism," CH, XXXVII, 1 (March, 1968), p. 72. Cf. also his "Quest for Authority."
111. Cf. Thomas F. O'Dea, *The Mormons* (Chicago: University of Chicago Press, c. 1957), p. 28, where he discusses the "slightly concealed revival meetings" in the Book of Mormon. He concludes that its revivalism is that of dignified New England. Wesley P. Walters, however, has called to the writer's attention the nature of Presbyterian revivalism during the 1820s, and the differences between it and the "New School" emotionalism that Charles Finney introduced after 1830. The pattern of the revival as James Hotchkin describes it is dignified and not at all the wild rantings and other emotional excesses depicted by Whitney Cross. The quieter pattern was at hand for Smith in western New York.

4

The Stage:
The Palmyra Region

Joseph . . . used to help us solve some portentous questions of moral or political ethics, in our juvenile debating club, . . . and subsequently, after catching a spark of Methodism in the camp meeting, away down in the woods, on the Vienna road, he was a very passable exhorter in evening meetings.

Orasmus Turner[1]

. . . some of us natives of Manchester have always been ashamed that Manchester gave Mormonism to the world . . .

Mitchell Bronk[2]

THE SMITH FAMILY[3]

The family of Joseph Smith, Jr. showed the same kind of religious dissent and political leaning that kept religious interest alive in western New England before, and during, after the first third of the 19th century.[4] Contrary to the reports that pictured them as an irreligious family, the Smiths showed a steady interest.

Asael Smith, grandfather of the Mormon prophet, was a Congregationalist in Topsfield, Massachusetts. When he moved his family to Tunbridge, Vermont, he left the Congregational Church and became a Universalist. This was 1797. This was the region where John Murray was establishing his brand of Universalism before and after the Revolutionary War. By this time Asael Smith found the churches' teachings irreconcilable with reason and scripture. When his son, Joseph, Sr., wanted to join the Methodist Church in Trumbull, Vermont, Asael threw Paine's *Age of Reason* at him and told him to read it.[5] In a letter to his children Asael Smith showed that he had a typical rationalistic viewpoint: he would not recommend a particular religious denomination to his children. Whatever church they might ultimately join, he wanted them to see if it were both scriptural and reasonable.[6]

Joseph Smith, Sr. joined the Universalist Church in Tunbridge along with his father and Jesse, his brother.[7] In spite of once inclining toward the Methodists, Joseph, Sr. had a vision that fully convinced him that no denomination "knew any more concerning the kingdom of God, than those of the world, or such as made no profession of religion whatever."[8]

The Mormon prophet's maternal side was Scotch Dissenter stock. Solomon Mack, his grandfather, came from a long line of clergymen. He saw visions in his old age and published his memoirs when he was 78. Jason, one of his sons, became a Seeker and established a semi-communistic community in New Brunswick with himself as economic and spiritual director.[9]

Before her marriage to Joseph Smith, Sr., Lucy Mack was pious, but unable to choose one church above another. She tried a Presbyterian church after she married Joseph, but was disappointed. Finally she was baptized, but only by a minister who did not insist upon her joining a particular denomination.[10]

Joseph, Jr. was almost eleven years old when the Smiths moved to Palmyra, N. Y. in 1816. Palmyra was then a town of almost 4000 people, prospering because of the construction of the Erie Canal.[11] Two years later they moved to a 100 acre farm two miles south of Palmyra and five miles northwest of Manchester. Manchester had a 600 volume library and a private circulating library.[12] Eight miles south of Manchester was Canandaigua, a county-seat. Through the years Palmyra boasted several book stores.[13]

The Smiths reflected that dissatisfaction with the standard churches so common among the pietistically trained, socially displaced population noted by De Pillis.[14] Critical of church divisions and the failure of the clergy to meet certain standards of piety, they satisfied their religious impulses apart from existing churches at times, at times uneasily within them.

UNIVERSALISTS AT LARGE

Palmyra was just above the Finger Lake region, right in the heart of that territory where the Universalists had planted 90 congregations. Their Unitarian argument generated so much concern that Abner Chase, the presiding Methodist Elder, spoke of Unitarian efforts in the Ontario District as almost successful enough to overthrow the entire "work of God in some Circuits on this District."[15] That was in 1820.

Joseph Smith, Jr. knew the Universalist argument from his father, and between his father and mother he got the pros and cons of rationalism and traditional Protestant orthodoxy. The arguments were also of public interest and were available in several forms. The *Universalist* was advertised in the *Wayne Sentinel* in the spring of 1825.[16] And although the young Joseph spent some of his time in 1825-26 in the Colesville, New York—Harmony, Pennsylvania area, the Newel Knight family, with whom he stayed in Colesville, was Universalist.

The charges tying Universalists to public discord seemed far fetched to many local inhabitants, but the indictment seemed well founded when it was applied to Robert Owen's colony at New Harmony, Indiana. When the *Wayne Sentinel* printed Owen's "Declaration of Mental Independence" speech, the fruits of half-way infidelity like Universalism seemed fully ripened, for Owen declared monstrous both private and individual property, and pronounced absurd the systems of religion (Christianity), and marriage (when it has some aspects of the first two evils).[17] Some were aware that this was a new generation of free thought, but the average person in the burned-over district took it as a resurgence of deism, a la Paine.

THE CHRISTIAN CONNECTION

It has been argued that Joseph Smith was greatly influenced by Campbellite theology through his association with Sidney Rigdon, a Campbellite minister.[18] John Locke's theology was thought to have found its way into Smith's thinking by way of Rigdon. Smith, however, picked up Locke's themes before he knew Rigdon through his familiarity with the arguments of deism, Universalism, and perhaps Locke himself.[19] Just as important was Smith's probable exposure to the Christians, or, as they were called, the Christian Connection.

Nearly one third of Christian Connection ministers were in New York in 1823. Twenty-five miles from Palmyra in West Bloomfield, the next township west, David Millard pastored a Connection church and edited the *Gospel Luminary*, whose greatest circulation was in the Finger Lakes area. By 1833 over 100 congregations were in New York.[20] Another congregation was located in Williamson, Wayne County, 15 miles from Palmyra. Oliver True was the minister at Winchester in 1826.[21] The *Gospel Luminary* also listed churches at Canandaigua (Philip Sanford, pastor); West Bloomfield (Millard); Mendon (Joseph Badger, pastor, assisted by Reuben Farley and James M'Grigor), Phelps (Benjamin Farley, pastor), and Rochester—all within a 25 mile radius of Palmyra.[22] Mendon, just ten miles from Palmyra, may have been a missionary base for Farley and M'Grigor.

Because a Presbyterian minister named Luckey attacked his views on the Trinity in 1818, David Millard responded with a 38 page tract and expanded it five years later into a book.[23] He held that Christ was a being separate from the Father (as our children are separate from us), but bore the nature of the One who begot him (as our children bear our nature). This "proper Son of God" existed and came into being before creation, and at the incarnation was *made* flesh. Therefore, he has only one nature, not both human and divine. Although the argument sounded like the Universalist or Unitarian view, it was a rejection of the Unitarian position.[24]

The Christian Connection influence disturbed David Marks, the Free-will Baptist itinerant evangelist, who had a recurring dread of the arguments for a uni-personal God. He visited the Connection church at Mendon when Badger, Farley and M'Grigor were there and heard a well-reasoned Unitarian argument in the sermon that left him in despair.

> I knew not what to believe of Jesus Christ. For the Unitarian arguments had so influenced my belief, and so formed the connection of my thoughts, that I supposed the doctrine that Jesus Christ is the true God, could not be proved from the scriptures.[25]

"My trials originated solely from my *Unitarian views* of the *character of Christ*."[26] Marks survived and returned to the orthodox position, but his experience illustrated the upsetting confusion that flourished in the region of Palmyra. This was Marks's territory.[27]

Joseph Smith's Unitarian position, then, may well have been his rejection of David Millard's emphasis. The purpose of the Book of Mormon, as stated on the Title Page, was to convince Jew and Gentile "that JESUS is the CHRIST, the ETERNAL GOD," a position that David Millard attacked and denied.

CORPSE OF DEISM

The fears of European meddling in American affairs subsided with the collapse of Napoleon, the defeat of Britain in the War of 1812, and the confident assertion of the Monroe Doctrine. Deism had been dispatched by the churches' counterattack, but the clergy continued to flay the corpse long after deism's demise.[28] The ghost of Tom Paine, as a result, kept turning up in the burned-over district. Each sighting of the ghost, as in the teachings of the Unitarians and Universalists, recalled the dreaded barbarity of the Jacobins. Newspaper editors in Palmyra and church journal editors passed them along.

The grim results of deism were spelled out in the "dying infidel" stories. One young man, beyond comfort because he had "rejected the Gospel," cried out on his deathbed:

> "Some years since, I unhappily read Paine's Age of Reason; it suited my corrupt understanding; I imbibed its principles; after this, wherever I went, I did all that lay in my power to hold up the Scriptures to contempt. . . . Paines's Age of Reason has ruined my soul."[29]

A year later a story with a happier outcome appeared. Paine's "'profane pages of "The Age of Reason," his plausible style . . . infused too successfully the poison of infidelity into the minds of many Americans.'" A New Jersey deistical society, for example, was enraged when the Second Great Awakening countered their messsge. The local society president persecuted the Christians, but his wife began to attend revival meetings. In 1808 he went with her. "'The infidel was reclaimed,—his society was broken up, and all around were obliged to confess this was the finger of God.'"[30]

Paine appeared again in the Palmyra paper after a five-year lapse, after the celebration of his birthday had begun. The *Wayne Sentinel* published an item about an unpublished manuscript of Paine's entitled *The Religion of the Sun* that turned up in the papers of Thomas Jefferson.[31] It also ran Benjamin Franklin's letter to "Thomas Payne" in which Franklin urged Paine not to publish *Age of Reason* because the country needed religion to keep it going.[32] These items were published in the same issues that covered the rising controversy over the disappearance of William Morgan, who had just published an expose of the Masonic Lodge.

Deism was also under attack from the tract societies. During the 1820s, auxiliary societies in western New York gave $14,732 for tracts from the American Tract Society.

> In the cities and large villages, and in many country towns, a systematic monthly distribution of tracts has been carried on, and the results have been highly

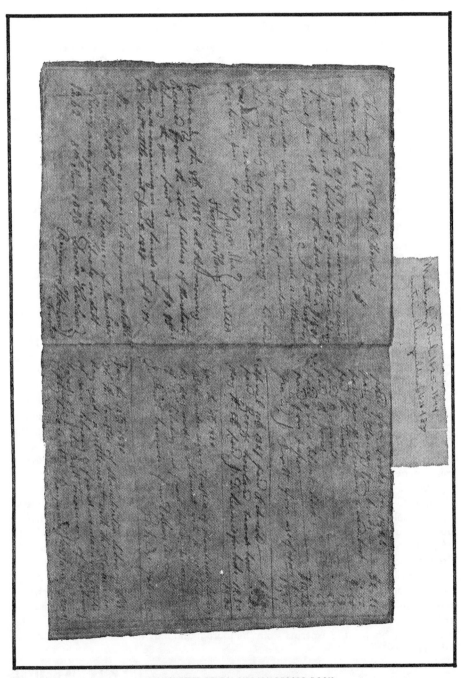

MANCHESTER RENTAL LIBRARY RECORD BOOK
Courtesy of Wesley P. Walters.

gratifying to the benevolent heart. . . . the system of *colportage* has to con-
siderable extent been adopted in Western New York.[33]

Palmyra had had an Auxiliary Missionary Society active at least since 1818.[34] The
Palmyra newspapers under Timothy Strong, Pomeroy Tucker, John Gilbert and Egbert
Grandin operated a bookstore and sold tracts. Tracts were printed for individual
distribution and also bound into annual volumes.

In July, 1824 the managers of the New York Tract Society (Methodist) issued a
report in which they described four new tracts published since the previous year. Tract
#46 was entitled "Three queries to deists."[35] The first query asked the deist reader how
he happened to renounce Christianity for deism. It suggested that the deist was living
an immoral life and used deistic thinking to justify himself.[36] He bolstered himself and
his position by winning others over to his way of thinking. But could this deist actually
promise peace of mind to those friends he might win to his side?

The second question had to do with consistency. Almost all deistic writers, it was
asserted, wrote favorably about Christianity.

> *Paine*, perhaps, has said as little in this way as any of your writers, yet he has
> professed respect for the character of Jesus Christ. "He was," says he, "a
> virtuous and an amiable man. The morality that he preached and practised was
> of the most benevolent kind."

Christian writers, the tract concluded, are not bothered with "these fits of inconsis-
tency."

The third query: why do deistical principles fail in the hour of death? Many
infidels, like Voltaire, died tormented that they might be facing judgment. But no
Christian, *"at the approach of death, was troubled or terrified in his conscience for
having been a Christian."* [37]

After its organization in 1825, the American Tract Society published 12 tracts
dealing with deism. It chose its selection from the publications of many tract societies
and some were extracted from anti-deistic books. Tract 123, "Leslie's Method with the
Deists," and Tract 374, "Short Method with A Skeptic," were based on Charles
Leslie's *A Short and Easy Method with Deists* (1805). This work emphasized the use of
miracles as an offensive weapon in the battle.[38]

In 1824 a revival surged through Palmyra, eventually involving the Palmyra Presbyterian Church and its pastor, Benjamin Stockton. On December 16, 1824, a meeting was held at the church to see about organizing a tract society.[39] Finally it was
done. As a testimony to Stockton's use of tracts during the revival that lasted into
1825, the women of his congregation made him a life-long member of the American
Tract Society.[40]

One of the journals cited by Whitney Cross was *The Methodist Magazine*, begun
in New York in 1818 and named after a counterpart in London. It offered articles,
missionary reports, statistics, testimonies, obituaries and theology. It covered the
revivals around the state and kept track of the fortunes of deism. The publishers of the
Palmyra papers printed excerpts from the journal and may have had it in their circulating library.

THE PALMYRA REVIVAL

Infidelity rose again. The favored response was still the revival, and from 1817 on revivals were a common feature of life in Palmyra.[41] In the 1820s the Palmyra news-papers printed reports of revivals throughout the state and elsewhere. Camp meeting notices, especially those of the Palmyra Methodist Church, were another indication of revival activity. In 1829 Methodist evangelist Lorenzo Dow preached to 3000 people in the field next to the Methodist Church, and in 1831 Charles Finney himself visited the community.[42]

The Methodists sponsored a revival in June, 1826, a mile from Palmyra. People came from as far as 100 miles away, so many that more than 100 tents were needed. From eight in the morning until nightfall, five sermons were preached. The five P. M. service featured a sermon that "contemplated the whole process of personal salva-tion, from its incipiency to its consummation in the world of light." The sermon electrified the crowd. Afterwards,

> the Rev. Goodwin Stoddard exhorted, and invited seekers within the circle of prayer in front of the stand. Hundreds came forward; some said nearly every unconverted person on the ground.[43]

The position of exhorter was a regular part of the service.

Orasmus Turner wrote of Joseph Smith that he had been a member of Palmyra's "juvenile debating club," helping to solve "some portentuous questions of moral or political ethics,"

> and subsequently, after catching a spark of Methodism in the camp meeting, away down in the woods, on the Vienna road, he was a very passable exhorter in evening meetings.[44]

Since Turner left Palmyra in 1822, this means that Smith had been involved in his middle teens and had participated in revival services right at home. The exhorter's job, to borrow terms from another vocation, was to "clinch the deal."

On September 15, 1824 a notice appeared in the *Sentinel* telling of a revival in progress.

> A reformation is going on in this town to a great extent. The love of God has been shed abroad in the hearts of many, and the outpouring of the Spirit seems to have taken a strong hold. About twenty-five have recently obtained a hope in the Lord, and joined the Methodist Church, and many more are desirous of becoming members.[45]

The Rev. George Lane, one of the leaders, wrote a report of this revival. It began in the spring of 1824 and broke out "afresh" on September 25-26, the time of the Methodist quarterly meeting. A young woman named Lucy Stoddard was converted and gave convincing testimony to many, but she died of typhus soon after. Many were with her at her death. She testified of her faith, sang a hymn, and died. Lane wrote: "The effect produced by this death was the happiest. While it confounded the infidel, it greatly strengthened believers, especially young converts."[46]

By October the Presbyterian Church was beginning to benefit from the revival. At that time the church was part of the Presbytery of Geneva, whose committee on the "State of Religion within the bounds of Geneva Presbytery" filed this report in February, 1825:

> In the congregation of Palmyra. . . . More than a hundred have been hopefully

METHODIST CAMP MEETING AT NIGHT IN THE 1830s
Courtesy of Cincinnati Historical Society

brought into the kingdom of the Redeemer. . . . Sabbath Schools, Bible classes, Missionary & Tract Societies are receiving unusual attention, & their salutary influence is apparent."[47]

It was this activity during this revival that led the Presbyterian Church to form a branch of the American Tract Society.

By September, 1825, the Palmyra revival brought 208 members to the Methodist Church, 99 to the Presbyterian and 94 to the Baptist.[48] It was only five years earlier that Methodist Elder Abner Chase had written that Unitarian (Universalist) efforts were about to swamp the entire "work of God" in the Palmyra vicinity.[49] The Palmyra revival, however, was another indication that infidelity could be defeated.

Charles Finney's estimate of what went wrong at the revivals held true in Palmyra, too. Joseph Smith found himself perplexed about the conflicting claims of who was right.[50] He was influenced by George Lane, but his mother, brothers Hyrum and Samuel, and sister Sophronia joined the Presbyterian Church. His father remained unaffiliated.[51]

Rather than choose the Methodist way, which would have judged the Presbyterian membership of the others as a gross error, Joseph Smith, Jr., like his father, remained apart. "Do not ask me to join them," he told his mother. "I can take my Bible, and go into the woods, and learn more in two hours, than you can learn at meetings in two years, if you should go all the time."[52] Nor could his father forget that when his eldest son, Alvin, died in November, 1823, the Presbyterian minister who conducted the funeral—probably Benjamin Stockton—strongly suggested that Alvin had gone to hell.[53]

That provides an easily understood reason for father and son to resist being swept along by the Palmyra revival of 1824. On September 25, the very day that George Lane reported that the revival "appeared to break out afresh," Joseph Smith, Sr. and some friends exhumed the body of Alvin—dead some ten months. Father Smith had heard rumors that Alvin's body had been "removed from the place of his interment and dissected." After proving to his satisfaction that the rumors were false he ran an ad to stop them.[54]

This could only reopen the wounds made by the insinuation that Alvin had gone to hell. It may explain why Joseph, Sr. and Joseph, Jr. did not join the Palmyra Presbyterian Church with the others.[55] It is also the probable reason why, when Joseph, Jr.'s mind was "awakened" by the revival preaching, it was the Methodist George Lane who aroused him, not the Rev. Benjamin Stockton of the Palmyra Presbyterian Church. The future prophet would attend many churches, but he shied away from committed membership.[56]

Revival sermons were designed to pull the brand from the burning. Testimonies (how sinners were led to faith); stories of Christians dying in hope of eternal life and of infidels dying in fear without hope; admonitions to forsake the evils of the day;[57] stories showing the dangers of unbelief—these were the grist for the revivalists' sermon mills. George Lane's preaching, according to Oliver Cowdery in his brief history of Smith, "was calculated to awaken the intellect" and Smith's mind "became awakened."[58] The anti-deistic polemic was part and parcel of the sermon material. From his report in *The Methodist Magazine*, Lane shows himself to have been very interested in confounding "the infidel." An earlier report shows him to have been capable of doing it.[59]

SUMMARY

The Palmyra papers reflect other developments during the period from 1818 to 1830. There is an emphasis on churches to minimize doctrinal differences, on clergy to be true to their calling, a mild but noticeable anti-Catholic polemic, and a rising interest in and finally obsession with the Masonic Lodge.

If the Morgan case could fan the fires of fear of Jacobin activity in an organization that seemed but a relic of the Infidel International, the reports of Robert Owen's debate with Alexander Campbell in Cincinnati in 1829, as featured in the *Wayne Sentinel*,[60] were further evidence that a defense based upon biblical revelation was necessary to preserve American and Christian freedoms.

The issues raised by Thomas Paine and others were to evoke from Joseph Smith an appeal to extra-biblical evidence to defend historical reporting and secondary testimony as valid revelation. That evidence would show the possibility of personally experienced revelation being available to all. It would demonstrate that the contents of biblical history were revealed as predictive prophecy and, therefore, were true revelations of that which was unknown to man.

The little town of Palmyra was not deaf to the voices of the times, for newspapers, church journals, sermons, tracts, and daily conversation were filled with items of current interest, and one of those items was the perceived menace of infidelity in its many forms.

FOOTNOTES

1. *Phelps and Gorham's Purchase*, p. 214.
2. Mitchell Bronk,"The Baptist Church at Manchester," *The Chronicle: A Baptist Historical Quarterly*, XI, 1 (January, 1948), p. 24. Bronk reported the memories of an old townsman.
3. This is not meant to be a complete coverage of the Smith's fortunes while they lived in the Palmyra area, but a tracing of the ways by which Joseph Smith would have become familiar with the influence of skepticism. For the complete coverage see Brodie and Lawrence Cardon Porter, "A Study of the Origins of the Church of Jesus Christ of Latter-day Saints in the States of New York and Pennsylvania, 1816-1831," unpublished doctoral thesis, Brigham Young University, 1971.
4. O'Dea, *The Mormons*, p. 7.
5. Hill, "Secular or Sectarian History," pp. 89-90 for citations of evidence.
6. *Ibid.*, p. 89.
7. Porter, p. 13, reproduced the articles of incorporation of the Tunbridge Universalist Church, which include the signatures of Asael, Joseph, Sr., and his brother Jesse. The document was attested December 6, 1797. Asael was the moderator of the congregation.
8. Lucy Mack Smith, *Biographical Sketches*, p. 58. This vision, however, is not in the earlier Lucy Smith manuscript transcribed by Martha Jane Coray.
9. *Ibid.*, p. 37.
10. *Ibid.*
11. Cf. the description of Palmyra, PH, June 19, 1822, p. 3, or in Brodie.
12. Brodie, p. 10. The remains of the old Manchester Rental Library with its Membership Record Book is in the basement of the Ontario County Historical Society in Canandaigua. The Record Book includes the date and book number of each book checked out to each number from 1826 into the 1840s. Each book has a number written on the Library Book Plate, so that one can discover who checked out what book and on what date. Some book titles are: William Wilberforce, *A Practical View of the Prevailing Religious System . . . Contrasted with Real Christianity*, 1799 edition, first published in England in 1797. It was in this book that the English evangelical dubbed Unitarianism a "half-way house" to "absolute infidelity." Another was Andrew Fuller's, *The Gospel Is Its Own Witness . . . Christian Religion Contrasted with the Absurdity of Deism*, Boston, 1803, the work of a noted Baptist theologian and pastor of the church at Kettering, England.
13. The T. C. Strong bookstore was operating in 1818 and ran a two column ad listing its books; PR, September 15, 1818. Leonard Westcott opened a store in 1821 and offered to take rags in payment for

books; WF, April 11, 1821. E. F. Marshall opened a new store in December, 1822; PH, December 4, 1822. Ads for bookstores in Canandaigua and Rochester also appeared. J. D. Evernghim operated a bookstore from October 1, 1823 to May, 1824; WS, October 1, 1823; May, 1824. Publishers of the Palmyra paper that went through a succession of name changes—Timothy C. Strong, Pomeroy Tucker, John H. Gilbert and Egbert G. Grandin—all operated a book store along with the printing business and also ran a circulating library.

14. De Pillis, "The Quest." Cf. also his "The Social Sources of Mormonism," CH, XXXVII, 1 (March, 1968), 50-79.

15. "Revival of Religion on Ontario District," MM, VII (November, 1824), p. 435.

16. WS, April 13, 1825.

17. WS, August 25, 1826.

18. Arbaugh, Revelation in Mormonism, passim.

19. Locke's works, particularly his Essay on Human Understanding which sets forth his view on revelation, were on sale in Palmyra bookstores. The work was also in the Manchester Rental Library and is recorded in the Record Book as one of its holdings. On January 31, 1844, Joseph Smith donated many books to the Nauvoo Library and Literary Institute. Among them were the essay by Locke and Parker's Lectures on Universalism. Cf. Kenneth W. Godfrey, "A Note on the Nauvoo Library and Literary Institute," BYUS, XIV, 1 (Spring, 1974), 389.

20. Cross, p. 263.

21. WS, October 8, 1823 carried a notice that True performed a marriage in Williamson.

22. Gospel Luminary, August, 1826.

23. David Millard, The True Messiah (Canandaigua, N. Y.: n. p., 1823).

24. Millard also held the Christian Connection emphasis that the Church of Christ was the only correct name for the Church.

25. Life of David Marks, p. 217.

26. Ibid., p. 219.

27. Marks and his wife were also befriended by Rachel Malin, successor to Jemima Wilkenson; Cross, p. 35.

28. Martin E. Marty analysed the usefulness of the "infidel" concept to the churches in his second chapter of The Infidel.

29. PR, July 12, 1820. Cf. also PH, July 17, 1822 for the miserable death of a profane man.

30. PR, February 7, 1821.

31. WS, August 25, 1826.

32. Ibid., August 4, 1826.

33. Hotchkin, pp. 261-62.

34. PR, August 19, 1818.

35. MM, VII (1824), p. 437.

36. This tract was reprinted under the title "Three Queries to the Rejecters of Christianity" and published as Tract #258 in The Publications of the America Tract Society (New York: American Tract Society, n. d. [1833?]), Vol. VIII.

37. WS, March 24, 1826. Tucker and Gilbert advertised tracts from the New York Tract Society. Christian Almanacks for 1824, reprinted from the Boston edition and published by the American Tract Sociaty were on sale at the J. D. Evernghim & Company book store, 48 pages for ten cents. This makes it likely that the store also carried tracts from the same firm; WS, October 8, 1823.

38. Charles Leslie, A Short and Easy Method with Deists, wherein the Certainty of the Christian Religion is Demonstrated by Infallible Proofs from Four Rules, in a Letter to a Friend, New American Edition (Cambridge: n. p., 1805).

39. WS, December 15, 1824.

40. Ibid., December 15, 1826.

41. Hotchkin, p. 378, records revivals for the Palmyra Presbyterian Church for 1817, 1824, and 1829. There were others in neighboring towns in other years. Wesley P. Walters has presented the most thorough discussion of the revivals during this period and in this region in "New Light on Mormon Origins from the Palmyra Revival," Dialogue, IV, 1 (Spring 1969), 60-81. Another important study, though less well researched, is Milton V. Backman's "Awakenings in the Burned-over District: New Light on the Historical Setting of the First Vision," BYUS, X, 3 (Spring, 1969), 301-20.

42. WS, August 28, 1829; Palmyra Reflector, February 1, 1831.

43. Z. Paddock, ed., Memoir of Rev. Benjamin G. Paddock (New York: Nelson & Phillips, 1875), p. 181; cf. pp. 177-81. In 1819 a camp meeting was held in Carpenter's Notch:

> Among the effective efforts from the stand of this meeting was a sermon from M. Pearce and an exhortation from G. Lane. The sermon was well argued, and closed under a high degree of excitement which electrified the whole encampment. The exhortation was a melting and overwhelming appeal to the unconverted. Many hardened sinners yielded to the call and were converted.

George Peck, *Early Methodism within the Bounds of the Old Genesee Conference from 1788 to 1828* (New York: Carlton & Porter, 1860), pp. 314-15. Cf. also MM, V (1822), 474-75 for the account of camp meetings where the sequence is preaching followed by exhortation and prayer.

44. Turner, p. 214. In "An Account of a Camp-Meeting Held in Telfair County, Geo.,"MM, VII (1824), 436, another note in the role of the exhorter is struck:

> It was common for these young converts, as soon as they felt the pardoning love of God, to rise and declare what God had done for their souls, and conclude by exhorting sinners to seek salvation. Among others, there were several children from twelve to fourteen years of age, earnestly engaged in exhorting their friends to fly to Jesus.

Smith's exhorting may have been closer to the Georgia camp meeting. His age range would have matched, and the unofficial nature of the children's exhorting was acceptable because it fit into the structure of preaching, exhortation, and prayer.

45. WS, September 15, 1824.
46. MM, VIII (1825), p. 160. Cf. the entire letter pp. 158-61.
47. Geneva Presbytery, "Records," October 5, 1824 and February 1, 1825, Book D, pp. 16, 27ff. Cited in Walters, "New Light on Mormon Origins," pp. 64-65, 76, nn. 25, 29.
48. Cf. n. 51, p. 66; cf. pp. 64-67 for full report. Walters produced a definitive report in his article.
49. Cf. n. 15 above.
50. He wrote into his DHC, I, 3 that when the revival was over and the

> converts began to file off, some to one party and some to another, it was seen that the seemingly good feelings of both the priests and the converts were more pretended than real; for a scene of great confusion and bad feelings ensued—priest contending against priest, and convert against convert . . . in a strife of words and contest about opinion.

Joseph's mother wrote that it was this that caused her son to reflect seriously upon divided Christendom: "While these things were going forward, Joseph's mind became considerably troubled with regard to religion"; *Biographical Sketches*, p. 74.

This sentence may not be hers. Her history of her son was transcribed by a Nauvoo school teacher, Martha Jane Coray The first manuscript of Lucy Smith's history is all but vanished. A fragment is in the Brigham Young University Library vault. A second manuscript is in the LDS Church Archives in Salt Lake City. In 1975 it was closed to public view to all but Dr. Richard L. Anderson, who was preparing to publish it, but this writer was allowed to check a few things. It appears that Orson Pratt published a third and later version, written mostly by Howard Coray with some sections probably in Martha's handwriting, which became *Biographical Sketches* in 1853.

The second manuscript is quite different from the published version. For example, the published version places Joseph's anxiety over religion after a notice of a revival that raised religious contention to a fevered pitch and which followed Joseph, Sr.'s seventh vision. By contrast, the second manuscript does not refer to the elder Smith's visions. And instead of a revival introducing the comment on the son's anxiety, the setting is a family discussion on the diversity of churches. *There is no revival in the second manuscript!*

Finally, the comment on Joseph, Jr.'s anxiety in the 1853 edition is followed by the story of the First Vision, where two personages appear to the future prophet. This is simply inserted from the 1838 *History* at this point in the 1853 edition. Again by contrast, the First Vision is *missing entirely* from the second manuscript. Instead it has the family discussion about the diversity of churches followed by the *1823 vision of the angel Moroni.*

Dr. Jan Shipps first alerted this writer to this feature of the second manuscript, and now this writer confirms it: where Martha Jane Coray's second manuscript differs from Smith's *History*, it appears that Howard Coray chose the DHC and set aside the words of Lucy Mack Smith. If Dr. Anderson should publish the entire second manuscript rather than just edit it, this feature should be prominent.

The story Joseph Smith, Jr. told about his anxiety over sectarian rivalry seen during a revival, followed by his prayer of faith and then the First Vision, has traditionally been dated in 1820. This has become one of the more important aspects of Mormon origins challenged by Walters's study. He contends that no such revival took place in 1820 as Smith described it, but that it did in 1824.

Walters was answered in a roundtable discussion by Richard L. Bushman, "The First Vision Story Revived," *Dialogue*, IV, 1 (Spring, 1969), 82-93; also by Backman, "Awakenings," and by Hill, "Secular or Sectarian History," pp. 82-83. Walters replied back to Bushman in the same issue of *Dialogue*, pp. 94-100. Unfortunately, Bushman, Backman, and Hill all seem to have responded to an earlier version of Walters's article, apparently unaware that Walters had revised the earlier version for this roundtable, anticipating their arguments and responding to them.

51. According to his wife, he continued to contend "for the ancient order, as established by our Lord and Saviour Jesus Christ, and his Apostles," *Biographical Sketches*, pp. 56-57.

52. *Ibid.*, p. 90.

53. In an interview with E. C. Briggs, DN, January 20, 1894, the prophet's younger brother, William, said it was Stockton. The DHC in the manuscript version carries a dedication at the very beginning: "In Memory of Alvin Smith Died this[?] 17[?]th Day of November In the 25t year of his age year 1823," and is signed by Joseph Smith. Cf. "Manuscript History of the Church," Book A-1, located in the LDS Church Archives, Salt Lake City. That, and a statement that he had been assured that Alvin had been saved, DHC, II, p. 380, are indications that Stockton's charge had bothered him even in his later years.

54. WS, September 29, 1824.

55. Another factor may have been the way people in the burned-over district perceived Universalists, and vice-versa. Presbyterians who regarded his father's views as worthy of an outlaw could only create conflict. Still another aspect may have been spelled out in a romantic novel based on the diaries of a woman who lived in Palmyra during this period and whose grandson used them to construct the novel. In it the Palmyra Presbyterian Church is pictured as the church attended by the town leaders who controlled the economic destiny of the community. Cf. Samuel Hopkins Adams, *Canal Town* (Toronto: Random House, 1944).

56. The old townsman of Manchester told Mitchell Bronk, p. 24, that

> Joe occasionally attended the stone church; especially the revivals, sitting with the crowd—the "sinners"—up in the gallery. Not a little of Mormon theology accords with the preaching of Elder Shay.

Note that this could well have been during the Palmyra Revival of 1824-25. The Rev. Anson Sha was a charter member of the Manchester Rental Library and likely had read Andrew Fuller's *The Gospel Is Its Own Witness* noted above, for Fuller was a prominent Baptist theologian who also authored the "Three queries to deists" noted above. It was another way for the anti-deistic message to be absorbed. In support of the old townsman's recollection, Fayette Lapham visited Joseph Smith, Sr. in 1830. Smith told Lapham that Joseph, Jr. had been baptized in the Baptist Church. Cf. "The Mormons," *Historical Magazine* (New Series), VII, 5 (May, 1870), p. 306.

57. Such evils as drinking beer and liquor, sabbath breaking, gambling, spiritual sloth, levity, and free thought.

58. MA, December, 1834, p. 42. This history was written with Smith's cooperation.

59. Cf. n. 47 above.

60. "Mr. Owen and Mr. Campbell," WS, June 19 & 26, 1829.

5

Lost: The Indians' Book of God

They have two flat sticks about one foot long, tied together, on which are several characters, which they say, the Great Father gave to their prophet, and mean as much as a large book.

W. W. Phelps[1]

. . . his fathers in this country had not long since had a book which they had *for a long time preserved*. But having lost the knowledge of reading it it . . . they buried it with an Indian chief.

Ethan Smith[2]

When a white missionary brought a request to the Six Nations for permission to work among the Indians in the region, the chiefs called a council to consider it and asked Seneca Chief Red Jacket to speak for them. "You have got our country, but are not satisfied; you want to force your religion upon us," he told the missionary. "We understand that your religion is written in a book," Red Jacket continued.

If it was intended for us, as well as you, why has not the Great Spirit given to us . . . and to our forefathers the knowledge of that Book, with the means of understanding it rightly? If there is but one religion, why do you white people differ so much about it?[3]

The year was 1805.

Thomas Paine had asked some of the same questions in his critique of Christianity. In the Book of Mormon Joseph Smith offered some answers to such questions as he tried to convince the Indians that "Jesus is the CHRIST, the ETERNAL GOD." But why did he write a scripture with the Indians cast in the starring roles? How could they be used to defend God against the forces of popular deism? Why did he use them to project his theology? When seen against Smith's environment and the sources on which he drew, these questions are thrown into sharp relief. But even as the sources are considered, the main concern is the "why."

THE ONLY GOOD INDIANS ARE DEAD

The growth of America has always involved the fate of the original inhabitants and has often made the Indian factor of international importance. The Indians wiped out an American force of 1400 men at a battle on the Wabash River in the Northwest Territory in 1791 and exposed the Canadian border. In 1811 the Indian leader Tecumseh led his forces to defeat at the Battle of Tippecanoe. When Tecumseh sought refuge with the British in Canada, many American politicians blamed the British for the Indian uprising. This became one of the factors that led to war with Britain in 1812.

Once a region became U. S. territory, a period of upheaval and relocation set in. Land agents bought land from Indian tribes. Reservations were established for those Indians who wished to remain within U. S. boundaries. White settlements sprang up around the Indians and cultural contact brought pressure upon the Indian way of life. Eventually, if not as soon as the transition began, the majority of tribes moved west of the U. S. borders.

In western New York of the 1820s, the process had almost been completed. Immediately after the Revolutionary War the Phelps and Gorham Purchase carved out the future home of the Smith family.[4] The land abounded in Indian relics. This was the country of the Six Nation Federation of the Iroquois tribes: Mohawks, Oneidas, Inondagas, Cayugas, Senecas, and the Tuscaroras further south. Centuries before, after a series of fearful battles that failed to determine supremacy, they united to end the almost constant state of warfare. They left in their wake palisaded forts, one chain of which extended to Pennsylvania 50 miles away. The Palmyra region also had Indian mounds. Through the 1820s the Indian fortunes were featured in the Palmyra papers.

The burial mounds excavated near Cuyahoga River in Ohio, another in Virginia, and still others in Fredonia, N. Y. and Worthington, O.; rock inscriptions found in or near Dighton, Mass., Pompey, N. Y., and Washington County, Missouri; a tomb in Tennessee and an excavation near Schenectady, N. Y. provided both concrete knowledge of Indians and much room for speculation.[5]

From the mounds came skeletal remains of a man judged to be 7'4" tall, an embalmed corpse with auburn hair and facial contours that were neither Indian nor Spanish,[6] artifacts that were both Indian and European.[7] Rock inscriptions revealed a public edict of Pope Leo X dated in 1520 inscribed in Latin with strange symbols,[8] hieroglyphics on Dighton's Writing Rock only much later translated,[9] and artwork in Missouri that little resembled "the rude sketches made by the Indians of the present day."[10]

A Mr. Miller opened the mound at Worthington, O. in 1810. Indians living nearby told Miller that the mounds had been there longer than anyone could remember, even the tribes that had been there before them. The writer of the article conjectured that the human remains "found in these mounds must have been . . . of human beings inhabiting the country, of whom the Indians had no knowledge."[11]

The reporter who wrote of Pope Leo's edict speculated concerning the first settlers of North America. They were probably Asiatics, descendants of Shem, son of Noah, who crossed the Pacific to settle in North America. The descendants of Japheth, Shem's brother, settled in Europe and then crossed the Atlantic, driving the Shemites into South America. He supported this with the observation that the language, manners, and customs of the South American Indians resembled those of Europeans. "What wonderful catastrophe destroyed at once the first inhabitants, with the species of the mammoth, is beyond the researches of the best scholar and greatest antiquarian."[12]

What wonderful catastrophe? The reporter concluded from the Latin inscription and other discoveries

> that this country was once inhabited by a race of people, at least, partially civilized, & that this race has been exterminated by the forefathers of the present and late tribes of Indians in this country.[13]

Dr. Edmund James of the U. S. Army, who reported the inscribed rocks in Missouri, wrote of the

> departure of that forgotten race of men who left their emblematic inscriptions to commemorate some event in their history; perhaps, "Their own heroic deeds, and hapless fall," and the commencement of the flight to the west before the barbarians who have exterminated their arts and remembrance.[14]

The reality of the current Indian tribes did not match what the mounds, tombs and inscriptions seemed to reveal.

In his four volume *Travels in New England and New York,* Timothy Dwight's description of the Iroquois reflected this picture. From the information he gleaned, the Mohicans considered themselves the original inhabitants and the Iroquois interlopers. The Iroquois admitted it and gloried in it, "asserting that they had fought their way to their present possessions, and acquired their county by conquering all who had resisted them."[15] Their savage spirit was enough for them to conquer any tribe, according to Dwight. This fall to the Iroquois was celebrated by James Fenimore Cooper's *The Last of the Mohicans* in 1826, available in the *Wayne Sentinel* bookstore in Palmyra.[16]

As they watched the remnants of once powerful tribes straggle westward to relocation areas, the whites of western New York compared their pitiful condition with what they thought the former inhabitants were like. The *Wayne Sentinel* reprinted an article from the *Batavia Peoples' Press* that summed up the speculation. It seemed that the former civilization was nearly as developed as that of the whites. It was pictured as a powerful, civilized, politically advanced nation that God or disease had decimated for some heinous, national sins. But who really knew? "There appears to be a gap in the history of the world, as far as relates to them, which can never be closed up."[17]

Thomas Jefferson said of the corpse from the Tennessee tomb, that it was "a relic of a civilized people who formerly inhabited this country—but who, ages since ceased to be."

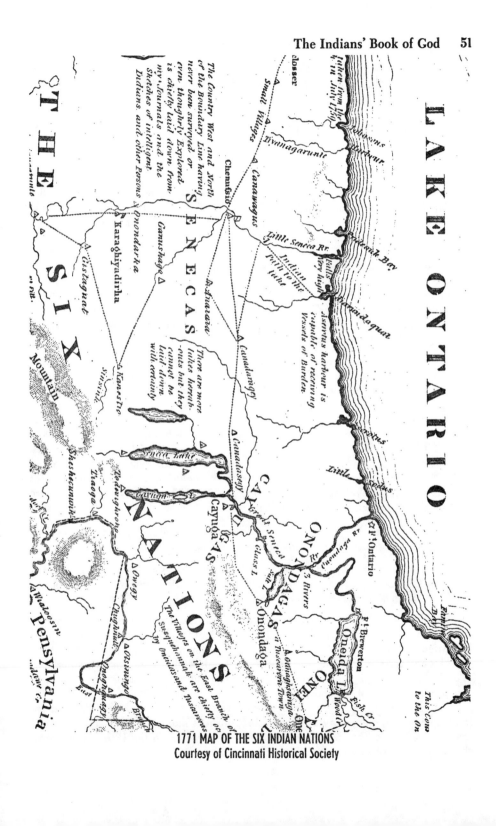

1771 MAP OF THE SIX INDIAN NATIONS
Courtesy of Cincinnati Historical Society

Who they were—from whence they sprung—and what was their destiny—remains locked up in the womb of the past, one of those inscrutable events which defy human ken or human examination; which loom up on the far-off ocean of by-gone years, with enough of reality about them to convince us that they are no fiction, but yet clothed with an indistinctiveness which defies investigation. The origin, the history, the destiny of that people, together with the cause of their extinction, is . . . "consigned to the receptacle of things forever lost upon earth."[18]

Civilized Indians wiped out by the barbarians that remain! That lent truth to the frontier axiom given a slight twist: all the good Indians were dead. The Indian as a hostile savage is painted clearly in the Palmyra press.[19] Indians massacre whites.[20] It is tragic for white women to fall captives to Indian savages, but wonderful if they are rescued.[21] Children captured and raised by Indians might be returned to their parents, but will always remain Indian.[22] Indians fought with each other so much on the river heading west out of Pittsburgh to the Mississippi that it was called the "Ohio," which means the "Bloody," or "War River."[23] Even the Cherokees, who had long been regarded as one of the most Christianized Indian nations, threatened to kill their own delegates to a peace conference upon their return from Washington, because they did not like the treaty the delegates had signed.[24]

Colonial attitudes toward the Indians were still present in the 19th century. There was the desire to get their lands and not have them around: kill or drive them away. But there was also a guilty awareness that this was wrong, and a sense of obligation was felt: convert and civilize them, or at least civilize them.[25]

In the early 19th century the government tried first to civilize the Indians. Christian missions were the means. If that failed, there was always the alternative. In 1820 John C. Calhoun, Secretary of War, held up to Congress the Cherokees, Choctaws, Wyandots, Senecas, and Shawnees as prime examples of what civilization could do.[26] In 1820-21 Congress granted over $16,000 to establish mission schools in several states and carried that policy through the twenties.[27] By 1824 twenty-one schools were supported in this manner and by 1826 there were thirty-eight.[28]

The readers of the Palmyra papers followed the civilizing process. In 1821 a report from the Brainard mission among the Cherokees concluded:

It no longer remains a doubt whether the Indians of America can be civilized— the Cherokees have gone too far in the pleasant path of civilization to return to the rough and unbeaten track of savage life.[29]

Another report from the same tribe urged Christians to "pursue the labour of love which we have commended, . . . and the Indian will become temperate and industrious."[30] As proof of the gospel's power to civilize, an article reported that the Oneidas had formed an agricultural society.[31] A notice that Bibles were being printed in an Indian language, and that they were bringing Indians to Christianity, was therefore printed with a note of approval.[32]

The motivation for this missionary effort was that the whites had mistreated the Indians by driving them away, and the best reparations that could be offered was what the missionaries had to give.[33] Another motive—prominent in the 19th century—was that Christ had ushered in "the millennial morn."

Why are kings become nursing fathers and queens nursing mothers,—why are the nations flinging away their gods and asking for the True God and the Bible, and why are all civilized nations aroused to relieve the miseries of the heathen, if the set time to favour Zion is not come?[34]

Still, there were some disclaimers. Red Jacket had opposed missionaries among his people, but others invited them in. He wrote his assessment of the results in a letter in 1821. The introduction of preachers "has created great confusion among us, and is making us a quarrelsome and divided people." Whenever the Black Coats get their consent to come in, he wrote, "confusion and disorder are sure to follow; & the encroachments of the whites upon our lands, are the invariable consequences." The preachers "were the forerunners of their dispersion." Indians quarreling, whites plundering, Indian population decreasing—all this happened in "proportion to the numbers of preachers that came among them." Red Jacket feared "that these preachers, by, and by, will become poor, and force us to pay them for living among us, and disturbing us."[35]

Contact with Indian tribes and antiquities led some to conclude that no one would ever discover the origin of the Indians and the lost race. Others were more optimistic. In September, 1825 Mordecai M. Noah, prominent in publishing and political circles in New York, dedicated the City of Ararat as a refuge for world Jewry. He issued a proclamation to that effect and delivered a speech setting forth the rationale of the enterprise. He had an answer as to the origin of the Indians and their predecessors.

In their manners, customs and "admitted Asiatic origin," he proclaimed, the Indians were "in all probability the descendants of the lost tribes of Israel."

Measures will be adopted to make them sensible   of their origin, to cultivate their minds, soften their condition and finally re-unite them with their brethren the chosen people.[36]

His speech was printed in the two following issues of the *Wayne Sentinel* and provided further comment:

The discovery of the lost tribes of Israel, has never ceased to be a subject of deep interest to the Jews. That divine protection which has been bestowed upon the chosen people . . . has, without doubt, been equally extended to the missing tribes, and if, as I have reason to believe, our lost brethren were the ancestors of the Indians of the American Continent, the inscrutable decrees of the Almighty have been fulfilled in spreading unity and omnipotence in every quarter of the globe. . . . It is . . . probable that from the previous sufferings of the tribes in Egyptian bondage, that they bent their course in a northwest direction, which brought them within a few leagues of the American continent, and which they finally reached.

Those who are most conversant with the public and private economy of the Indians, are strongly of opinion that they are the lineal descendants of the Israelites, and my own researches go far to confirm me in the same belief.[37]

Then Noah listed the similarities between the Indians and Jews that tended to support the identification. He concluded his point as follows:

Should we be right in our conjecture, what new scenes are opened to the nation

—the first of people in the old world, and the rightful inheritors of the new? Spread from the confines of the northwest coast of Cape Horn, and from the Atlantic to the Pacific.

If the tribes could be brought together, could be made sensible of their origin, could be civilized, and restored to their long lost brethren, what joy to our people, what glory to our God, how clearly have the prophecies been fulfilled, how certain our dispersion, how miraculous our preservation, how providential our deliverance.[38]

Mordecai M. Noah drew upon a theory that had been believed for several hundred years.[39] Jewish sailors on Columbus's ships took the belief back to Spain. It was picked up by a rabbi in the mid-17th century, promulgated in English,[40] believed by both Catholics and Puritans, accepted and acted upon by prominent American clergymen, and set forth in a series of books in the first part of the 19th century.[41] It was almost always tied into some aspect of belief in the millennium. It was a subject of current debate among members of the New York Historical Society[42] and was currently available in books by Elias Boudinot and Ethan Smith.

Ethan Smith's ministerial career from 1750 to 1840 was enlisted in the struggle against Thomas Paine's brand of popular deism. His *View of the Hebrews*[43] was his major contribution to the cause of biblical revelation's validity. The book came out first in 1823 and then, revised and enlarged, in two printings in 1825. It was widely available in New England and New York.

Ethan Smith made his book a tract presenting the millennial hope that the conversion of the Indians would help usher in the thousand year reign of Christ. It was a sermon urging Christian America to evangelize the Indians. A literalistic approach to the restoration passages of the Old Testament, particularly those of Isaiah and Jeremiah, led the author to look for their fulfillment just before the impending millennium.

Smith thought he had discovered the fate of Israel's lost tribes, where they were and what had befallen them. By distinguishing between the Jews as *dispersed* and the ten tribes as *outcast*,[44] God "surely must have provided a place for their safe keeping as a distinct people, in some part of the world, during that long period."[45] But where were they?

He found many clues as to their present location in the Old Testament and Apocrypha. Jeremiah 30-31 speaks of Ephraim (the ten tribes) as scattered to the "coasts of the earth" in the "north country." Ephraim was in the "isles afar off," which signifies any land over "great waters."[46] 2 Esdras 13 declares that the ten tribes went north from Palestine past Armenia, bound for a land where no man had dwelt since the Flood.[47] Amos 8:11-12 speaks of the tribes' wandering from the north to the east, from sea to sea, when the famine of hearing the words of the Lord is in the land.[48]

Smith drew such tight parallels between the Indians and the Hebrews that no other conclusion could be drawn: they were one and the same. The parallels are made to show that the same conclusion he drew from a speech by Montezuma might be applied to the North American Indians; namely, events in pagan mythology may be confused and blended with fable, yet some of them "can easily be traced to ancient revelation."[49]

Smith concluded that those Israelite tribes which cultivated civilized ways separated from those which depended on hunting. The hunters gradually forgot about their common ancestry and waged frightful wars upon the others. After many centuries, the civilized tribes were finally overcome and destroyed. Thus would be explained the forts, mounds, and vast enclosures that pre-dated Columbus's discovery—ruins that had no connection with the current Indian population. In this way Ethan Smith accounted for abandoned Indian cities along the Ohio to the Mississippi, estimated by Caleb Atwater to be almost 5000 in number.[50] The ruins and artifacts were eloquent witnesses of the builders' extirpation.

> And nothing appears more probable than that they were the better part of the Israelites who came to the continent . . . while the greater part of their brethren became savage and wild. No other hypothesis occurs to mind, which appears by any means so probable.[51]

Sure of the Indian-Israelite identification, Smith argued for their literal restoration to Palestine to correspond to their literal expulsion. Zechariah 8:7 speaks of the Lord saving His people from the east country and west country. Since none in a west country were restored to the land of Israel in the return from Babylon, Smith deduced that the west country must refer to America. This showed, he thought, "that the thing predicted was distinct from and future of that event."[52]

The restoration is both future and literal, for that following the Babylonian Captivity was followed centuries later by expulsion at the hands of the Romans. "But after the restoration here promised," Smith reminded, "God says 'They shall no more be pulled up out of their land.'"[53] Ethan Smith, accordingly, awaited a restoration for the lost tribes of Israel—the Indians—that was both future and literal.

One of the most important traditions used to prove this theory was that of a lost book. The Indians told of

> a book which God gave, was once theirs; and then things went well with them. But other people got it from them, and then they fell under the displeasure of the Great Spirit; but that they shall at some time regain it.[54]

He quoted Elias Boudinot, who derived from good Indian authority

> that the book which the white people have was once theirs. That while they had this book, things went well with them; they prospered exceedingly; but that other people got it from them; that the Indians lost their credit; offended the Great Spirit, and suffered exceedingly from the neighboring nations; and that the Great Spirit then took pity on them, and directed them to this country.[55]

Smith cited the Indian tradition that once they lived "away in another country, had the old divine speech, the book of God; they shall at some time have it again, and shall   then   be happy."[56] He passed along the report of a conversation between a missionary and the wife of a Cherokee chief, who told him when she was old,

> that when she was a small child, the old people used to say that good people would come to instruct the Cherokees at some future period; and that perhaps she and others of her age would live to see the day. And now she thought that, perhaps, we and the other missionaries had come to give them that instruction. This traditionary opinion, among the different tribes . . . it seems, must have been handed down from ancient prophecy of their restoration.[57]

The Pittsfield Parchment story was the most important evidence produced to support the stories of the Indians' lost book.[58] Joseph Merrick of Pittsfield, Massachusetts owned land on "Indian Hill" where he discovered a blank leather strap, sewn with sinews, containing dark yellow leaves of an old parchment. He brought them to the Rev. Mr. Sylvester Larned of Pittsfield in 1815.[59] Larned discovered the standard texts of a Jewish phylactery on the leaves. He wrote Merrick a letter with his translation of the Hebrew script[60] and then took the leaves to Cambridge for further examination. There he left them with a Dr. Eliot, who died soon after.

When Ethan Smith learned of this, he visited Pittsfield to find evidence that a Jew had lived there, but found none. So he went to Boston to have the leaves' existence verified by the scholars who had seen them. The Rev. Mr. Jenks told him that the leaves were in the care of the Antiquarian Society of Worcester and that Dr. Holmes, the Hebrew professor, had examined them.

Holmes told Smith of his careful examination and the correctness of Larned's translation. And Worchester's Dr. Thomas, president of the society, knew of such a leaf and assumed that it was in the society archives. Several hours' search, however, failed to uncover it. As a result, Ethan Smith had only an interview and an interesting story to show for his wild goose chase.

He believed in the existence of the parchment leaves, but it could be proved only by the testimony of their discoverer, by the three who examined and translated them, and by six men who had heard of them. The six were: Dr. Griffin, president of Williams College, who heard the story from Elias Boudinot, first president of the American Bible Society,[61] who related it by letter to Ethan Smith; Dr. Humphrey, Larned's successor at the church in Pittsfield; Mr. J. Everts of Boston, who told Smith that the leaves were at the Worcester location; Dr. James, who was living in Pittsfield when the leaves were found; and Dr. Thomas of the Worcester Antiquarian Society, who conducted a fruitless search for them.

The last report of a lost book immediately followed the Pittsfield Parchment story. An old Indian told the Rev. Mr. Stockbridge

> that his fathers in this country had not long since had a book which they had *for a long time preserved.* But having lost the knowledge of reading it . . . they buried it with an Indian chief.[62]

Smith combined the two accounts of the Pittsfield Parchment and the Stockbridge book buried with the chief. He concluded that this was the kind of evidence one might expect to connect the Indians with Israel. The parchment leaves seemed obviously Indian, for Jews buried their old or illegible phylacteries and Bible pages in a sheet of paper. They would never have used animal sinews for thread. The whole episode, Smith thought,

> might have been thus safely brought down to a period near to the time when the natives last occupied *Indian Hill,* in Pittsfield; perhaps in the early part of the last century.[63]

The Israelite identity of the American Indians offered America a profound opportunity. According to Smith's view of Isaiah 18, Isaiah was appealing to the future European Christian stock in America to restore the Gospel to the outcast Israelite-Indian tribes.[64] After such restoration, which included the return of the Bible to the

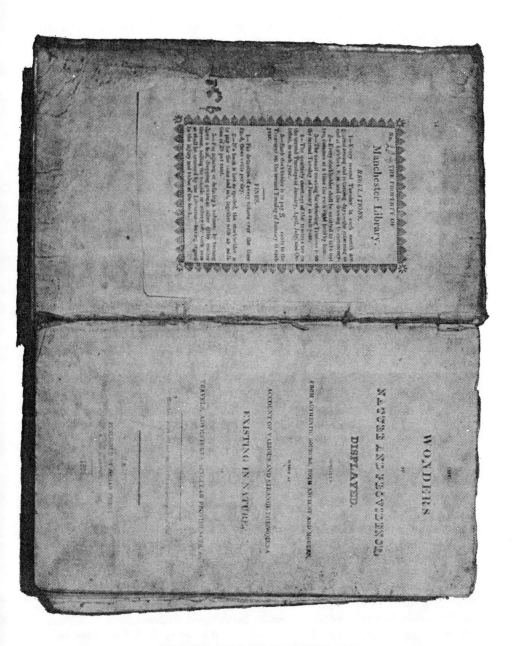

Josiah Priest's 1825 book with excerpt from Ethan Smith's *View of the Hebrews*. Courtesy of Wesley P. Walters.

Indians, the American Christians would be able to Christianize them. Smith had God say through Isaiah:

> were not your fathers sent into that far distant world, not only to be (in their posterity) built up a great protecting nation; but also to be the instruments of gathering, or recovering the miserable remnant of my *outcasts* there, in the last days?[65]

By converting the Indians, the Christians could help inaugurate the millennium.

Smith spelled out the theory's apologetic value in the on-going debate with the skeptics. "New evidence is hence furnished of the divinity of our holy scriptures . . . striking characteristics are found of the truth of ancient revelations."[66] Smith had met the infidel on what he considered fair ground and challenged him to explain the phenomena otherwise.

> Whence their ideas that their ancestors once had the book of God; and then were happy; but that they lost it; and then became miserable; but that they will have this book again at some time?[67]

Israel's outcast state is new evidence of the divinity of the Old Testament, Smith claimed, and also of the New. The restoration of the ten tribes would confound infidelity. Indian traditions were beginning to exhibit the new evidence, "a powerful evidence of the truth of revelation."[68] The preservation of the Jews was a

> kind of standing miracle in support of the truth of revelation. . . . But the arguments furnished from the *preservation and traditions* of the tribes, in the wilds of America from a much longer period, must be viewed as furnishing, if possible, a more commanding testimony.[69]

The Indian-Israelite identification confounded popular deism. God is vindicated! The Bible is true!

The Pittsfield Parchment story seemed to prove that the Indians had once possessed the Old Testament, and the story may well have circulated in the Palmyra region years before Ethan Smith's second edition of 1825. Sylvester Larned and Elias Boudinot were the two men responsible for the story's getting to Ethan Smith. Larned was a young, well-known preacher in the Congregational Church. In 1817 and 1818 he preached in the Canandaigua Congregational Church,[70] raising the possibility that the Pittsfield Parchment story was used and passed along by word of mouth seven to eight years before Ethan Smith's 1825 edition reached the Palmyra area.

Elias Boudinot, long active in Indian affairs before he came to head the American Bible Society in 1816, visited Palmyra for a lecture at the City Hotel in 1820.[71] In 1816 he had used the Indian-Israelite identification in his *Star in the West* to combat deism. His lecture, his probable use of the Pittsfield Parchment story to bolster the Bible, and the possible sale of his book could have gotten the story circulating at least five years before Ethan Smith's book. Abner Chase had reported that the Palmyra vicinity was in danger of being overrun by Unitarianism (Universalism), and Boudinot well knew the potential impact of the story for increasing the value of the Indian-Israelite theory as a weapon for battling skepticism.

Joseph Smith in his teens was, according to his mother, a thoughtful young man, and was inclined to ponder life's issues. He could take current topics of interest and

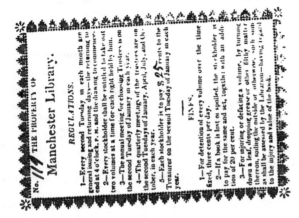

PERSONAL NARRATIVE

OF

TRAVELS

TO

THE EQUINOCTIAL REGIONS

OF THE

NEW CONTINENT,

DURING THE YEARS

1799—1804.

BY ALEXANDER DE HUMBOLDT

AND

AIMÉ BONPLAND.

Written in French by

ALEXANDER DE HUMBOLDT,

And translated into English by

HELEN MARIA WILLIAMS.

PHILADELPHIA:

PUBLISHED BY M. CAREY, NO. 121 CHESNUT STREET.

Dec 23 1815.

entertain others with them. He recited stories of the Indians, their fortifications, customs, and life as if he had lived among them all his life.[72] He had access to Humboldt's *New Spain,*[73] the weekly newspapers and the people who produced them.

SMITH'S INDIAN POLICY

Smith made the Book of Mormon a morality play with the American Indians cast in the leading roles. This is particularly evident in the book of Alma. The name of God given there is the Great Spirit, who is identified with the God of the Bible — the world's Creator. There we read of Indians waging endless tribal warfare. They had tremendous battles in which tens of thousands were slain (Al 28:2). One aspect of their fighting ways was the practice of scalping (Al 44:13-15). They built fortification mounds topped with palisades and towers with moats in front.

The issues of their warfare were religious and moral. Once a tribe was converted to belief in Christ, it had to decide to continue fighting or to throw down its arms and risk being slaughtered. "They became a righteous people; they did lay down the weapons of their rebellion, that they did not fight against God any more, neither against any of their brethren" (Al 23:6). "They began to be a very industrious people; yea, and they were friendly" (Al 23:17-18). They repented of their past murderous ways and refused to wage war even in self-defense (Al 24:7-16).

> Now there was not one soul among all the people who had been converted unto the Lord that would take up arms against their brethren; nay, they would not even make any preparations for war; yea, and also their king commanded them that they should not. (Al 24:6)

The people of Anti-Nephi-Lehi carried out this "no fight" policy when they were attacked by the Lamanites. One thousand of them offered themselves as sacrificial lambs in a massive passive resistance movement and shamed the slaughtering Lamanites. Repenting Lamanites "threw down their weapons of war, and they would not take them again, for they were stung for the murders which they had committed" (Al 24:25). More than 1000 were brought to the Christian faith as a result of this supreme act of love on the part of those who were willing to die to show their murderers that war was not the way.

Preaching to the Indians led them "to disbelieve the traditions of their fathers, and to believe in the Lord" (Al 25:6). They joined "themselves to the people of God, buried their weapons, and became a righteous people" (Al 25:13-14). They also showed the fruits of their sincerity. "They had rather sacrifice their lives than even to take the life of their enemy"; they loved their enemies by burying their weapons, and not even the believing Nephites had that much love or faith (Al 26:32-34). "They were perfectly honest and upright in all things; and they were firm in the faith of Christ, even to the end" (Al 27:27).

The script which Smith wrote for the Indians to play out was the fulfillment of the government's dream for an ideal Indian policy. Christian mission efforts among the Indians had had some results, but these efforts were too few and too slow. As Smith envisioned what was needed to speed up the civilizing and christianizing of the Indians, he thought that could best be done by making the Book of Mormon *their* book. It gave them a past and an identity as the people of God, and held that out as a worthwhile reason to make peace with each other and the whites and become exemplary Christians.

The Book of Mormon is filled with speculations about the Indians, duplicating what appeared in books and newspapers.[74] The apologetic value that Ethan Smith saw in the Indian-Israelite theory against deists and rationalists appears in full measure in the Book of Mormon.[75] The Pittsfield Parchment story finds a striking parallel in Joseph Smith's setting up the consultation between Martin Harris and Charles Anthon, and in his interpretation of Isaiah 29.[76]

SUMMARY

By using parallels at hand, Joseph Smith wrote a book "which is to shew unto the remnant of the House of Israel how great things the LORD hath done for their fathers; and that they may know the covenants of the LORD, that they are not cast off forever."[77] It was this book, not the Bible, that he wanted the Indians to accept as their long lost book of God.

FOOTNOTES

1. W. W. Phelps, "Israel Will Be Gathered," EMS, II, 13 (June, 1833), p. 101.

2. *View of the Hebrews: or the Ten Tribes of Israel in America* (2nd ed.; Poultney, Vt.: Smith & Shute, 1825), p. 223.

3. Lewis Copeland, ed., *The World's Great Speeches* (New York: Garden City Publishing Co., Inc., c. 1941), pp. 266-68.

4. The development of the region is described by Orasmus Turner's *History of the Pioneer Settlement*.

5. PR, May 26, 1819; WF, September 18, 1821; PH, November 14, 1822; July 24, 1822; October 30, 1822; WS, November 3, 1824; July 24, 1829.

6. PH, October 30, 1822; WS, July 24, 1829.

7. WF, September 18, 1821.

8. PH, February 19, 1823.

9. PR, June 2, 1819.

10. WS, November 3, 1824.

11. PH, October 30, 1822.

12. *Ibid.*, February 19, 1823.

13. PH, May 26, 1819.

14. WS, November 3, 1824.

15. Timothy Dwight, *Travels; in New-England and New-York* (4 vols.; New Haven: S. Converse, Printer, 1821-22), IV, 131.

16. WS, March 3, 1826. "It is exclusively an American work—descriptive of American scenery, and American aboriginal character." Cooper pictured one of the Indian villains as a deist.

17. *Ibid.*, July 24, 1829.

18. *Ibid.*

19. Cf. PR, September 27, 1820.

20. *Ibid.*, May 3, 1820.

21. *Ibid.* Cf. WS, August 17, 1824.

22. PR, July 3, 1822.

23. *Ibid.*, July 19, 1820.

24. WS, August 15, 1828.

25. This ambivalence is traced historically by R. Pierce Beaver, *Church, State, and the American Indians* (St. Louis: Concordia Publishing House, c. 1966), chap. I, pp. 7-52.

26. *Ibid.*, p. 73.

27. *Ibid.*

28. *Ibid.*, p. 76.

29. WF, April 4, 1821.

30. PH, October 30, 1822.

31. PR, July 7, 1818.

32. *Ibid.*, October 4, 1820.

33. *Ibid.*, August 25, 1818.

34. PH, October 30, 1822.

35. WF, April 4, 1821.

36. WS, September 27, 1825.

37. *Ibid.* October 11, 1825.

38. *Ibid.*

39. Lynn Glaser, *Indians or Jews? An Introduction to a Reprint of Manasseh Ben Israel's The Hope of Israel* (Gilroy, Cal.: Roy V. Boswell, c. 1973), surveys the changing shape of that belief over the centuries. Robert Wauchope, "Lost Tribes and the Mormons," *Lost Tribes & Sunken Continents: Myth and Method in the Study of American Indians* (Chicago: University of Chicago Press, c. 1962), chap. 4, pp. 50-68, gives a broader and more scholarly survey. The best treatment is that of Robert Silverberg, who presents the archaeological evidence and evaluates the Indian-Israelite identification in the on-going sweep of archaeological understanding in its development from the 16th through the 20th centuries; *Mound Builders of Ancient America: The Archaeology of A Myth* (Greenwich, Ct.: New York Graphic Society Ltd., c. 1968).

40. Cf. Manasseh Ben Israel's *The Hope of Israel.*

41. Ethan Smith's *View of the Hebrews* was only one of many.

42. Elias Boudinot, *A Star in the West; or A Humble Attempt to Discover the Long Lost Ten Tribes of Israel Preparatory to the Return to their Beloved City, Jerusalem* (Trenton, N. J.: D. Fenton, S. Hutchinson, and J. Dunham, 1816) made the identification. Samuel Latham Mitchill spoke for an Asiatic origin in his "The Original Inhabitants of America Shown to Be of the Same Family with Those of Asia," *American Antiquarian Society Transactions*, Vol. I (1820).

Samuel Farmer Jarvis challenged James Adair and Elias Boudinot in "A Discourse on the Relations of the Indian Tribes of North America: Delivered Before the New-York Historical Society, December 20, 1819," in *Collections of the New York Historical Society, for the Year 1821* (New York: Bliss & White, 1821), pp. 183ff. After citing Boudinot's book and judging James Adair's *The History of the American Indians* (London: Edward and Charles Dilly, 1775) of "little use," Jarvis acknowledged Boudinot's advocacy, saying that his "exalted character renders every opinion he may defend a subject of respectful attention." Boudinot, Mitchill, M. M. Noah, and Jarvis are listed as members in the *Collections* on pp. 11, 17.

43. His 1811 book on millennialism also spoke against deism.

44. E. Smith, pp. 70-71. This distinction is found throughout the work. He cites Isaiah 49:18-22; 56:8; 63:1-6 as proof passages.

45. *Ibid.*, p. 75.

46. *Ibid.*, pp. 230-31.

47. *Ibid.*, pp. 74-75. 2 Esdras 13:40-42 reads:

> Those are the ten tribes, which were carried away prisoners out of their own land in the time of Osea the king, whom Salmanesar the king of Assyria led captive, and he carried them over the waters, and so came they into another land. But they took this counsel among themselves, that they would leave the multitude of the heathen, and go forth into a further country, where never mankind dwelt. That they might there keep their statutes, which they never kept in their own land.

Joseph Smith used the passage in Ether 2:4, "the Lord commanded them that they should go forth into the wilderness, yea, into that quarter where there never had man been."

48. E. Smith, p. 81.

49. *Ibid.*, p. 206.

50. *Ibid.*, pp. 198-99.

51. *Ibid.*, p. 173.

52. *Ibid.*, p. 234. In chap. 11 he contends for a literal restoration on the grounds that their expulsion was literal, citing Isa. 14; 18; 49:18-23; 60; 65; 66:20; Jer. 16:14-15; 23:6, 8; 30:3; Deut. 30; Hos. 2-3; Zeph. 3:10.

53. E. Smith, p. 60.

54. *Ibid.*, p. 77.

55. *Ibid.*, p. 115.

56. *Ibid.*, p. 130.

57. *Ibid.*, p. 131.

58. The Pittsfield Parchment story is found in E. Smith, pp. 217-25 in the 1825 edition. That year

Josiah Priest, *The Wonders of Nature and Providence* (Albany: n. p., 1825), p. 290, began a chapter "extracted from the Rev. E. Smith's *View of the Hebrews*, with some additional remarks." In 1837 Parley P. Pratt cited parts of the story and the Hebrew biblical quotations in *A Voice of Warning and Instruction to All People* (Independence, Mo.: Zion's Printing and Publishing Company, 1943), p. 79. Mormon historian B. H. Roberts pointed to the Pittsfield Parchment story as proof for the Book of Mormon in *New Witnesses*, II, pp. 49-50. Cf., however, his later studies in Ethan Smith as discussed in Appendix I below.

59. Larned's involvement is dated in 1815. This is based upon the notation that he "was living in Pittsfield, Mass.— his native place—after he left college," E. Smith, pp. 212-13, and that he was a "graduate then in town," p. 220. That means that Larned had just finished Andover and was preparing to enter Cambridge. By the time he preached in Canandaigua in 1817 and 1818, he had known the story for several years. Cf. Wm. Sprague, *Annals of the Congregational Pulpit*, Vol. II, *Annals of the American Pulpit* (New York: Robert Carter & Brothers, 1869), pp. 556-71.

60. The letter in E. Smith, p. 220, reads as follows:

Sir, I have examined the parchment manuscripts which you had the goodness to give me. After some time and with much difficulty and assistance I have ascertained their meaning, which is as follows; (I have numbered the manuscripts.) No. 1 is translated by Deut. vi. 4-9 verses inclusive. No 2, by Deut. xi. 13-21 verses inclusive. No 3, Exod. xiii, 11-16 verses inclusive. I am, &c.

SYLVESTER LARNED

61. Boudinot (1740-1821) was an attorney active in the Revolutionary War. He served in Congress from 1777-84 and was a strong Federalist supporter of Washington. His three books before *A Star in the West* involved him in the deistic controversy, and his millennial views and acceptance of the Indian-Israelite identification made him an attractive candidate for the presidency of the American Bible Society formed in 1816. Cf. "Elias Boudinot," DAB, II, 477-78.

62. E. Smith, p. 223.

63. *Ibid.*, p. 224.

64. *Ibid.*, pp. 229-30, 237. Boudinot wrote in the same vein: " Who knows but God has raised up these United States in these latter days, for the very purpose of accomplishing his will in bringing his beloved people [the Israelites] to their own land." Boudinot, p. 297.

65. E. Smith, p. 248; cf. pp. 246-55, *passim*.

66. *Ibid.*, p. 253. Boudinot, pp. 279-80, appreciated this earlier than Ethan Smith. He wrote:

What could possibly bring greater declarative glory to God, or tend more essentially to affect and rouse the nations of earth, with a deeper sense of the certainty of the prophetic declarations of the holy scriptures, and thus call their attention to the truth of divine revelation, than a full discovery, that, these wandering nations of Indians are the long lost tribes of Israel . . , ?

67. E. Smith, p. 264.

68. *Ibid.*, pp. 266-67.

69. *Ibid.*, p. 267.

70. Cf. n. 59.

71. PR, June 7, 1820.

72. Lucy Mack Smith, pp. 84, 90. The second Lucy Smith manuscript, transcribed by Martha Jane Coray, originally had "16." The "6" has been crossed out or written over, but it is clearly visible.

73. Humboldt's *New Spain* is listed for sale in a two-column ad for the T. C. Strong bookstore, PR, September 15, 1818. Strong published the *Palmyra Register*. Orasmus Turner, p. 214, wrote that Joseph Smith came to the newspaper office every week to get his father's copy of the *Palmyra Register*, and was there often enough to be described as a "meddling, inquisitive lounger," who used "to put himself in the way of the working of the old fashioned Ramage press," and earn the retribution of the printshop workers. It is likely that Smith had access to *The Methodist Magazine* at Strong's establishment, since Strong often printed its material and also ran a circulating library. The journal was filled with reports of mission activity among the Indians.

74. Cf. Brodie, pp. 44-49, for the way Smith wove Indian lore into the Book of Mormon. David Marks showed the impression created by the Book of Mormon upon those who had heard of it, because it seemed to offer insights into Indian antiquities. "When I was in Ohio," he wrote,

I had quite a curiosity to know the origin of the numerous mounds and remains of ancient fortifications that abound in that section of the country; but could not find that any thing satisfactory was known on the subject. Having been told, that the *'Book of Mormon'* gave a history of them, and of their authors, some desire was created in my mind to see the book, that I might learn the above particulars.

Marks, p. 341. Cf. chap 1, nn. 19, 21 above and accompanying text.
    75. Cf. chaps. 9-11.
    76. Cf. in chap. 8, "The Real Purpose of the Consultation," and Appendix II below.
    77. Title Page, Book of Mormon, 1830 ed. Cf. in chap. 2, Smith's goal to "Christianize the Indians."

6

Identified:
Ezekiel's Two Books

Say, our Savior came through the tribe of Judah, and the Jews kept the record of the bible . . . and then, that the Redeemer shall come the second time, in the tribe of Joseph; and they have also written and kept a record, called the Book of Mormon, . . . and who can mistake what Ezekiel meant by the Two Sticks? They are the Lord's reading sticks (or records) for the benefit of Israel.

W. W. Phelps[1]

WESTERN RENDEZVOUS

"Go west, young man," guided young America long before Horace Greely offered his famous advice. Immediately after the Revolutionary War west meant to New Englanders the stretch of terrain from New York to Niagara Falls. By the 1820s, the horizon embraced the Mississippi. Destiny beckoned from the west.

Out there the Indians were fighting the ever-encroaching whites. Out there the boundaries of a surging nation claimed still more land. Out there, beyond the Falls, was Cincinnati and St. Louis—gateway to the new frontier. By the late 1820s the westernmost boundary had moved 250 miles from St. Louis to what is now the Kansas-Missouri border. Beyond that lay Indian territory.

Government policy toward the Indians headed more and more toward their removal. One church official advised their displacement beyond the Mississippi where the whites would leave them alone, and vice versa.[2] Treaties made with the red men would not be kept. Tribes from the south and north over the years left the settled eastern regions—themselves to settle and displace other Indians.

In Palmyra this process was carefully watched. People read of Indian uprisings in the south due to government disregard of treaty obligations.[3] Seminoles, Creeks and Cherokees left their lands.[4] Senecas sold over 80,000 acres near Buffalo to begin their pilgrimmage—or retreat—to a better place.[5]

Many missionaries saw the retreat as a pilgrimmage. Since the whites could not be trusted, it was said, the Indians would be better off beyond the reach of the United States.[6] Whatever part of the east they came from, the Indians were going to the center of the continent. Such a gathering had millennial overtones.

Another kind of gathering took place in the west in 1825. Mordecai Manuel Noah, self-appointed guardian of the Jews, founded a City of Refuge for oppressed Jews around the world. Situated on Grand Island in the Niagara River, the City of Ararat was dedicated in September, 1825 as the reestablishment of the Jewish people as a nation. Laws were proclaimed, relations with the U. S. government were set up, and Noah's arms were opened to oppressed Jews everywhere.[7] The long story was printed in the *Wayne Sentinel*, together with the claim that Indians and Jews were all descendants of Abraham. Ararat was to be temporary. The Jews would stay there until they could return to Palestine—to Jerusalem.

The Jewish influx had already begun, according to the Palmyra press. They came from the oppressive European governments which denied Jews their rights. Christian missionaries opened missions in Jerusalem.[8] Bible societies sent them Jewish New Testaments.[9] The millennial picture was coming into focus, and the lens through which many saw it was Ezekiel 37.

Ezekiel 37 deals with the restoration of the Jews to their land following their captivity in Babylon. It views them as a nation dead and gone that would take flesh and live again (verses 1-10), like the bones in a grave stepping forth to new life (verses 11-14). Ezekiel pictured it still another way:

> The word of the LORD came again unto me, saying, "Moreover, thou son of man, take thee one stick, and write upon it, for Judah, and for the children of Israel his companions; then take another stick and write upon it, For Joseph, the stick of Ephraim, and for all the house of Israel his companions. And join them one to another into one stick; and they shall become one in thine hand. (Verses 15-17)

Then Ezekiel was to tell the people that they would return to Jerusalem and be reunited with the tribes of Israel, just as he held the two sticks united in his hand—as one.

ETHAN SMITH: RESTORATION DISCOVERED

Elias Boudinot earlier had found the restoration theme of Ezekiel 37 useful in developing the Indian-Israelite identity,[10] but Ethan Smith used it to advantage. He quoted 37:11-14 as something to be fulfilled in the millennium, but not simply by the conversion of the Jews. "The re-union of the two branches of that people follows, by the figure of the two sticks taken by the prophet," he wrote.

> Lest any should say, the prediction which here seems to foretel the restoration of the ten tribes, as well as that of the Jews, were accomplished in the restoration of that few of the Israelites, who clave to the Jews under the house of David, and the ten tribes are irrevocably lost; it is here expressed that the Jews and those Israelites, their companions, were symbolized by one stick; and Ephraim, all the house of Israel (the whole ten tribes,) by the other stick.[11]

Smith pointed to the continued existence of the Jews as an argument for a literal restoration. If the preservation of the Jews was literally intended by God—as their present existence showed that it was—then Israel shall be literally restored to one land, receive a new heart and spirit, and "the two sticks in the prophet's hand shall become one.[12] "Yes, the stick of Ephraim is to become one in the hand of the prophet, with the stick of the Jews."[13]

Smith further observed:

> America was the land of Israel's outcast state. It was Israel's huge valley of dry bones . . . a literal wilderness of thousands of miles, where the dry bones of the outcasts of Israel have for thousands of years been scattered . . . the most essential *pile* of the prophet Ezekiel's valley of dry bones.[14]

Israel's outcast condition presented a "volume of new evidence of the divinity of the Old Testament,"[15] and therein lay the apologetic appeal of America as the valley of the dry bones.

The restoration symbolized by Ezekiel's joining of the two sticks in his hand, Smith cautioned, had received neither a partial nor a complete fulfillment.[16] None of the tribes, whose names were

> written on the second stick, in the hand of the prophet, have ever yet been recovered. The whole passage is intimately connected with the battle of that great day, which introduces the Millenium; . . .[17]

Finally, Smith related the "way-preparer" of Isaiah 40 to Ezekiel 37. John the Baptist may have primarily and typically fulfilled the former passage, but if the American Indians were the lost tribes of Israel, then its fullest completion would be in connection with the millennium. "The voice, which restores Israel, is heard in the *vast wilderness of America*," and "is to have a kind of literal fulfillment upon a much greater scale, in the missions, which shall recover the ten tribes."[18]

JOSEPH SMITH: RESTORATION TRANSFORMED

Ethan Smith's literalistic application of Old Testament prophecies of restoration for Judah *and* Israel was grounded in the fact that Israel was not yet restored. The Book of Mormon presents the same view of the Indians, where they are to be restored in fulfillment of God's promise to Israel. The Indians, however, are presented as members of only *one* Israelite tribe—that of Joseph as represented through the half-tribes of his sons Ephraim and Manasseh.[19]

Joseph Smith identified the Indians as the tribe of Joseph from Ezekiel 37:16-17. The use made of it by Ethan Smith, the way "Ephraim" is used in the Old Testament restoration chapters, and the "stick" of Ephraim in Ezekiel 37:16 led Joseph Smith to designate the Indians as the tribe of Joseph in America. Another innovation came in his interpretation of the "sticks" of 37:16 as "books" or "records" of the tribes of Joseph and Judah.[20]

When Joseph Smith began dictating the Book of Mormon in 1829, he had the idea of equating "stick" with "record," and the stick of Ephraim as a record on a par with the Bible. This is evident from the use he made of Ezekiel 37, although he never literally quoted it.

In the vision of I Nephi 13, Nephi beheld among the Gentile nations a great and abominable church, devilish and corrupt. Nephi's brethren were separated from the Gentile nations by an ocean; that is, the Indians were separated from the European nations by the Atlantic. When Europeans came to America, they scattered the Indians, but they humbled themselves before the Lord. They had God's power and were instruments of His wrath upon those who opposed them. The Gentiles had a book which was the record of the Jews,

> which contains the covenants of the Lord, which he made unto the house of Israel; and it also containeth many of the prophecies of the holy prophets; and it is a record like unto the engravings which are upon the plates of brass, save there are not so many; nevertheless they contain the covenants of the Lord, which he hath made unto the house of Israel; wherefore, they are of great worth unto the Gentiles. And the angel of the Lord said unto me: Thou hast beheld that the book proceedeth forth from the mouth of a Jew; and when it proceedeth forth from the mouth of a Jew it contained the plainness of the gospel of the Lord, of whom the twelve apostles bear record; and they bear record according to the truth which is in the Lamb of God. Wherefore, these things go forth from the Jews in purity unto the Gentiles. (I Ne 13:23-25)

After the book reached the Gentiles, the great and abominable church removed many precious covenants from it and it reached all nations of the Gentiles in its emasculated form. The Europeans brought the truncated Bible to America, subdued the future descendants of Lehi (the Lamanites, or Indians), who were to have restored to them many of the missing portions of the Bible. After the Nephites' downfall the book was hidden "to come forth unto the Gentiles" (verse 35).

Nephi's vision permitted him to see the Gentiles bring the decimated Bible to the Indians. Later on, more books were to come to them from the Lamb (Christ) through the mediation of the Gentiles (verse 39). They would be books of testimony to the Son, the only Savior, to whom all people must come (verse 40).

> And they must come according to the words which shall be established by the mouth of the Lamb; and the words of the Lamb shall be made known in the records of thy seed, as well as in the records of the twelve apostles of the Lamb; wherefore they both shall be established in one; for there is one God and one Shepherd over all the earth. (I Ne 13:41)

So the Nephites would be given a separate record through which Christ would make known his words. It would parallel and equal the record of the apostles and prophets of historic Christianity and Judaism. Both records would be used as one unit, but the Old and New Testaments are to be viewed as one book that came from a Jew. I Nephi 14:23-27 reinforces the identification of the entire Bible as the book of the Jew by including in it the Revelation of John.

2 Nephi begins with the death-bed blessings that Lehi bestowed upon his sons. He addressed Joseph, his last-born son, and recalled a lengthy prophecy of his own forebear, the biblical Joseph. Joseph was told by God that one of his descendants would minister to the rest of mankind. He would be another Moses.

> But a seer will I raise up out of the fruit of thy loins; and unto him will I give power to bring forth my word unto the seed of thy loins—and not to the

bringing forth of my word only, saith the Lord, but to the convincing them of my words, which shall have already gone forth among them. Wherefore, the fruit of thy loins shall write; and the fruit of the loins of Judah shall write; and that which shall be written by the fruit of thy loins, and also that which shall be written by the fruit of the loins of Judah, shall grow together, unto the confounding of false doctrines and laying down of contentions, and establishing peace among the fruit of thy loins. (2 Ne 3:11-12)

Like the biblical Joseph, the seer would be named Joseph, as would his father. Like Moses, he would receive the writing of God and have a spokesman (verses 17-18). The writing to come from biblical Joseph's descendant would refute false doctrine, settle disputes, and establish peace among Joseph's posterity.

In 2 Nephi 29 God assures Nephi that He will remember Nephi's posterity "and that the words of your seed should proceed out of my mouth unto your seed" (the words of the Nephites would go to the Lamanites-Indians, verse 2).

And because my word shall hiss forth—many of the Gentiles shall say: A Bible! A Bible! We have got a Bible, and there cannot be any more Bible. . . . O fools, they shall have a Bible; and it shall proceed forth from the Jews, mine ancient covenant people. (2 Ne 29:3-4)

Thou fool, that shall say: A Bible, we have got a Bible, and we need no more Bible. Have ye obtained a Bible save it were by the Jews? Know ye not that there are more nations than one? Know ye not that I . . . bring forth my word unto the children of men, yes, even upon all the nations of the earth? Wherefore murmur ye, because. . . . that I remember one nation like unto another? Wherefore, I speak the same words unto one nation like unto another. And when the two nations shall run together the testimony of the two nations shall run together also. (2 Ne 29:6-8)

The Bible does not contain all the words of the Lord; more is to come. Every nation shall have its own book out of which it shall be judged (verses 9-11).

For behold, I shall speak unto the Jews and they shall write it; and I shall also speak unto the Nephites and they shall write it; and I shall also speak unto the other tribes of the house of Israel, which I have led away, and they shall write it; and I shall also speak unto all the nations of the earth and they shall write it. And it shall come to pass that the Jews shall have the words of the Nephites, and the Nephites shall have the words of the Jews, and the Nephites and Jews shall have the words of the lost tribes of Israel; and the lost tribes of Israel shall have the words of the Nephites and Jews. And it shall come to pass that my people, which are of the house of Israel, shall be gathered home unto the lands of their possessions; and my word also shall be gathered in one. (2 Ne 29:12-14)

In the Book of Mormon, then, Joseph Smith used Ezekiel 37 to mean that the Bible was to come from the Jews, the tribe of Judah. The Old and New Testaments were to be viewed as one book. The Nephites would be given a separate record through which Christ's words would be made known. It would equal and parallel the biblical record of the apostles and prophets. The Bible would be given to the Gentiles, and then the abominable church would remove some sections. After that, the Gentiles would bring the deficient book to the Indians.

A latter-day Joseph, of the tribe of Joseph, would write the Lord's words to give to the Indians. This writing, the Book of Mormon, would convince the Indians of the Bible's authenticity and would be used with the Bible together as one unit. Two nations, then, would become one, and their respective records one record. Their united testimony would make more of an impact than the testimony of only one people and of only one record. Every nation will have its own God-given record, or scripture. All the tribes of Israel will produce scriptures. In Israel's restoration all the different scriptures, including the records of the Jews and the tribe of Joseph, will be joined together into one great scripture.

Joseph Smith's development of Ezekiel 37 had an apologetic value for his defense of God. He gained the benefit of proof for God's existence, as he saw it, for there were two records in different parts of the world testifying to God's being and activity. He upheld God's justice and impartiality by making provision for each nation and tribe to have its own God-given record. God's unchanging way of dealing with humanity was maintained by having the different records contain the same essential message ("I speak the same words unto one nation like unto another," 2 Ne 29:8). Ongoing revelation was asserted. By calling all who fought to uphold the Bible as the only written revelation of God fools, the idea of a closed biblical canon was denied.

Designation of the Indians as the tribes of Joseph, and the Book of Mormon as the stick of Joseph was a distinctive feature of the early Mormon message, as it remains yet today. Its early use was amply attested,[21] and where the Book of Mormon did not literally quote Ezekiel 37:16-17, the early Mormons did. Joseph Smith himself made explicit use of the text in a revelation that was amended after 1833 and before 1835. Jesus spoke to Smith about communing with him and the angel Moroni, who was sent to Smith "to reveal the Book of Mormon, containing the fulness of my everlasting gospel, to whom I have committed the keys of the record of the stick of Ephraim" (DC 27:5).[22]

Joseph Smith's interest in the restoration of the Indians continued in early Mormon history.[23] Signs that his interpretation of "stick" to mean "book" or "record" corresponded to Indian life were often printed.[24]

The fact that Smith frequently interwove Ezekiel 37:16-17 with passages from Isaiah 29, is further indication of his purpose in writing the Book of Mormon. Now that the lost book of the Indians had been identified and given its character of equality with the Bible, its recovery and translation needed to be provided for. That leads into Smith's use of Isaiah 29.

FOOTNOTES

1. EMS, November, 1932.

2. Beaver, pp. 95ff.; cf. chap. III, "The Missions and Indian Removal," pp. 85-122.

3. WS, February 14; March 17; June 9, 23, 1826; February 8, August 15, 1828.

4. WS, April 6, July 19, August 16, 1825; February 2, 1827.

5. WS, September 8, 1826.

6. Beaver, chap. III.

7. WS, September 27, October 4, 11, 1825. Cf. "Mordecai Manuel Noah," DAB, XIII, 534-35; and Abram Leon Sacher, A History of the Jews (4th ed., rev. & enlarged; New York: A. A. Knopf, c. 1953), p. 306, for a description of the dedication ceremony; and WS, November 15, 1825.

8. Letters from Levi Parsons and Pliny Fisk, Presbyterian missionaries to Jerusalem, were often featured: PR, December 9, 1818; October 11, 1820; WF, June 20, August 1, 1821; February 13, 1822; PH, July 17, 1822; WS, December 24, 1823. Articles on modern Jerusalem appeared in WF, June 20, 1821— and the Holy Land, August 1, 1821—to provide general information.

9. PR, December 10, 1817; October 11, 1820. Cf. "The Converted Jew," two columns about a dying girl who asked her father to grant one request. She knew little about Jesus, but saw him in vision on her deathbed. She asked her orthodox, well-educated, cultured, Jewish father: *"I beg you never again to speak against JESUS of Nazareth."* He converted after her death; WF, August 29, 1821.

10. Cf. Boudinot, p. 46, where he comments upon Ezekiel 37:16:

It appears by this chapter, that there are some few of the Israelites still with Judah; but all are again to become one people at a future day. It also appears that the body of the house of Israel are remote from Judah, and are to be brought from distant countries to Jerusalem, when they are to become one nation.

11. E. Smith, p. 53.

12. *Ibid.,* p. 279.

13. *Ibid.,* p. 247.

14. *Ibid.,* pp. 79, 257, 266.

15. *Ibid.,* p. 266.

16. Ezekiel 37:19-22.

17. E. Smith, p. 54. Both the writer and Wesley P. Walters misread this passage, thinking that Ethan Smith, from the context, used "stick" to refer to prophecies rather than tribes. This was caused by the way Ethan Smith used the term. Walters suggested that Joseph Smith could easily have made the same mistake, and that it was this that led him to think of "stick" as a book; or record. In his entire discussion on pp. 53-55, however, Ethan Smith used the word as symbolic of a tribe, not a book. Cf. in chap. 8 below, "The Pillars," for another possible link that led Joseph Smith from "stick" to "record."

18. *Ibid.,* p. 257. The Shakers had identified Ann Lee as the voice in the wilderness. Mormons were to see Joseph Smith as the voice. Parley Pratt wrote of him that he was "the Elias, the Restorer, the presiding Messenger, holding the keys of the 'Dispensation of the fulness of time.'" *Key to the Science of Theology* (Liverpool: By the author, 1855), p. 77.

19. Lehi, patriarch of the Book of Mormon, came from a family of the tribe of Joseph that escaped the dispersion of the ten tribes in 721 B. C. by fleeing to Egypt. Lehi returned to Jerusalem, only to flee again with his family as the Babylonian invasion was imminent. He was of the half-tribe Manasseh. Ishmael went with Lehi. The Book of Mormon does not give his genealogy, but it was later determined that he was of the tribe of Ephraim. Still another fugitive, Zoram, was of unknown tribal origin.

By marrying Ishmael's daughters, Laman and Nephi provided America with a branch of the tribe of biblical Joseph. The restoration of the ten tribes of Israel will take them back to Jerusalem, but the restoration of the tribe of Joseph—including those of Ephraim and Manasseh and the Mormon tribes of Laman and Nephi—will gather them together upon the American continent.

Joseph Smith made a mistake in his treatment of Ezekiel 37:15-17. The Nephites needed to have come through the line of Manasseh. Cf. Jerald and Sandra Tanner, *Mormonism— Shadow or Reality?* (Salt Lake City: Modern Microfilm Company 1964), p. 61.

20. The best explication of this view is that of Hugh Nibley, "The Stick of Judah," IE, Vol. 56, Nos. 1-6 (January-June, 1953), which is a somewhat technical treatment of the anthropological evidence of the use of writing sticks in several cultures. A simplified version of the series is found in *An Approach to the Book of Mormon,* (Salt Lake City: Deseret News Press, c. 1964), chap. 24, pp. 257-72. Hundreds of years of French missionary influences, however, must be considered for the Indians of the northeastern region of the North American continent; likewise, Spanish missionary influence for the South American continent.

21. Cf. DHC, I, 84; II, 41, 390; III, 53. EMS, June, 1832, p. 6. These are representative. There are many more.

22. Other allusions are found in DC 33:16; 35:17; 128:19-20.

23. Mormon publisher Phelps started a tradition that was continued in early Mormon newspapers. In EMS, December, 1832, he reported that 400 Shawnees "passed this place for their inheritance a few miles west, and the scene was at once calculated to refer the mind to the prophecies concerning the gathering of Israel in the last days." From his vantage point in Independence, Missouri, Phelps rejoiced "that the great purposes of the Lord are fulfilling before our eyes." Routine reports of Indian movements were occasions to consider the fulfillment of ancient prophecy.

24. "Israel Will Be Gathered," EMS, June, 1833.

7

Recovered:
Isaiah's Book,
Buried and Sealed

"If anyone of them can explain it," said Alice, "I'll give him sixpence. *I* don't believe there's an atom of meaning it it. . . ." "If there's no meaning in it," said the King, "that saves a world of trouble, you know, as we needn't try to find any. And yet I don't know," he went on, spreading out the verses on his knee . . . "I seem to find some meaning in them."

Lewis Carroll, *Alice in Wonderland*

ISAIAH IN THE BOOK OF MORMON

The relationship of a new Church to American culture in the early 19th century, Eduard Meyer maintained, had to be formed by a book because of the Reformed churches' preoccupation with the Bible.[1] It is now becoming clear that a generation of speculation had prepared the way for a book that would disclose the origin of the Indians and confirm the revelatory activity of God.

Ethan Smith drew extensively upon texts from Isaiah to show that a literal restoration was predicted for the last days.[2] Joseph Smith made even greater use of Isaiah. In number of words the Book of Mormon uses Isaiah for one-tenth of its content, as demonstrated in Table II.

Isaiah 29 stands out above all others in importance because it gave rise to Joseph Smith's claims and seems to validate them. In Ethan Smith's *View of the Hebrews* Ezekiel 37 dominated, with no use made of Isaiah 29. In the Book of Mormon, however, Isaiah 29 is the most reworked chapter of the Bible. See Appendix II for a full comparison. Table III compares Smith's use of Isaiah 29 in the Book of Mormon and his Inspired Version[3] with the text of the King James Version.

TABLE II

ENTIRE CHAPTERS OF ISAIAH
IN THE BOOK OF MORMON

ISAIAH	BOOK OF MORMON
2-14	2 Nephi 12-24
29	2 Nephi 27
48-49	1 Nephi 20-21
50-51	2 Nephi 7-8
52	3 Nephi 30
53	Mosiah 14
54	3 Nephi 22

TABLE III

ISAIAH 29 IN THE INSPIRED VERSION, BOOK OF
MORMON, AND KING JAMES VERSION

INSPIRED VERSION	BOOK OF MORMON	KING JAMES VERSION
Isaiah	2 Nephi	Isaiah
29:1-2		29:1-2
29:3-5	26:15-18	29:3-5
29:6-10	27:1-3a	29:6-10
29:11-16		
29:17-24	29:19-35	29:11-12
29:25-30		29:13-19
29:31-32		29:20-24

ISAIAH 29:4 AND THE BURIED BOOK

The Book of Mormon applies Isaiah 29:3-5[4] to the destruction of the Nephites (2 Ne 26:15-18) and also to Jerusalem's destruction. In 3 Nephi 8-9 the tempest, earthquake, whirlwind and fire that attested the crucifixion are described. Cities were demolished, roads and highways disrupted, people killed—all because of the peoples' abominations and killing of the God-sent prophets.

Joseph Smith indicated his intent to make the Book of Mormon a subject of prophecy by his use of this text. In Nephi's famous vision Jesus tells him:

> I will manifest myself unto thy seed, that they shall write many things which I shall minister unto them, which shall be plain and precious; and after thy seed shall be destroyed, and dwindle in unbelief, and also the seed of thy brethren, behold, these things shall be hid up, to come forth unto the Gentiles: by the gift and power of the Lamb. (1 Ne 13:35)

The "hiding up" of the "writing" after the Nephites' destruction incorporates verses 3-5, with the speech from the dust interpreted as what men might read in a "record" or "book." The point is made again by making biblical Joseph say:

> and the Lord said unto me also: I will raise up unto the fruit of thy loins; and I will make for him a spokesman. And I, behold, I will give unto him that he shall write the writing of the fruit of thy loins, unto the fruit of thy loins; and the spokesman of thy loins shall declare it. . . . And it shall be as if the fruit of thy loins had cried unto them from the dust. . . . even after many generations have gone by them. (2 Ne 3:18-21)

Although Smith intermingled the text of Isaiah 29:4 with Ezekiel 37:15-16, the point is the same: the Nephite offspring of biblical Joseph shall write for the sake of still future descendants. The writing shall speak from the "dust."

Smith introduced and ended the KJV rendition with material that makes it impossible to miss the point of a buried book. The speaker is Nephi, who says:

> After my seed and the seed of my brethren shall have dwindled in unbelief, and shall have been smitten by the Gentiles. . . . thus saith the Lord God: They shall write the things which shall be done among them, and they shall be written and sealed up in a book, and those who have dwindled in unbelief shall not have them, for they seek to destroy the things of God. (2 Ne 26:15, 17)[5]

Smith identified the Lamanites (Indians) with those who have "dwindled in unbelief," who sought to destroy—and thus were without—the things of God. The element of time future from Nephi is brought in by the prospect of Joseph's seed being smitten by the Gentiles. The new element here is the defeat of both Nephite and Indian factions before the time of uncovering the written and buried book.

Finally, Smith made Mormon describe the latter days in which the eternal purpose of God would be fulfilled, as Isaiah said (Morm 8:22-23):

> Yea, behold I say unto you, that those saints who have gone before me, who have possessed this land, shall cry, yea, even from the dust will they cry unto the Lord; and as the Lord liveth he will remember the covenant which he hath made with them. And no one need say that the promises of the Lord shall not come,

ISAIAH 29 IN THE "E MS," OLIVER COWDERY'S PRINTER'S COPY

Used by permission of the Research Library and Archives, Reorganized Church of Jesus Christ of Latter Day Saints, The Auditorium, Independence, Missouri.

for they surely shall, for the Lord hath spoken it; for out of the earth shall they come, by the hand of the Lord, and none can stay it. (Morm 8:23,26)

America's former inhabitants would speak from their graves⁶ in the form of a book and fulfill from the ground the promises of God in the latter days.

In these examples Smith used Isaiah 29:3-5 as an extension of Ezekiel 37:1-14 (national resurrection) and Ezekiel 37:15-21 (the sticks of Judah and Joseph). He made Isaiah's text a prediction of people speaking to future generations through a book buried with them in their destruction. It was a book written by a descendant of biblical Joseph to future descendants and buried in the ground, the dust, not to be recovered until the Gentiles would defeat the Indians. Long before the recovery both Lamanite and Nephite would fall from faith. The Nephites would be wiped out. The remaining Lamanites would be left without the book. In the latter days the book would come forth to fulfill the promises of God as they appear in Isaiah—those that deal with the restoration of Israel and Judah.

Smith also found Isaiah 29:4 useful as a closing verse of the Nephite writers to their intended readers. This reinforced the interpretation of this verse as a reference to a buried book. Nephi says:

and now, my beloved brethren, all those who are of the house of Israel, and all ye ends of the earth, I speak unto you as the voice of one crying from the dust: Farewell until that great day shall come. (2 Ne 33:13)

Moroni speaks of the record he and Mormon, his father, have made:

I am the same who hideth up this record unto the Lord. . . . And blessed be he that shall bring this thing to light for it shall be brought out of darkness unto light, according to the word of God; yea, it shall be brought out of the earth, and it shall shine forth out of darkness, and come to the knowledge of the people; and it shall be done by the power of God. (Morm 8:14-15)

Finally, Moroni wrote parting words to the Lamanites:

I exhort you to remember these things; for the time speedily cometh that ye shall know that I lie not, for ye shall see me at the bar of God; and the Lord God will say unto you: Did I not declare my words unto you, which were written by this man, like as one crying from the dead, yea, even as one speaking out of the dust? (Moro 10:27)

Smith, then, used his Nephite writers to make positive identification between the Book of Mormon and the "voice of one crying from the dust." The voice was the record of the Nephites, a book buried in the earth, containing the words of God written by men long dead. By the power of God, the book came forth unto the house of Israel, the Indians (Lamanites), to speak "as one speaking out of the dust."

There is a decided change in meaning in the above usage of "dust" from that of Isaiah, where it is associated with physical destruction. In this change Smith once again revealed his intent, for he used the term elsewhere in accordance with biblical usage.

In the Book of Mormon "dust" is associated with man's creatureliness, referring to that out of which he was formed.⁷ It is often used to express spiritual unawareness⁸ of the terrible humiliation that is its consequence.⁹ It may refer to the physical destruction brought on by war that results because of spiritual unawareness.[10] From that usage "dust" may refer to dying, or to the state of death. In all these ways man's lowliness and the transitory nature of his life stands in contrast to God's transcendence.[11] So far the Book of Mormon usage parallels the biblical.

In Isaiah 29:4 "dust" denotes destruction brought on by war that is the result of spiritual ignorance. In their contexts three examples show that Joseph Smith knew of this usage and adopted it in line with the biblical usage. *Mormon 8:32* refers to the slaughtered, pious Nephites, lost in the war with the Lamanites, crying from the dust to the Lord. *2 Nephi 26:15* refers to that destruction almost a thousand years before the event and predicts that the Nephites will be destroyed by the Lord's waging war against them. Finally, *1 Nephi 22:14* promises that all who battle against Mount Zion will fall, especially the "great and abominable church." In that destruction all false churches will be "consumed as stubble."[12]

All this strongly signals that Smith was aware of Isaiah's meaning for 29:4, that it referred to Jerusalem's destruction; that even in its tomb Jerusalem would testify to its humiliation. His use of the text to predict a book that would be discovered in future ages is an intentional variation. It strengthened his claim for the book's divine message.

ISAIAH 29:11 AND THE SCHOLARS' COUNSEL

A book buried by Hebrew forefathers and discovered in the 1820s needed translating to be of use. Isaiah 29:11-12 provided a pattern to follow in getting the American scripture written and published. No passage of the Bible was so strongly handled as these two verses.[13]

The passage depicts God as denouncing the prophets and seers of Jerusalem. Because of their apostasy He closes their eyes so they can no longer see Him. So completely do they lose their vision that they are like a scholar trying to read a sealed book. Impossible!

> And the vision of all is become unto you as the words of a book that is sealed, which men deliver to one that is learned, saying, Read this, I pray thee: and he saith, I cannot; for it is sealed: And the book is delivered to him that is not learned, saying, Read this, I pray thee: and he saith, I am not learned. (Isaiah 29:11-12)

To determine what Joseph Smith intended in using this text, one must see how the early events of Mormon origins were shaped by it. But there is a bewildering flood of conflicting evidence bearing on Smith's use of the text and the episode that it inspired. Discovering the historical kernel requires peeling back layer upon layer of accumulated folklore. Smith created this difficulty, for his last telling of the episode was quite different from that which he first told.

Joseph Smith dictated the Official Version ten years after the event. He said that Martin Harris gave him $50 to move from Manchester, N. Y. to Susquehanna County, Pennsylvania in December, 1827. Once there, Smith copied a considerable number of characters from the newly-found golden plates and translated them. Harris came in February, 1828 to take a transcript and sample translation to New York City for scholarly evaluation. When he returned, according to Smith, Harris told this story:

I went to the city of New York, and presented the characters which had been translated, with the translation thereof to Professor Anthony, a gentleman celebrated for his literary attainments;—Professor Anthony stated that the translation was correct, more so than any he had before seen translated from Egyptian. I then showed him those which were not yet translated, and he said they were Egyptian, Chaldeac, Assyriac, and Arabac; and he said they were true characters. He gave me a certificate, certifying to the people of Palmyra that they were true characters, and that the translation of such of them as had been translated was also correct. I took the certificate and put it into my pocket, and was just leaving the house, when Mr. Anthony called me back, and asked me how the young man found out that there were gold plates in the place where he found them. I answered that an angel of God had revealed it unto him'

He then said to me, "let me see that certificate." I accordingly took it out of my pocket and gave it to him, when he took it and tore it to pieces, saying that there was no such thing now as ministering of angels, and that if I would bring the plates to him he would translate them. I informed him that part of the plates were sealed, and that I was forbidden to bring them. He replied, "I cannot read a sealed book." I left him and went to Dr. Mitchill, who sanctioned what Professor Anthony had sdid respecting both the characters and the translation.[14]

The account gave no motivation for Harris's visit either to Smith or to the scholars, nor did it say whose idea it was.

Source analysis,[15] however, indicates that the Official Version evolved over a ten year period, and yields quite different results. Harris in fact took only a transcript of the golden plate characters to the scholars, who failed to translate them. Their failure is required by the Mormon story and only such failure makes Harris's reaction to the consultation intelligible.

The Scholars Consulted

One name would have drawn Martin Harris to New York: that of Dr. Samuel Latham Mitchill. Mitchill was known throughout the state and nation from his service in state and national legislatures from 1791 through 1813. Dating from his appointment in 1798 as a commissioner to purchase land in western New York from the Six (Indian) Nations, he was a noted authority on Indians. Further, he won renown in science, history, higher education, medicine, and land development.[16]

Readers of the Palmyra papers understood the references to Dr. Mitchill (or Mitchell) of New York as the person connected with medicine, exploration, politics, Indians, and the Erie Canal.[17] His name was never explained. It was unnecessary. It is far more likely that Martin Harris set off to consult Dr. Mitchill rather than Professor Anthon.[18]

In contrast to Mitchill, Charles Anthon was known primarily in New York City. He was admitted to Columbia College when just a boy and recognized as a genius when he was 14. The state supreme court accepted him before the bar when he was 22. A year later in 1820 he became adjunct professor of Greek and Latin at Columbia College. He was also proficient in French and German. Although he was well-known in

SAMUEL L. MITCHILL, L. L. D.
From *History of the Western Canals* by E. Watson, p. 172. Courtesy of New York State Library.

educated circles for his edition of Lempriere's *A Classical Dictionary*, in 1828 his fame lay in the future.[19]

Another person Harris consulted was Luther Bradish, who went abroad as a special trade emissary of U. S. Secretary of State John Quincy Adams in 1820. He visited in countries bordering the Mediterranean and traveled in Turkey, Egypt, Syria, Tunesia and Europe, studying closely the "language, manners, and antiquities" of those nations. In 1827 he was elected to the state assembly as a Whig.[20]

Joseph Smith, Sr., Pomeroy Tucker, and John Gilbert said that Harris consulted Bradish enroute to New York.[21] W. W. Phelps indirectly supported that claim.[22] Bradish was known in the Palmyra area because he had relatives there.[23] Harris probably tried to see him in his home in Utica, a stopping place on the Erie Canal, but went on to Albany when he found him absent.

Why They Were Consulted

The Official Version gave no reason for the consultation but the sources do. Many charged that Harris was after a profit from the enterprise. It is more likely that he was concerned about getting back the money he was going to advance, but no more.[24]

Religious Motives

Harris first heard about the plates when his brother, Preserved Harris, spoke of them "about the first of October, 1827."[25] Soon afterwards Smith sent his mother to tell Harris that he wanted to see him. According to an angel, Smith claimed, translating the plates was "God's work." At the angel's direction, therefore, Smith looked into the spectacles that were found with the plates and saw the man who was to help get the translation before the world. Harris was the man.

Harris was cautious. "If the Lord will show me that it is his work," he told Smith, "you can have all the money you want." He went home to pray about it, and then God

> showed me that it was his work, and that it was designed to bring in the fulness of the gospel. . . . He showed this to me by the still small voice spoken in the soul. Then I was satisfied that it was the Lord's work, and I was under a covenant to bring it forth.[26]

Thus Harris followed Smith to Pennsylvania, got the transcript, returned to Palmyra,[27] and called on Father John A. Clark of Palmyra's Episcopal Church before heading east.[28]

Clark heard that "a great flood of light was about to burst upon the world, and that the scene of divine manifestations was to be immediately around us." A Golden Bible had been found "as would settle all religious controversies and spsedily bring on the glorious millenium."[29] Charles Anthon later heard the same story. The contents of the golden book "would, as he had been assured, produce an entire change in the world and save it from ruin." It contained "very great truths, and most important revelations of a religious nature."[30]

Harris was even more convinced of Smith's divine commission after his visit with the eastern sages. Smith's obscurity and lack of education confirmed it. Clark reported that Harris was willing to "take of the spoiling of his goods . . . though it consumed all his worldly substance" to help Smith publish the book, because Harris thought it was "the work of the Lord."[31]

Practical Motives

Anthon wrote that Harris was under pressure to publish the translation and came to him "as a last precautionary step."[32] Harris had to convince himself more

> clearly that there was no risk whatever in the matter, and that the work was actually what it claimed to be . . . and satisfy him as to the perfect safety of the investment.[33]

Harris told Pomeroy Tucker at the *Wayne Sentinel* office that the forth-coming translation would be of God, but that he did not want to bear alone the publication costs. Nevertheless, Harris "sought out the 'wisdom of learned men'" to see if the discovery and revelation were genuine.[34]

Environmental Reasons

Martin Harris followed a well-worn route for those who had hieroglyphic writings in hand. In 1819 the *Palmyra Register* told of a rock in Dighton, Mass. which had hieroglyphic inscriptions. Two copies of the characters were sent off to several U. S. universities and to the University of Edinburgh, but were not deciphered until much later.[35] In 1823 the *Palmyra Register* printed the translation of a facsimile of a rock in Pompey, N. Y. and explained several symbols of the inscription. The article concluded that the inscription was written by a Roman Catholic in 1520 and suggested ways by which the stone might have gotten to Pompey.[36]

"Deciphering of Hieoglyphics" appeared in the *Wayne Sentinel* in 1827, describing the work of Professor Seyffarth of Leipzig, who was translating Egyptian antiquities in Rome. Seyffarth

> found the picture of a Jew in bonds, and other allusions to the state of slavery to which the Jews were reduced. He adds, that he had found the old and new testaments in the Sefitic, and the Pentateuch in the Memphitic dialect; and a Mexican manuscript in hieroglyphics, from which he infers, that the Mexicans and Egyptians had intercourse with each other from the remotest antiquity, and that they had the same system of mythology.[37]

Here were models for Harris to follow when he wanted to find further proof that the proposed translation of hieroglyphics on the golden plates was "God's work." The news that the golden plate characters told of the lost "House of Israel," identified as the forefathers of the American Indians, would lead him straight to the foremost Indian authority, Dr. Samuel L. Mitchill.

Whose Idea?

Lucy Smith wrote that Harris's intense interest in the plates led her son to agree

CHARLES ANTHON OF COLUMBIA COLLEGE
From *Harper's Weekly,* 1867, photographed by Brady.

to the consultation even before he left for Pennsylvania. To get the translation started, he was "instructed" to set up the trip and secure an interview.[38] Edward Stevenson, Smith's close friend in later years, said that it "was manifested" to Smith to send Harris east.[39] In 1875 Harris told Simon Smith that he went east "by command."[40]

Joseph Smith's testimony is ambiguous. 2 Nephi 27:15-18 says that the Lord commanded Smith to send Harris. When he began a draft of his history in 1832, however, Smith credited Harris with a vision in which Christ told him to get the characters and consult the scholars.[41] According to Oliver Cowdery's brief history of the Church, the angel in Smith's 1823 vision said that the "scripture must be fulfilled before it is translated, which says that the words of a book, which were sealed, were presented to the learned.[42]

Harris, therefore, pressed for the consultation and Smith let him go to gain his support. Smith's accounts in the Book of Mormon and Cowdery's 1835 history, plus those of his mother, Harris and Stevenson, mean that Smith was told from on high to arrange the interview, that it was needed before the translation could begin.[43] But if Harris wanted the consultation, it is even more certain that Smith also wanted it, for the way he read the prophet Isaiah demanded it.

Prophetic Fulfillment

Smith fleshed out Isaiah 29:11-12 with his interpretation of the details of the Harris-Anthon consultation. It provided for Smith ("him that is not learned") to read what Anthon ("one that is learned") could not; namely, the transcribed characters ("the words of a book that is sealed").[44]

In his 1832 draft Smith told of the consultation, the scholars' failure, Harris's return and request that Smith translate the characters, and his reply to Harris: "I cannot for I am not learned." Smith went on to tell of his translating the characters with the aid of the spectacles and then commented: "and thus the prophcy of Isiah was fulfilled which is writen in the 29 chapter concerning the book."[45] This evidence that Smith was trying to fulfill prophecy is strengthened by the Cowdery account three years later, where emphasis is placed on appropriate procedure: first the scholars had to see the characters, and then the translating could begin.[46]

Harris was ignorant of Isaiah 29's relevance to the consultation as he set out for New York. Anthony Metcalf asked him in 1873 if he had known about the passage, and Harris replied that "Joseph Smith had shown that chapter to him after his return."[47] Ever after Harris explained the scholars' failure to translate the characters by a paradox: since the scholars failed, Smith must be right.[48]

The intent to fulfill prophecy gave Smith a different perspective of the consultation from that of Harris's pragmatic and religious need to see if the proposed translation was of God or Satan, and if he should invest the money. Smith saw the consultation as a way to take a first step on the road to the millennium. That is clear both from the descriptions of the forth-coming book that Harris gave Clark, Anthon and Tucker, and also from later Mormon testimony.[49]

The Harris-Anthon Consultation

Were the Characters Identified?

The Official Version has Anthon and Mitchill say that the transcript characters

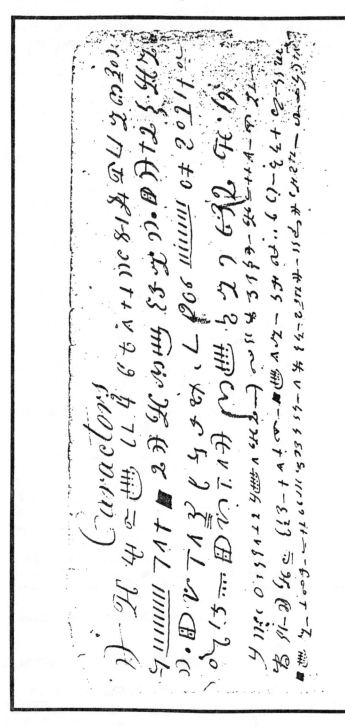

THE ANTHON TRANSCRIPT, CHARACTERS SAID TO HAVE BEEN COPIED FROM THE GOLDEN PLATES

Used by permission of the Research Library and Archives, Reorganized Church of Jesus Christ of Latter Day Saints, The Auditorium, Independence, Missouri.

were "true characters": Egyptian, Chaldaic, Assyriac, and Arabic. In 1829 Smith had identified them simply as "reformed Egyptian," an altered form of Hebrew. Hebrew writing had been changed by the ancient Nephites so that "none other people knoweth our language" (Morm 9:32-34). The question is, did the scholars identify either the characters or the language?

Some sources did identify some characters. John Clark saw one letter that might have been the Hebrew letter **ה**, but otherwise was ignorant "of the characters in which this pretended ancient record was written."[50] In 1834 Charles Anthon spoke of Greek, Roman, and Hebrew letters, but by 1841 concluded that "the marks in the paper appeared to be merely an imitation of various alphabetical characters." Joseph Smith, Sr. report Anthon as saying that, "with few exceptions, the characters were Arabic," but there could not have been many since there was "not enough to make anything out."[51]

W. W. Phelps and David Whitmer supported Smith in saying that the scholars identified the characters as "shorthand" or "reformed" Egyptian.[52] But the scholars would not have known reformed Egyptian if they saw it, since knowledge of it had disappeared with the Nephites. Besides, in 1834 Anthon wrote that the characters were "anything but 'Egyptian hieroglyphics,'" and in 1841 denied that he had pronounced "the Mormonite inscription to be 'reformed Egyptian hieroglyphics.'" But when Smith claimed Anthon as the authority for identifying the characters as Egyptian, Chaldaic, Assyriac and Arabic in the 1838 Official Version, he ignored Anthon's denial.

Smith also repudiated Anthon's statement that the characters were Greek, Roman and Hebrew. Smith ruled out Hebrew in 1829 when the Book of Mormon described reformed Egyptian as an "altered" form of Hebrew, unknown to any but the Nephites. In 1843 he wrote that "there was no Greek or Latin upon the plate from which I. . . . translated the Book of Mormon."[53] Anthon and Mitchill might have compared the characters to different alphabets, as Kimball suggested,[54] but Smith excluded those that Anthon named.

Martin Harris finally supported the Official Version in 1853 and again in 1859.[55] But just as Phelps and Whitmer followed the Book of Mormon's identification of the characters as "reformed Egyptian," so Harris may have followed the Official Version, which has been the story the Church has presented to the public since 1842.

The language of the transcript characters is the other aspect of the question. It has already been established that the Book of Mormon ruled out knowledge of reformed Egyptian to anyone in 1828. Smith supported that several times. In the summer of 1829 he told Martin Harris's brother, Henry, that the transcript was taken from "italic letters written in an unknown language."[56] In 1835 Cowdery wrote that Smith was denied the plates in 1823 "because they cannot be interpreted by the learning of this generation."[57] And in 1843 Smith wrote James Arlington Bennett that "I translated the Book of Mormon from hieroglyphics, the knowledge of which was lost to the world."[58]

Charles Butler, an attorney in Geneva, said that Harris told him that Mitchill thought the characters were "of a nation now extinct which he named," but which Harris did not name.[59] But Harris also told Butler that Anthon "did not know what language they were,"[60] just as he had earlier told John Clark that Anthon "could not decide exactly what language" the characters "belonged to."[61]

The Scholars—Success or Failure?

If the scholars could not identify the language or the characters, they could not translate the transcript. Yet the Official Version has Anthon declare that Smith's sample translation of the transcript "was correct, more so than any he had seen before translated from the Egyptian." This claim finds even less support in the sources.

JOSEPH SMITH, SOURCE OF CONFUSION

Joseph Smith did not deal with the scholars' facility with the transcript characters in the Book of Mormon, but did introduce extraneous features that distract from the progress of the Harris-Anthon consultation story. In 2 Nephi 27 it is the words "which are not sealed" (15) that are delivered to Anthon; the words "which are sealed" (10) were not delivered.

Smith made "sealed" a fluid word. Sometimes it means part of the plates that not even he was allowed to see (8, 21, 22b). At other times it refers to those plates that he and some witnesses were allowed to see (10-11, 17, 19-20). These are the "words which are not sealed" from which the Book of Mormon would be translated. They were not sealed to Smith, the one who was "not learned," but remained sealed to the "learned."

The Book of Mormon, however, says nothing at all about Anthon's ability with the transcript characters. The "learned" (Anthon) neither confirms nor denies that he *can* read them Instead, he asks to see the "book" (plates) before he will *try* to read the characters. Harris (identified only as "another" in verses 9 and 15) tells "the learned" (Anthon) that the "book" (plates) is "sealed" to all but the one who is "not learned" (Smith). "The learned" (Anthon) then responds that he "cannot read" a book he cannot see, but he is referring to the "book" (plates), not to the transcript.

Smith gave his clearest portrayal of the Harris-Anthon consultation in the unfinished history he began in 1832. He wrote that the Lord directed Harris to

> go to New York City with some of the characters so we proceided to copy some of them and he took his Journey to the eastern City and to the learned saying read this I pray thee and the learned said I cannot but if he would bring the plates they would read it but the Lord had forbid it and he returned to me and gave them to me to translate and I said I cannot for I am not learned but the Lord had prepared spectacles for to read the Book therefore I commenced translating the characters.

There is no confusion here. Harris asked Anthon to translate the characters. Anthon could not decipher them and asked to see the plates. They were denied him. Harris brought the transcript back to Smith and asked him to translate it. Smith admitted that he could not translate the characters by his own ability, but found that he could after he donned the spectacles. The transcribed characters, not the plates, are the reference throughout.

Cowdery's 1835 history of the Church has "the words of a book, which were sealed, were presented to the learned." "Sealed" is used to mean that the *language* was sealed to the learned, but not to the unlearned. Orson Pratt used "sealed" in that way when he wrote that the characters were a "sealed writing to the learned professor —the aboriginal language of Ancient America could not be deciphered by him."[63]

The 1832 account is clearer in still another way. The presentations of the Book of Mormon and the Official Version *do not* quote Anthon as saying that he cannot read the transcript, but only that he asked to see the plates, which he was denied. If his reading ability in connection with the transcript was tested at all, both versions say nothing about it. Only in Smith's 1832 account is anything said about Anthon's ability with the Egyptian characters: he could not read them.

There was another factor, however, which also denied to scholars the ability to translate the transcript. Only Smith had the spectacles needed to get the meaning of the characters. Since the reformed Egyptian was known to "none other people," the Lord "hath prepared the means for the interpretation thereof" (Morm 9:32-34). The "interpreters" enabled their user to "translate all records that are of ancient date . . . and no man can look in them except he be commanded" (Mos 8:13). If the scholars had performed according to the Official Version, the purpose for Harris's trip would have been only to fulfill scripture, but Harris actually sought their translation. Moreover, if the scholars had translated the transcribed characters, that would have struck Harris as a real problem, since only Smith had the needed spectacles.

OTHER SOURCES

When the Smith party returned to Palmyra in June, 1829 to find a printer, *Wayne Sentinel* publisher E. B. Grandin refused the contract, but published the Book of Mormon title page, along with his comment:

> much speculation has existed, concerning . . . an ancient record, of a religious and divine nature and origin, written in ancient characters, impossible to be interpreted by any to whom the special gift has not been imparted by inspiration.[64]

This note rules out Anthon's ability to decipher the characters.

In August, 1829 the *Palmyra Freeman* reported that Harris

> took some of the characters interpreted by Smith, and went in search of some one, besides the interpreter, who was learned enough to *English* them; but all to whom he applied (among the number was Professor Mitchell, of New York,) happened not to be possessed of sufficient knowledge to give satisfaction![65]

A week later a similar report in the *Rochester Gem* concluded that Harris "found that no one was intended to perform that all important task but Smith himself."[66]

David Whitmer, one of the Three Witnesses of the Book of Mormon, told *Palmyra Reflector* publisher Abner Cole that when Smith opened the unsealed portion of the plates he discovered "divers and wonderful CHARACTERS; some of them large and some small, but beyond the wisdom of men to understand without supernatural aid."[68] Fifty years later Whitmer said that after Anthon and Mitchill had examined the transcript, "they pronounced the characters reformed Egyptian, but were unable to read them."[68]

In 1830 Joseph Smith, Sr. said that Luther Bradish "could not read the strange characters," and that Anthon could not "make any thing out" of the "Arabic" letters.[69] John Gilbert, Book of Mormon typesetter, wrote that "Martin returned from his trip satisfied that 'Joseph' was a 'little smarter than Professor Anthon,'"[70] which means that Smith could read what Anthon could not. Gilbert's colleague, Pomeroy Tucker, wrote that the scholars "scouted the whole pretense as too depraved for serious attention."[71] Attorney Charles Butler reported Harris as saying that Anthon "admitted that he could not decypher them," and Mitchill gave a "learned dissertation" upon the characters, but did not translate them.[72]

In 1837, Parley Pratt said that Anthon examined the characters, "but was unable to decipher them correctly,"[73] and in 1838 he said that Isaiah 29:11-12 was fulfilled because the "learned" (Anthon) received "the words or characters" but "could not read them."[74] In 1840 Orson Pratt duplicated his brother's words of 1837[75] and noted in 1848 that the characters were "a sealed writing to the learned professor—the aboriginal language of Ancient America could not be deciphered by him."[76] In a debate with Parson Hall in Johnson County, Tennessee in 1841, John Doyle Lee said that the Book of Mormon had been intended to appear "in a language unknown to men."[77] The characters

> were taken to Professor Anthon, of New York City, for translation. He replied that he could not translate them, that they were written in "a sealed language, unknown to the present age." This was just as the prophet Isaiah said it should be.[79]

Charles Anthon expressly denied that the transcript could be translated. According to the 1834 letter, "Dr. Mitchell confessed that he had been unable to understand. . . . I soon came to the conclusion that it was all a trick." And in 1841 he wrote that the characters "had, in my opinion, no meaning at all connected with them."

Support for the Official Version first came from W. W. Phelps in a letter dated January 15, 1831 to E. D. Howe, in which he wrote that the characters "were shown to Dr. Mitchell, and he referred to professor Anthon, who translated them and declared them to be the ancient shorthand Egyptian."[79] A few years later Joseph Knight, Sr. wrote that Martin Harris found men in Albany, Philadelphia and New York who could translate some of the characters, although he said of Anthon and Mitchill, "there were some caricters they could not well understand."[80] In 1870 Martin Harris finally did say that "the characters were translated correctly,"[81] which means that Anthon also could translate. And when Anthony Metcalf interviewed him in 1873, Harris told him that Anthon "said the characters were translated correctly."[82] But the nearly unanimous witness, from Mormon and Gentile, is that the scholars could not translate the transcript.[83]

Was There A Transcript Translation?

According to the Official Version, Anthon declared that Smith's transcript translation "was correct, more so than any he had before seen translated from the Egyptian." On the other hand, Charles Anthon wrote in 1834 that "no translation had been furnished at the time by the young man with the spectacles."

Support for the Official Version came from the Pratt brothers in 1837 and 184J, when they wrote that "a few of the original characters were accurately transcribed and translated by Smith, which, with the translation . . . were presented to . . . Anthon."[84] Tucker wrote that Harris took the transcript "together with the translation in his possession" to New York, but noted that he may not have given Anthon the translation.[85] If Tucker was reporting the actual words of Harris, then as early as the summer of 1829 the transcript translation was becoming part of the Mormon story.

Indirect support might be found in the two letters of Anthon. In the first he wrote of *copies* of the characters whereas the second has *copy*. John Clark wrote that Harris had left him "with some of the manuscripts that Smith furnished him."[86] Anthon's accounts could explain the differences in the paper he saw and that which exists today as the Anthon Transcript, but no translation can be seen. Only from Clark's testimony can one conjecture that a translation was one of the manuscripts.

Not until 1870 did Martin Harris write anything about the sample translation: "the translation that I carried to Prof. Anthon was copied from these plates."[87] Here there appears to be some confusion between the translation and the transcript. In 1873 he finally spoke clearly when he told Anthony Metcalf that Anthon "said the characters were translated correctly."[88] After Simon Smith spoke with Harris in 1875, he wrote that Harris "by command, took part of the manuscript with the translation thereof to one Professor Anthon . . . to get his opinion in regard to the language and translation."[89]

Joseph Smith denied the truth of the 1838 story, however when he said in the 1832 account that Anthon could not translate the characters. Many who knew Smith and Harris in the early years—including family members, close associates, and non-Mormons as well—made no mention of the transcript translation when they spoke or wrote of the consultation. The sample translation was not an element of the original story that Mormons told in the quest for converts. If Harris made the claim of the Official Version, then one must choose between that and the opposite word of Anthon. It is more likely, however, that Smith changed the story and that Harris, years later, accommodated himself to that change.

Anthon's Palmyran Certificate

The bulk of the Official Version deals with a certificate that Anthon wrote to the citizens of Palmyra to verify the characters and the transcript translation. It is mentioned nowhere else by Smith and only once, indirectly, by Harris, when he told Simon Smith that the Official Version was true,[90] yet Harris had every reason to tell it if it were true.

Smith's 1832 account particularly militates against the claim because he wrote that Anthon could not translate the characters. If Anthon could not identify the characters or language and could not translate, then there could be no certificate.

The Official Version has Anthon tear up the certificate. This served the same purpose as having an angel remove the plates from Smith: it made comparison impossible and kept the focus on the message that Smith brought rather than on the medium through which it came. Against the claim is Charles Anthon, who, in a written opinion he gave to Harris,[91] wrote that the marks on the transcript were meaningless.

Joseph Knight, Sr. recalled the Harris-Anthon consultation and said that Anthon could translate a few characters but not others. Therefore he "rote a very good piece to Joseph and said if he would send the original he would translate it."[92] It was this that Anthon tore up, according to Knight. Both Knight's and Anthon's versions are plausible, whereas Smith's Official Version is contradicted by Smith himself.

The Consultation's Purpose

Martin Harris's Strange Reaction

Harris's enthusiasm to publish the book seems strange in view of the nearly unanimous witness that the scholars could not translate the transcript characters. It is strange, also, that little attention has been given to his response.

At the start of his eastward journey, Harris viewed John Clark's ignorance of the characters as "new proof that Smith's account of the divine revelation made to him was entirely to be relied on."[93] Luther Bradish told Harris that there was not enough "to make anything out." Anthon told him that the transcript was a "trick, perhaps a hoax," that it was "part of a scheme to cheat the farmer of his money and I communicated my suspicions to him" that "some cunning fellow had prepared the paper in question, for the purpose of imposing" upon him.[94]

When Harris returned to Palmyra he told Clark that Anthon could not pinpoint the language of the characters.

> Martin had now become a perfect believer. He said he had no more doubt of Smith's commission, than of the divine commission of the apostles. The very fact that Smith was an obscure and illiterate man, showed that he must be acting under divine impulses. It was in vain I endeavoured to expostulate. I was an unbeliever, and could not see afar off.[95]

"My intimations . . . in reference to the possible imposition that was being practiced upon him . . . were indignantly repelled."[96]

If he were looking for scholarly confirmation of the characters' authenticity, Harris should have been discouraged. But he was convinced by their failures and warnings. He had wanted the Lord to show him "that it is his work." Now he "was satisfied that it was the Lord's work," and he "was under a covenant to bring it forth." Such sentiment is behind John Gilbert's report that "Martin returned from his trip east satisfied that 'Joseph' was a 'little smarter than Professor Anthon.'" Smith could "read" the characters that were "sealed" to the "learned." According to Pomeroy Tucker, Harris regarded

> these untoward results merely as "proving the lack of wisdom" on the part of the rejecters, and also as illustrating the truth of his favorite quotation, that "God hath chosen the foolish things of the world to confound the wise." This was always his self-convincing argument in reply to similar adversity in his fanatical pursuit.[97]

There is no way to explain his joy at scholarly ignorance, or disregard for their warnings, except that he had been primed for their failure.

It is probable, then, that Smith forewarned Harris that the scholars would fail, and that such failure would be a sign that Smith's story was true. Harris said that he did not know that he was fulfilling Isaiah 29 until he returned from the consultation. Smith had told him—and he believed it—"that Smith was to prepare the way for the conversion of the world to a new system of faith, by transcribing the characters from the plates and giving translations of the same."[98]

Smith's Purpose

Smith sent Harris to Mitchill and Anthon, therefore, not to get their translation, but to convince Harris to go through with financing the publication of the translation, and to fulfill prophecy. Hugh Nibley suggested that it was to give the leading scholars the opportunity "to speak their piece," so that no one could charge that Smith was afraid to display "his mythical manuscript to *real* scholars."[99] But Smith knew that they would not, could not—as Nibley also admits—translate the characters.[100]

Smith used the schema of Isaiah 29:11-12 as a step-by-step blueprint to launch his restoration. That is, to fulfill the conditions of Isaiah's pericope, first the "sealed" words had to be presented to the "learned" before the "sealed" book could be translated. He had been talking about it since his marriage to Emma in January, 1827, and his 1832 account and Cowdery's 1835 account particularly accent this feature.

The Harris-Anthon consultation was suggested by Isaiah 29, but another source meshed with it and indicated that evidence in hand was not needed to incite faith. Ethan Smith's Pittsfield Parchment story told of his belief that there was an Indian parchment with Hebrew characters on it, but he never found the parchment. He believed it only on the basis of a translation and the testimony of two sets of witnesses.[101]

Thus the Harris-Anthon consultation connected the translation of the Book of Mormon and the launching of the restoration church to prophetic fulfillment. It was a prior step in the commonly accepted progression of events that millennialists believed would signal the second coming of Christ.

Evolution of the Official Version

The first change from the 1828 consultation is found in the Book of Mormon's presentation of the event, for Joseph Smith changed the identity of what Anthon could not read from the transcript characters in his hand to the plates that he was not allowed to see. From 1829 to 1838 there are four further discernible steps in the story's evolution.

Harris visited the scholars, found that they could not translate the characters, and went home. (2) Harris visited the scholars, found that they could authenticate, but not translate, the characters. This was possibly as early as the summer of 1829. (3) Harris visited the scholars and found that they could identify and translate the characters. This was by late 1830 or early 1831. (4) Smith completed the evolution in 1838. Harris visited the scholars, found that they could authenticate the characters, identify the language, and verify Smith's sample translation. He received Anthon's certificate to the Palmyrans and then saw Anthon tear it up. The many sources can be seen to be at different stages along the line of progression, but most stayed at a pre-1838 version even into old age.

The evolution of the Harris-Anthon consultation story was to be only one of many changes made in Joseph Smith's developing theology. Unitarian theology of the Book of Mormon became the polytheism of the Doctrine and Covenants. Book of Mormon monogamy became Nauvoo polygamy. After the Mormons purchased Egyptian mummies in 1835, Smith arranged "a grammar of the Egyptian language as practiced by the ancients"[102] and brought forth the Book of Abraham. The Official Version gave scholarly support to Smith's current activity in the late 1830s and projected it back to his first efforts with the reformed Egyptian on the golden plates.

The developments of the 1830s also shed light upon the transformation of the reformed Egyptian characters of 1828-35 into characters of the Egyptian, Chaldaic, Assyriac and Arabic alphabets. Before his 1828 imprisonment in Liberty, Missouri,

TABLE IV

SOURCE ANALYSIS OF HARRIS-ANTHON CONSULTATION

	Main Contact (Harris / Both / Smith)			Contact Year	Publication Year	Language Known?		Scholars Translate?		Transcript Translation		Any Palmyra Certificate?	
	H	B	S			Y	N	Y	N	Y	N	Y	N
PRIMARY SOURCES													
C. Anthon#	H			1828									
1834 Letter					1834		X		X	X			/
1841 Letter				1841	1841		X		X				/
M. Harris Letter				1828	1870	/?		X?		X?			
J. Smith, Jr.	H			1828									
Bk. Mormon					1829		X	/					/
1832 Hist.					1832	/			X				/
Insp. Vers.					1833		X	/					/
Off. Vers.					1838	X		X		X		X	
Letter to JAB					1843		X	/					/
OTHER SOURCES	H												
J. Clark#	H			1828	1840		X		X				/
J. Smith, Sr.		B		1828	1870	X			X				/
J. H. Gilbert	H			1828	1892				X				/
J. Knight, Sr.			S	1828	1835(?)			X	X				X
W. R. Hein			S	1828	1888				X				
E. B. Grandin#*		B		1829	1829			/	X				/
Pal. Freeman#	H			1829	1829				X				/
Roch. Gem#	H			1829	1829				X				/
C. Butler#	H			1829	1831	X	X		X				/
D. Whitmer		B		1829	1831				.X				/
"					1881	X			X				/
W. W. Phelps			S	1830	1831	X	X						
P. Pratt		B		1830	1837				X	X			/
"					1838				X				/
O. Pratt		B		1830	1840				X	X			/
J. D. Lee			S	1838	1841		X		X				/
D. B. Dille	H			1853	1853	X							
J. Tiffany#	H			1859	1859	X							
A. Metcalf#	H			1873	1888	/		X		X			
S. Smith	H			1875	1881	X		X		X			

NOTES ON SOURCE ANALYSIS TABLE

* Source is not referring to the Harris-Anthon consultation, although it bears upon it.

\# Non-Mormon source.

/ Answers in other columns imply an answer in a column, the question of which is not directly answered.

Main Contact. The source heard about the consultation from Smith, or Harris, or both. If the source knew Smith as well as Harris, there may be some indication of it if it is known from whom the source got the story.

Contact Year. When the source first heard of the consultation.

Publication Year. The year that the source appeared in print, or the year that the manuscript, letter, or dictated notes are known to have taken form. Example: the Book of Mormon manuscript was dictated in 1829, but the book appeared in 1830.

Language Known? Refers to the naming of the characters or the language, or to the claim that the language was known or unknown.

Scholars Translate? Yes or no. Evidence indicates that they did or did not. If it is claimed that the scholars corroborated Smith's sample translation, then that implies that they translated. If Joseph Smith told someone that the knowledge of the language in which the characters were written had been lost, then that implies that they did not translate.

Transcript Translation? By testimony or implication, the source indicates that there was or was not a sample translation.

Any Palmyran Certificate? Yes or no. Indirect evidence indicates one or the other. Example: If the source said that the language was unknown, or that the scholars did not translate, then that rules out Anthon giving Harris the kind of certificate stated in the Official Version.

Smith stayed with George and Lucinda Morgan Harris.[103] Lucinda was the widow of William Morgan whose 1826 disappearance was the immediate cause of the anti-Masonic excitement in New York. Morgan had received only the Royal Arch degree of Masonry, and in 1829 David Bernard added the Royal Arch to his reprint of Morgan's expose of Masonry's first three degrees.

Bernard spoke of the Royal Arch word for God that was lost with the death of Masonry's legendary hero, Hiram Abiff, and restored when the temple was rebuilt in Jerusalem after the Jews return from the Babylonian exile. The word JAH-BUH-LUN was compounded from "three different languages, (i. e. Hebrew, Chaldaic, and Syriac."[104] He also added a secret alphabetical code, many letters of which correspond to characters on the Anthon Transcript.[105] The Harris family may either have had Bernard's book or revealed this aspect of the Royal Arch to Smith. By identifying the characters as he did in 1838, Smith may have been appealing to those with Masonic backgrounds. Later he did make that appeal more openly.[106]

Mormon Use of the Consultation

By 1834 if not earlier, Mormons used Anthon's name and authority to claim that the transcript characters were "reformed Egyptian hieroglyphics,"[107] and were still doing it in New York in 1841.[108] In Brooklyn in 1836 Mormons held a meeting in which "they were to prove by the scriptures that the Book of Mormon was of divine authority," and when they came to Isaiah 29, the speaker "strove to make his bearers believe that the prophet had this book in mind."[109] On a Mississippi steamer in 1842, according to Daniel Kidder, Mormons used the consultation story to make proselytes to Mormonism, saying "that the prophecy of Isaiah was literally fulfilled in the origin of the book before us."[110] Today it has become one of the staples of Mormon folklore.[111]

CONCLUSION

Contrary to Stanley Kimball's conclusion that the Harris-Anthon consultation had no important missionary use, no "great practical value," it convinced Martin Harris to finance the publication of the Book of Mormon, tied Smith's restoration to prophetic fulfillment, and gave Smith his credential as one foreseen in prophecy. The names of Samuel L. Mitchill and Charles Anthon were and are used to authenticate Mormon claims when Mormon missionaries call. The Harris-Anthon consultation is practical and far reaching, then, because it helps establish Joseph Smith's influence.

Joseph Smith used Isaiah 29:4 to claim that the Book of Mormon was the lost book of the Indians, buried through the ages, and recovered by himself from the side of Cumorah Hill near his home. Isaiah 29:11-12 was used to establish the rediscovered book as written in a lost script that defied the efforts of the best known scholars of New York. It provided for Smith himself to translate it and set the stage for the millennium.

FOOTNOTES

1. Meyer, pp. 28-34.
2. He cited in whole or in part chaps. 5, 7, 10, 11, 14, 18, 26, 42, 43, 48, 51, 60, 65, and 66. He

regarded chaps. 48-49 as predictions of the restoration in the "latter days." So did Joseph Smith as he expressed it through Nephi in I Nephi 20-21.

3. *Inspired Version of the Holy Scriptures.* An Inspired Revision of the Authorized Version, by Joseph Smith, Jr. A New and Corrected Edition (Independence, Mo.: The Reorganized Church of Jesus Christ of Latter Day Saints, c. 1944). Smith made this revision with the help of Sidney Rigdon from 1831-33, although he worked on it from time to time after that. Cf. Howard, *Restoration Scriptures*, pp. 70-193. The Inspired Version is the official Bible of the Reorganized Church, but the larger Utah Church has never accepted it as an officially authorized version. For their reasoning and a complete history of Smith's revision, cf. Reed Connell Durham, Jr., "A History of Joseph Smith's Revision of the Bible," (unpublished Ph. D. dissertation, Brigham Young University, 1960). Cf. also Arbaugh, *Revelation in Mormonism*, pp. 75-85 for a critique of the Revision.

4. It reads as follows:

> And I will camp against thee round about, and will lay siege against thee with a mount, and I will raise forts against thee. And thou shalt be brought down, and shalt speak out of the ground, and thy speech shall be brought low out of the dust, and thy voice shall be, as of one that hath a familiar spirit.

Cf. also Appendix II for the textual comparison with the Inspired Version and the Book of Mormon.

5. Cf. the KJV with the Book of Mormon rendition in Appendix II.

6. Cf. Ezekiel 37:1-14; Isaiah 29:3-5.

7. Jac 2:21; Mos 2:25-26; Morm 9:17.

8. Jac 2:15; Al 34:38; 42:30; 3 Ne 20:37; Moro 10:31.

9. I Ne 22:14, 23; 2 Ne 15:24; Jac 2:15.

10. I Ne 22:14, 23; 2 Ne 15:25; 26:15; 33:13.

11. I Ne 18:18; 2 Ne 3:19-20; 12:10; 27:9; Morm 8:16, 23, 26; Eth 8:24; Moro 10:27, 29.

12. The editors of the 1952 LDS edition of the Book of Mormon suggest in the index, p. 547, that the destruction of the "great and abominable church" and the false churches is a figurative usage. They support the writer's point, therefore, that Smith used "dust" figuratively and literally to mean "destruction."

13. Cf. Appendix II.

14. TS, May 2, 1842. Also in DHC, I, pp. 19-20. The professor's name, however, was Anthon, not Anthony.

15. Sources are the principals involved and the people who knew or interviewed them. Many who refer to the consultation did not speak with the parties involved and are therefore not cited.

16. "Samuel Latham Mitchill," DAB, XIII, 69-71.

17. Mitchill's name appeared in the *Western Farmer, Palmyra Herald*, and *Wayne Sentinel* more than 15 times from 1821-26.

18. At least eight sources do not refer to names of the scholars. Some mention only Anthon. Four have the order of Mitchill, then Anthon. Anthon specifically said that Mitchill sent Harris to him.

19. "Charles Anthon," DAB, I, 313-14.

20. "Luther Bradish," DAB, II, 567-68.

21. Lapham, p. 307, interviewed the prophet's father before 1831. Pomeroy Tucker, *The Origin, Rise, and Progress of Mormonism* (New York: D. Appleton and Company, 1867), p. 42; Memorandum of John H. Gilbert, Esq., September 8, 1892, Palmyra, New York (typescript copy, p. 4, located in LDS Church Archives in Salt Lake City).

22. In his January 15, 1831 letter to E. D. Howe, *Mormonism Unvailed*, p. 273, Phelps said that Harris took the characters to Utica, Albany, and New York City. Bradish lived at Utica and was serving in the state legislature in Albany in 1828. Two additional sources mention Philadelphia as one of the cities visited: Joseph Knight, Sr. and William R. Hein. Cf. Dean C. Jessee, "Joseph Knight's Recollection of Early Mormon History," BYUS, XVII, I (Autumn, 1976), 29-39; and "W. R. Hine's Statement," *Naked Truths About Mormonism*, I, I (January, 1888), p. 2. Knight's recollection was written in the 1830s. Both Knight and Hein lived in Colesville, N. Y. and knew Smith before publication of the Book of Mormon. Knight became a follower. Hein did not.

23. Stanley B. Kimball, "The Anthon Transcript: People, Primary Sources, and Problems," BYUS, X, 3 (Spring, 1970), 330, points out that Harris may have known about Bradish's travels, may have known Bradish himself, since Bradish had relatives around Palmyra.

24. The sources reveal different estimates of Harris. The first was that Harris was deluded but absolutely honest in his persuasion. The second estimate, including that of his wife, was that Harris saw his

involvement as a financially profitable venture. The third was a blending of the first two estimate. Clark, p. 224, reported Harris as "intent upon the pecuniary advantage . . . as upon the spiritual light" the newly discovered Nephite book "would diffuse over the world." Cf. also Tucker, p. 55 and Turner, p. 215.

25. Joel Tiffany, "Mormonism, No. II," *Tiffany's Monthly* (August?, 1859), V, 167. The prophet's mother said that her husband told Harris about the plates at least a couple years before; Lucy Mack Smith, p. 109.

26. Tiffany, p. 168. Turner, p. 215, supported Harris's story that Smith made the first contact in seeking Harris's support. Lucy Smith, pp. 113-14, said that her son asked her to arrange a meeting between him and Harris. Joseph Knight, Sr. also credits Smith with the initial impetus to contact the scholars; cf. Dean C. Jessee, "Joseph Knight's Recollection," p . 33. It is clear that Smith wanted the meeting.

27. Clark, pp. 228-29, is the source for Harris's return to Palmyra before he left for New York City.

28. Clark, p. 222, wrote that Harris had occasionally "attended divine service in our church."

29. *Ibid.,* pp. 223-24.

30. From a letter to E. D. Howe in Howe, pp. 270-72. Often reprinted and cited hereafter as the 1834 letter.

31. Clark, p. 230.

32. Letter to Rev. T. W. Coit, Rector of Trinity Church, New Rochelle, West Chester County, New York; published in *The Church Record* (Vol. I; Flushing, N. Y., April 24, 1841), pp. 231-32. It appeared in Clark, pp. 233-38 and will be cited hereafter as the 1841 letter.

33. Tucker, pp. 41-42.

34. *Ibid.,* p. 55.

35. PR, June 2, 1819. The Smiths subscribed to the *Palmyra Register* and its successors *Western Farmer, Palmyra Herald,* and *Wayne Sentinel.*

36. PH, February 19, 1823.

37. WS, June 1, 1827. After their marriage on January 18, Smith and Emma stayed at the Smith home in Manchester until the middle of December, 1827. DHC, I, 20.

38. Lucy Smith, pp. 109, 113-14.

39. *Reminiscences of the Prophet Joseph* (Salt Lake City, 1893), pp. 28-29. Cited in William E. Berrett and Alma P. Burton, *Readings in L. D. S. History from Original Manuscripts* (3 vols.; Salt Lake City: Deseret Book Company, c. 1953), I, 26.

40. Simon Smith's letter to President Joseph Smith, III, dated December 30, 1880, SH, February 1, 1881.

41. This first came to public view in Paul R. Cheesman's "An Analysis of the Accounts Relating to Joseph Smith's Early Vision," (unpublished Masters thesis, Brigham Young University, 1965), Appendix D. Dean C. Jessee published an authoritative account of portions of it in "The Early Accounts of Joseph Smith's First Vision," BYUS, IX, 3 (Spring, 1969), 275-94.

42. MA, February, 1835, p. 80. The trustworthiness of Cowdery's account on some particulars was debated by Wesley P. Walters and Richard L. Bushman in "The Question of the Palmyra Revival," *Dialogue,* IV, 1 (Spring, 1969), 59-100. Bushman criticized Walters's reliance on Cowdery's version because his evidence was "hearsay" and—because he was physically distant from Smith—"close cooperation was impossible," pp. 85-86. Walters, p. 95, reviewed the evidence showing the frequency with which Cowdery and Smith spent time together to support Cowdery's claim to have had "authentic documents" and Smith's help in the writing, MA, October, 1834, p. 13.

43. Forty of the first 72 revelations show the pattern. Some person or circumstance initiated—or presented—a question, challenge or need to Smith. To respond, Smith began a dialog with—or posed the problem to—God. God's response or revelation—the impression that came to Smith's mind—revealed the way to respond to the person, challenge or need.

44. 2 Nephi 27:15-19. This account does not have Smith translate the characters, but finally he can, since he translated the plates from which the transcript was taken.

45. Cheesman, Appendix D. Emily M. Austin, nee Colburn, wrote of Smith's coming to Colesville at the time he was married in January, 1827:

> He declared an angel . . . told him of golden plates . . . containing a history . . . which Isaiah the prophet had spoken of; a vision which should become as the words of a book that is sealed.

Mormonism: or Life Among the Mormons (Madison: M. J. Cantrell Book and Job Printer, 1882), pp. 33-35. More than a year before Harris went east to Anthon, therefore, Smith had been thinking about prophetic fulfillment in terms of Isaiah 29 and the golden plates.

46. The Pratt brothers spread this thinking: the *words* of a book had to be delivered to the learned (who would be unable to read them), while the book itself was delivered to the unlearned (who would be able to read it with the aid of the spectacles). That fulfilled the text. Parley P. Pratt wrote it in *Mormonism Unveiled—Truth Vindicated* in 1838. Cf. *Writings of Parley Parker Pratt* (Parker Pratt Robison, ed.; Salt Lake City: By the editor, c. 1952), pp. 205-06.

47. Anthony Metcalf, *Ten Years Before the Mast* (Mildad, Idaho: By the Author, 1888), p. 71.

48. Clark, p. 230, and Tucker, p. 42, noted the paradox.

49. Church benevolences, revival campaigns, communal experiments and newly formed religious groups had the millennium as a motivating factor.

50. Clark, p. 228.

51. Lapham, p. 307.

52. Phelps, in Howe, p. 273. Whitmer in an interview in the *Kansas City Daily Journal*, June 5, 1881.

53. TS; May 15, 1843.

54. Kimball, p. 335.

55. Cf. David B. Dille, MS, XXI, 34 (August 20, 1853), 545-46; Tiffany, p. 163.

56. Howe, p. 253.

57. MA, October, 1835, p. 198.

58. Joseph Smith to James Arlington Bennett, Nauvoo, November 13, 1843. *Reply of Joseph Smith to the Letter of J. A. B.—of A—n House* (New York. Liverpool, published by R. Hedlock & T. Ward [1844]); referred to in MS, February, 1844, p. 160. Copies are in the Yale University Library and the LDS Church Archives in Salt Lake City.

59. Leonard J. Arrington, "James Gordon Bennett's 1831 Report on 'The Mormonites,'" BYUS, X, 3 (Spring, 1970), p. 362. Arrington published the article referring to Butler along with the notes that Bennett took, p. 355, from which he wrote the article. The notes were dated August 7-8, 1831.

60. *Ibid.*, p. 352.

61. Clark, p. 229.

62. Cheesman, Appendix D.

63. Orson Pratt, "Divine Authority, or the Question, Was Joseph Smith sent of God?," *Doctrines of the Gospel* (Salt Lake City: Juvenile Instructor Office, 1884), p. 9. This is a reprint of *A Series of Pamphlets* published from 1848-51, with some portions deleted.

66. *Rochester Gem*, September 5, 1829. The similarity of wording suggests that the editor of the *Gem* took his account from the *Advertiser*, published a few days earlier, or from the *Freeman* itself.

67. *Palmyra Reflector*, March 19, 1831.

68. *Kansas City Daily Journal*, June 5, 1881.

69. Lapham, p. 307.

70. Gilbert, p. 4.

71. Tucker, p. 42.

72. Arrington, p. 362.

73. Parley P. Pratt, *Voice of Warning*, p. 72; *Writings of Parley Parker Pratt*, pp. 205-06; cf. n. 46 above.

74. *Ibid.*

75. Orson Pratt, *An Interesting Account of Several Remarkable Visions and of the Late Discovery of Ancient American Records* (New York City: By the Author, 1841), pp. 6-7. First published in Edinburgh in 1840.

76. "Divine Authority," p. 9.

77. John Doyle Lee, *Mormonism Unveiled: or the Life and Confession of the Late Mormon Bishop John D. Lee* (Omaha: F. H. Rogers, 1891), p. 119.

78. *Ibid.*, p. 120.

79. Howe, p. 273.

80. Jessee, "Joseph Knight's Recollection," p. 33.

81. Martin Harris to Mr. Emerson, Smithfield, Utah, November 23, 1870; SH, XXII (1875), p. 630.

82. Metcalf, p. 71.

83. Mormon scholars recognize that the Official Version claims too much. B. H. Roberts, *New Witnesses for God* (Salt Lake City: Deseret Book Company, c. 1926), II, pp. 95-96, n. c; Hugh Nibley, "A New Look at the Pearl of Great Price Part I. Challenge and Response," Vol. 71, No. 2 (February, 1968), p. 17; and Kimball, "The Anthon Transcript," pp. 335-36, have agreed that the scholars could not translate Egyptian at that time because the Rosetta Stone had only recently been decoded. There had not been sufficient time to learn the language. They suggest that Anthon and Mitchill may have compared the

characters to various styles of writing, or said that they were authentic characters, but nothing more. Kimball also suggests that Harris was eager to fulfill a prophecy and that he might have mistaken "translation" for "transcription." Harris, however, said that he did not know of the prophecy until Smith showed it to him upon his return from the east. Kimball's suggestions have the effect of removing from Joseph Smith the responsibility for claiming scholarly corroboration. Harris cannot be blamed, however, for Smith placed the Official Version into his *History*, and he had been the first to identify the language in the Book of Mormon. Seemingly unaware, Smith went against his own statements about the "reformed Egyptian" that he had made in the Book of Mormon, later writings, and interviews.

84. Cf. nn. 73, 75.

85. Tucker, pp. 42-45.

86. Clark, p. 229.

87. Martin Harris to Mr. Emerson.

88. Metcalf, p. 71.

89. Simon Smith to President Joseph Smith, III.

90. *Ibid.*

91. Two apparent contradictions in Anthon's two letters lead Mormon scholars to favor Harris's account over Anthon's. Kimball, p. 339, concluded that Anthon was an "uncritical, emotional man," not a "detached scholar." But Anthon cannot be dismissed like that, for this description fits no one so much as Martin Harris. Joseph Smith was contradictory very many times.

Wesley P. Walters offered a plausible explanation of the apparent contradictions. First, when Howe asked Anthon for his version of the consultation, he appeared not to have told Anthon it was for publication, since Anthon asked him "to publish this letter immediately, should you find my name mentioned again by these wretched fanatics." In his introduction to the 1841 letter, T. W. Coit wrote that he had asked Anthon for a public statement. Anthon, therefore, replied that no one had previously asked for his statement in "writing," and that he had not thought it "worthwhile to say anything publicly on the subject."

Second, the 1834 letter restates Harris's story about the spectacles enabling the person who used them to examine the plates to read and fully "understand their meaning." Harris came to get Anthon's opinion "about the meaning of the paper," but Anthon refused to give a "learned opinion" about a "hoax." Harris, however, may have wanted a written statement that the characters . . . "had in my opinion no meaning at all connected with them." Wesley P. Walters to Robert Hullinger, January 8, 1975. Note that this is likely, since Harris most probably expected the scholars to fail.

92. Jessee, "Joseph Knight's Recollection," p. 33.

93. Clark, p. 230.

94. 1834 letter.

95. Clark, p. 230.

96. *Ibid.*, p. 224. This was during Harris's first visit before he had seen Anthon.

97. Tucker, p. 42.

98. Clark, p. 228.

99. Nibley, "A New Look," p. 17.

100. Cf. n. 83 above.

101. Cf. Appendix I below and pp. 55 — 58 above.

102. DHC, III, p. 238.

103. *Ibid.*, p. 9. Smith arrived at Far West, Missouri on March 14, 1838 and began dictating his *History* on April 27; *ibid.*, p. 25. He was still dictating on May 1-4; *ibid.*, p. 26. He did enough to cover the material of the Official Version in the first few days after having been with the George Harris family for over a month. The Official Version is found in Smith's Manuscript History, Book A-1, p. 9, in the LDS Church Archives, Salt Lake City. Interestingly, the following was written between the lines, possibly as an afterthought or even at a later time: "I informed him that part of the plates were sealed, and that I was forbidden to bring them. He replied, 'I cannot read a sealed book.'"

104. David Bernard, *Light on Masonry* (Utica: William Williams, 1829), pp. 138-39. Also reproduced in the "Report of Seceding Freemasons, or, A Summary of Freemasonry," *The Proceedings of the United States Anti-Masonic Convention, Held at Philadelphia, September 11, 1830* (New York: Skinner and Dewey, 1830), pp. 45-46. Cf. "The Royal Arch Key" illustration on p. 109   since Bernard's book and the "Report" appeared during the years that Smith was dictating and publishing the Book of Mormon, and Bernard's book was widely available, Smith may well have seen it long before his stay with the Harris family at Far West.

It's an interesting sidelight that the ritual as Bernard knew it mentioned only three languages. Although the Official Version mentions four, as does modern Masonic ritual, it appears that this was one of the variations to be found in Masonry in the 1820s and 1830s. Martin Harris mentioned only three languages in his interview with David B. Dille in 1853, although he later spoke of four. For a modern ritual with the context of the four languages in the Mystical Lecture of the First Chair of the Royal Arch and its modern spelling of the Sacred Name as JAH-BUL-ON, cf. Walton Hannah, *Darkness Visible: A Revelation & Interpretation of Freemasonry* (London Augustine Press, c. 1952), p. 181.

105. Bernard, pp. 138-39; "Report of Seceding Freemasons," pp. 45-45. See "The Royal Arch Key" illustration on p. 109.

106. Reed Connell Durham, Jr., "Is There No Help for the Widow's Son," Presidential Address for the Mormon History Association, April 20, 1974, Nauvoo, Illinois. A typed copy was circulated by Prof. Mervin B. Hogan, Research Lodge of Utah, and since published in *Mormon Miscellaneous*, Vol. I, No. 1 (October, 1975), pp. 11-16. Durham finds many parallels between the developing Mormonism of the late 1830s and 1840s.

107. Howe, p. 273.

108. Coit, *The Church Record*, p. 231.

109. James McChesney, *An Antidote to Mormonism* (New York: By the Author, 1838), p. 21.

110. Daniel P. Kidder, *Mormonism and the Mormons: A Historical View of the Rise and Progress of the Sect Self-Styled Latter Day Saints* (New York: G. Lane and P. P. Sanford, 1842), p. 305.

111. It has become a faith-promoting story taught to children, even as the story of the Pilgrims teaches patriotism to American children. Cf. Austin and Alta Fife, *Saints of Sage and Saddle: Folklore Among the Mormons* (Bloomington, Ind.: Indiana University Press, c. 1956), pp. 38-39.

8

Exposed:
Masonic Ritual and Lore

In answer to our question, as to what it was that Joseph had thus obtained, he said it consisted of a set of gold plates, about six inches wide, and nine or ten inches long. They were in the form of a book. . . . On the next page were representations of all the masonic implements, as used by masons at the present day.

Fayette Lapham[1]

As the third decade of the 19th century began there was also the beginning of a resurgent anti-Masonic movement among some eastern churches. In 1820 the Baptists at Hamilton College in Clinton, New York mounted a resistance.[2] The Presbyterian Pittsburgh Synod declared the Lodge unfit for Christians in January, 1821 and the General Methodist Conference forbade its Pennsylvania clergy to be Masons.[3] Nevertheless, Freemasons were solidly fixed as part of the American establishment in the early 1820s. Fears of the previous generation, which led people to connect Freemasonry with deism and Jacobinism, were largely assuaged.[4] Significant numbers of the order were church members and many Protestant clergy served as chaplains of local lodges. Hence a Masonic sermon at the close of the 2nd decade could show the same regard for the Bible that pietistic Christians held:

Take from Masonry the validity of the Bible . . . and total darkness will ensue. If the unhallowed feet of the deist, presumes to step upon thy *pavement*, spurn him from thence. No DEIST OR STUPID LIBERTINE CAN BE A MASON.[5]

In 1825 the Masonic Lodge of New York had a membership of 20,000 in 480 lodges, and there were very many irregularly organized or not yet recognized lodges.[6] In the United States Masons represented nearly one ninth of American voters and nearly half of the lodges were in New York.[7] That is why the nation could hardly have anticipated the explosion of rage that followed William Morgan's abduction and disappearance. Fears lodged deeply in the American mind before the turn of the century resurfaced.

Governor De Witt Clinton, himself a high-ranking Mason, offered a reward for information leading to the arrest and conviction of the kidnappers and for information about the whereabouts of Morgan.[8] Clinton's abhorence of the affair was widely shared by Masons as they joined non-Masons in community meetings to draw up resolutions urging that justice be done.[9]

The kidnappers were tried in Canandaigua,[10] but the public was convinced that their sentences were too light and that others had been involved. The press covered the trial and every paper carried an increasing amount of news about the Masonic controversy.[11] Public interest was so intense, however, that 46 anti-Masonic papers sprang up in New York, and 70 others appeared in Pennsylvania, Ohio, Massachusetts and a few other states.[12] By 1829 anti-Masonic papers were in Lyons, Canandaigua, Waterloo, Troy and Seneca Falls. In 1828 the anti-Masonic *Palmyra Freeman* came on the scene.[13]

Anti-Masonic conventions convened already in 1826. Twenty such conventions were held in New York in 1827, and half of them were in West Bloomfield, Bloomfield, Manchester, Farmington, Seneca, Vienna and Victor—all hosting one, and Canandaigua—hosting three. Manchester and Farmington were close to the Smith home. In October an anti-Masonic convention appointed Martin Harris to the Palmyra "committee of vigilance"[15] and the Wayne County convention resolved not to elect to public office any Mason or one who did not treat seriously Morgan's abduction.[16] A distinct feature at the conventions was the enactment and parody of Masonic ritual by ex-Masons for the sake of lampooning Masonic "secrets."[17]

Lodges in western New York condemned the abduction and chapters in Canandaigua and Pultneyville disavowed it publicly.[18] Soon after, Palmyra Lodge No. 112 published its repudiation.[19] Manchester Lodge No. 269, with over 100 members, dissolved in December, 1828 when all lodges in Monroe County disbanded.[20] Lodges in Richmond and Naples, Ontario County, followed suit by March, 1829.[21] From 1827-34 only as many as 90 and as few as 50 lodges reported to the Grand Lodge of the state of New York.[22]

Church bodies and individual congregations divided over the Masonic question. Baptist churches convened at Milton, N. Y. September 27, 1827 and adopted a 15 point condemnation of the Freemasons.[23] The Baptist Society Convention at Le Roy, New York in January, 1828 resolved to ask all members who were Freemasons to leave the lodge or face eventual excommunication.[24] In June the Genessee Consociation resolved:

> That the Consociation will neither license, ordain, or install those who sustain any connexion with the institution of Masonry, or who will not disapprove and renounce it; nor will we give letters of recommendation in favor of such persons to preach in any of the churches in our connexion.[25]

Baptists around Palmyra were at war with each other.[26] Finally, revivalists who had united in camp meetings also divided over the lodge. Methodist Lorenzo Dow and Presbyterian Charles Finney were on opposite sides while others, like Free-will Baptist David Marks, were perplexedly undecided.

The first edition of Morgan's expose came out in 1826 from Batavia and in 1827 English editions were printed in New York City, Rochester, and York, Canada. A French edition was published in Boston in 1827 and a German edition in Waterloo, N. Y. (25 miles from Palmyra) in 1828. The *Rochester Daily Advertiser* said of the Canadian run on Morgan's book:

> McKenzie at York, published an edition, with a sort of historical preface, and sold a couple hundred copies the first day. M. McFarlane, of the Kingston Chronicle, had still greater success, having disposed of 1733 in four days.[27]

Appeals for Morgan's family were published far and wide. A letter published in Batavia several weeks after Morgan disappeared reappeared in a number of papers and expressed the typical sentiment:

> His distressed wife and two infant children, are left dependent on charity for their sustenance. . . . All person who are willing to serve the cause of humanity, and assist to remove the distressing apprehensions of his unfortunate wife are earnestly requested to communicate to one of the committee.[28]

McFarlane at the *Kingston Chronicle* intended to donate the proceeds from his printing to Mrs. Morgan.[29] The same concern surfaced in Joseph Smith's Book of Mormon:

> Yea, why do you build up your secret combinations to get gain, and cause that widows should mourn before the Lord, and also the blood of their fathers and their husbands to cry unto the Lord from the ground, for vengeance upon your heads? (Morm 8:40)

Secret combinations! That charge was hurled at the Masonic Lodge for years. In fact, there were several points developed against the Masons and repeated over and over in the anti-Masonic conventions, town assemblies, books and newspapers—most of which would reappear in the Book of Mormon. (1) The Masonic Lodge was one of those combinations about which President Washington had warned the country in his Farewell Address.[30] (2) The Masons were a secret society, but to what end now that their secrets were known?[31] (3) Masonic oaths were blasphemous in themselves, but also pledged Masons to carry out institutionally authorized murder.[32] (4) Masons had taken over the judicial system which meant that a Masonic judge could not be counted upon to mete out justice to any Mason who was guilty or party to a case.[33] (5) Masons claimed the right to judge and punish their members by their own laws.[34] (6) Freemason had usurped power, controlled the government and proposed to destroy it.[35]

All the fearful aspects of the Infidel International had been revived and Morgan's fate could be anyone's. The image of the Masonic Lodge as a deistic, subversive, and terroristic society with ritual focused clearly once again. The Jacobins were back and they wore lambskin aprons!

But Joseph Smith revealed that all this had happened before. A secret society had subverted the early Jaredite civilization, and the Gadianton band brought the later Nephite and Lamanite societies to ultimate ruin. Sworn to secrecy by oaths, known to each other by signs, loyal to each other even though guilty of heinous crimes, in control of the judiciary and making their own laws, the early secret societies destroyed good government and true religion.[36] Their secrets were so seductive that people easily could be tempted to want them for themselves. Neither their secrets or charitable works should be known among good people, but the consequences of their influence should be broadcast as a warning not to get involved.[37] And as an example that this devil-led[38] activity could not be assumed to be dead simply because it was ancient, he warned that when the Book of Mormon would come to light the same activity would be wreaking its havoc among the populace (Eth 8:18-26).

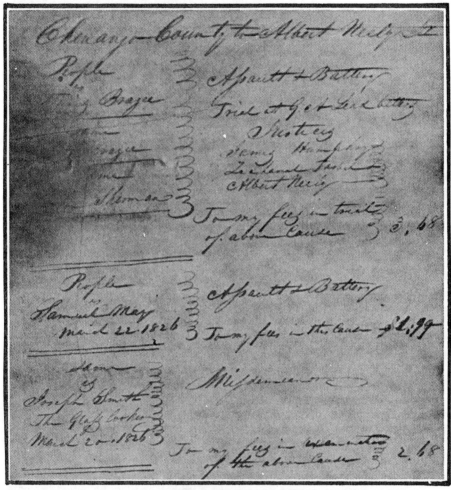

JUSTICE ALBERT NEELY'S BILL
Wesley P. Walters discovered this bill in July, 1971 in Canandaigua, N. Y. and established beyond question Joseph Smith's money-digging activity and the fact of his 1826 trial. The 5th item reads:

same [i. e., The People]
vs   Misdemeanor
Joseph Smith
The Glass looker
March 20, 1826

To my fees in examination
of the above cause 2.68

MASONRY, MAGIC, AND MORMONISM

At the time that the Morgan story broke and the anti-Masonic movement was building momentum in late 1826, Joseph Smith, Jr. was closing out a six-year career as a treasure hunter; or, as he was called then, a money-digger. Money-digging was an activity that people in New England and New York had pursued for some time. In 1825 Vermont's *Windsor Journal* complained that

> even the frightful stories of money being hid under the surface of the earth, and enchanted by the Devil or Robert Kidd, are received by many of our respect-able fellow citizens as truths.[39]

In the Smith's earlier home at Tunbridge, Vermont a man was told in a dream of a treasure chest buried on an island in Agre's Brook near Randolph. He took a crew to the site, dug a hole 15' square and 8' deep and found the chest lid. One of the crew pierced it and cried out: "'There's not ten dollars a piece.' No sooner were the words out of his mouth, than the chest moved off through the mud."[40] In the late 1840s the Smithsonian Institute and the New York Historical Society jointly sponsored an explor-ation of the mounds in western New York. The explorer reported that

> most of them have been excavated under the impulse of an idle curiosity, or have had their contents scattered by "money diggers," a ghostly race, of which, singularly enough, even at this day, representatives may be found in almost every village."[41]

The stories and court testimonies about the Smiths' money-digging activities show the same characteristics. Joseph Smith, Jr. used his peep-stone to locate a cache at some distance. Then he accompanied a crew that included his father and brother, Hyrum, to dig it up. They enacted a magic ritual consisting of drawing a circle around the site and marching around it, sacrificing a dog or sheep and sprinkling its blood on the ground to nullify the effect of the charm that kept them from the treasure. But someone in the crew usually spoke at the wrong time or enacted the ritual incorrectly, and the chest moved off through the ground out of their reach and sight.[41]

During 1825-26 young Joseph worked for Josiah Stowell at Harmony, Pa. in this activity and boarded with Isaac Hale nearby. He often spoke of his activities when he went to Colesville, N. Y., a little way across the state line. William R. Hein of Coles-ville recalled that Smith spoke about his peep-stone and money-digging activities, claiming

> that he could see lost or hidden things through it. He said he saw Captain Kidd sailing on the Susquehanna River during a freshet, and that he buried two pots of gold and silver. He claimed he saw writing cut on the rocks in an unknown language telling where Kidd buried it, and he translated it through his peep-stone.[43]

In later years Smith's mother recalled her son's use of magic rites in his youth and told her intended public:

> let not the reader suppose that . . . we stopt our labor and went at trying to win the faculty of Abrac, drawing magic circles, or sooth saying, to the neglect of all kinds of business. We never during our lives suffered one important interest to swollow up every other obligation.[44]

Abrac, from Abracadabra and Abraxis, is a magic word or formula used on amulets to work magic charms.[45] Eighteenth century Masons were said to know how to conceal "the way of obtaining the faculty of Abrac," which implied that they knew how to get it."[46] Hyrum Smith had been a member of the Mount Moriah Lodge, Palmyra Lodge No. 112, since 1823 and may have provided this Masonic connection in the pre-Morgan era.[47]

As 1827 dawned and the Morgan trials heated up, Joseph Smith returned to his father's house at Manchester with his new bride, Isaac Hale's daughter Emma. Within a few weeks anti-Masonic conventions came to Farmington and Manchester. Smith still practiced money-digging in 1827,[48] but he also spoke of some golden plates that he had located with his peep-stone.[49] By August Smith had decided to discontinue his money-digging.[50] In September he recovered the golden plates from which he would read in 1829 that God had cursed the land so that the riches, weapons and tools of long-ago people behaved just like the objects of New England treasure hunters: "Yea, we have hid up our treasures and they have slipped away from us, because of the curse of the land" (Hel 13:33-36); "the inhabitants thereof began to hide up their treasures in the earth; and they became slippery, because the Lord had cursed the land, that they could not hold them, nor retain them again" (Morm 1:18).

Oliver Cowdery preserved this aspect of Smith's treasure hunting lore when he recorded Smith's story of finding the plates in 1823. Smith tried three times to get the chest containing the plates, but his motives were impure and he was shocked away and deprived of his strength.

> What was the occasion of this he knew not—*there* was the pure unsullied record, as had been described—he had heard of the power of enchantment, and a thousand like stories, which held the hidden treasures of the earth . . .[51]

Elements of Smith's earlier activity of money-digging carried over to his later career as translator and prophet. In 1827 he began to shift his stories about his prowress with the stone to speak of seeing plates in the earth. After he had them his story of how he got them began to display other elements and their source can be found in Masonic ritual and lore.

OTHER MASONIC ASPECTS TO MORMON ORIGINS

When Cowdery described Smith's recovery of the chest containing the golden plates, he listed the contents of the box. There was a breastplate used as chest armor. Three small pillars stood upright and upon them "was placed the record of the children of Joseph and of a people who left the tower far, far before the days of Joseph." The pillars "were not so lengthy as to cause the plates and the crowning stone to come in contact."[52] Lucy Mack Smith spoke of four pillars.[53] Joseph Smith also listed the spectacles which he called the Urim and Thummim, the Sword of Laban, and the ball, or compass.[54]

The Pillars

In the Explanation of the First Degree Tracing Board the newly Entered Apprentice Mason learns that three pillars support the Masonic lodges. They are called

Wisdom, Strength, and Beauty and represent Solomon, King of Israel; Hiram, King of Tyre; and Hiram Abiff.[55] The Second Degree Tracing Board Lecture teaches that Solomon's Temple at Jerusalem had two great pillars at the entrance. They were cast from molten brass, made hollow, contained the constitutional rolls, served as the archives, and were topped by two spherical balls on which maps of the terrestrial and celestial globes were represented.[56]

One use of the pillars in Masonry is found in the Enoch Legend of the Royal Arch Degree.[57] In brief, the degree teaches that the Christian world is indebted to Masonry for the preservation of the Book of the Law (the five books of Moses) and its rediscovery when it was lost.[58] At the same time Masons had preserved the highest respect for the name of God, had preserved His *true* name in both its written and pronounced forms.

The Enoch Legend teaches that Enoch, the seventh from Adam, foresaw the Flood of Noah's time. He had an underground temple built according to a vision he had of it and then erected two pillars over the entrance to it. One was of brass to withstand water. The other was of marble to withstand fire. On the marble pillar Enoch engraved hieroglyphics that told of the treasure concealed in the underground temple. A variant ritual had the hieroglyphics identified as Egyptian, telling of the historical events connected with the Tower of Babel. On the brass pillar Enoch engraved "the principles of the liberal arts, particularly of Masonry."[59] The variant ritual specifies that it was the history of creation and the Secret Mysteries.[60]

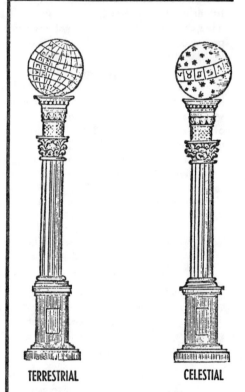

TERRESTRIAL   CELESTIAL

THE TWO PILLARS AND THEIR GLOBES
From Webb's *The Freemason's Monitor* (Cincinnati: Applegate & Company, 1860), p. 59.

The brass pillar survived the Flood but the marble pillar was broken up. When Solomon sent three Master Masons to explore the ruins of Enoch's temple they found some marble fragments engraved with hieroglyphics and took them to Solomon. Solomon sent for specialists in hieroglyphics, and they assured him that the pieces were from the marble pillar. Solomon had the pieces assembled and placed them in the Sacred Vault—a room beneath his temple known only to him, Hiram of Tyre, Hiram Abiff, and the three Master Masons.[61]

Cowdery's description recalls the Masonic materials which taught that the pillars were written histories: the history of the events surrounding the Tower of Babel; and the history of the creation and the Secret Mysteries. This may be the missing link between Ethan Smith's use of the Two Sticks of Ezekiel 37:16 and Joseph Smith's use. In Ezekiel the Two Sticks refer to the nations of the northern kingdom (the Ten Lost Tribes) and the southern kingdom (Judah). Ethan Smith used it like that, but Joseph Smith transformed the meaning to refer to the two nations' records or histories.[62]

In the Book of Mormon the plates of brass contain the history from the creation to the Tower of Babel, plus the "mysteries of God."[63] The plates of Lehi and his descendants were made into two sets of plates by Nephi, the larger set telling of the Nephites' secular history and the smaller set telling of their religious history (I Ne 9:1-5; 19:1-6). The two sets together also absorbed the brass plates, and the whole constituted the "record of Joseph."

The Spectacles, or Urim and Thummim

The Royal Arch taught that three Master Masons lived through the Babylonian Captivity and were released by Cyrus to return to Jerusalem. When they came to the pavillion near the temple ruins they offered themselves as assistants in rebuilding the temple to Haggai, Joshua and Zerubbabel. They set to work clearing away the ruins of Solomon's temple and discovered his Secret Vault. They found a box on a pedestal and took it to the Grand Council, who opened it and found it to be the Ark of the Covenant. On the lid in a triangular form were three characters. Inside the box were the long lost Book of the Law, the pot of manna from Sinai, Aaron's rod and a key to the characters on the lid. The Council used the key to decipher the box lid characters, which were the sacred characters spelling the name of God.[64]

In 1827 Joseph Smith began to speak of the spectacles in his story of the discovery of the chest containing the golden plates. They were the key to the unknown script on the plates, and only *he* had the key—the spectacles, or Urim and Thummim. In April, 1828 the Harris-Anthon consultation established that not even the language specialists of Smith's day could translate those characters. He alone had the spectacles and they served exactly the same function as his peep-stone did when he used it to translate Captain Kidd's unknown cipher cut on the rocks and thereby discovered directions to buried treasure. The spectacles were Smith's strong signal that he was drawing upon Masonic ritual and lore, but transforming it in the process.

The Curse of Death

The early stories from 1828-29 tell of Smith's translating from behind a curtain, hidden from the sight of his scribes. He warned all that any one who should see the plates would incur God's displeasure and probable death. In June, 1829 he revealed that three could see the plates and live (DC 17). This probably reflects his growing awareness of the Enoch Legend in the Royal Arch degree. After the three Master Masons were allowed to see the gold plate engraved with the forbidden name of God, a band of workers were impatient to discover the secret for themselves and went to the ruins of Enoch's temple, descended through the nine arches into the secret chamber, and died as the arches collapsed upon them.[65] Only three who were worthy could see the characters and live. So it was, also, with Smith and the golden plates.

The Sword of Laban

Late 1827 and early 1828 saw the introduction of the Urim and Thummim, the breastplate, the compass, and the Sword of Laban as chest relics—along with the plates. Smith had used a sword in the magic ritual to disenchant the treasure sites, but the Sword of Laban was a Masonic touch.[66] When Martin Harris returned to Palmyra from Pennsylvania in June, 1828, he told Willard Chase that Emma Smith was to have a child in June and that when the baby was two years old, Joseph Smith would be walking the "streets of Palmyra, with a Gold Bible under his arm, and having a breastplate on, and a gold sword hanging by his side."[67] Before Harris returned, both he and Smith informed Joshua M'Kuno "that 'Smith had found a sword, breastplate and a pair of spectacles, at the time he found the gold plates.'"[68]

Early in the Book of Mormon in April, 1829 Joseph Smith told of Laban having 24 brass plates that Nephi had to obtain. At first Laban agreed to accept Nephi's silver and gold for the plates, but then took it by force and kept the plates. Later, Nephi found Laban drunk, found his sword nearby and "smote off his head with his own sword" (1 Ne 4:7-18). The sword had a hilt of pure gold, was finely crafted, and had a blade of most precious steel (1 Ne 4:9), although when Smith found it in the chest the blade had rusted away.[69] The Book of Mormon witnesses were promised in June, 1829 a "view of the plates, and also of the breastplate, the sword of Laban, the Urim and Thummim . . . and the miraculous directors" (DC 17) by their faith. More than half a century later David Whitmer said that when he and Cowdery viewed the plates they were overwhelmed by a brilliant light. "In the midst of this light, but a few feet from us, appeared a table, upon which were many golden plates, also the sword of Laban and the directors."[70]

The Third, or Master Mason, Degree told of three loyal Masons who pursued those who had killed Hiram Abiff. One of them found one of the killers asleep nearby his sword, or knife, and the avenger used it to decapitate the killer. In Masonic ceremonies the words "strike off his head" were used, and in Revolutionary France they meant the tyrant King Phillipe le Bel—Philip the Fair, or Philip IV—who destroyed the Knights Templar.[71]

The Liahona—Called the Ball, or Directors, or Compass

The pillars of the Second Degree Tracing Board were topped by globes, one of the earth and one of the universe. In the Enoch Legend the brass pillar was topped by a metal ball containing maps, "directions of the world and of the universe, and which also acted as a sort of oracle."[72] The "directors" that Smith listed as one of the relics in the stone chest contained two spindles, one of which pointed the way for Lehi and his family through the wilderness (1 Ne 16:10). Writing appeared on the ball to inform the refugees of the Lord's ways as the occasion demanded. But the writing appeared and was changed, and the pointers pointed the way only when "faith and diligence" were present. This compass, then, was also an oracle.

Smith drew from the compass a lesson equally as good as any Masonic moral analogy of the meaning of their implements. In mid-ocean a rebellious group seized the ship and compass from Nephi's control, but they lacked the faith to believe that God worked the compass and had to ask Nephi to work it for them. From this Smith taught that when the fathers ignored a concrete thing like a compass simply because God

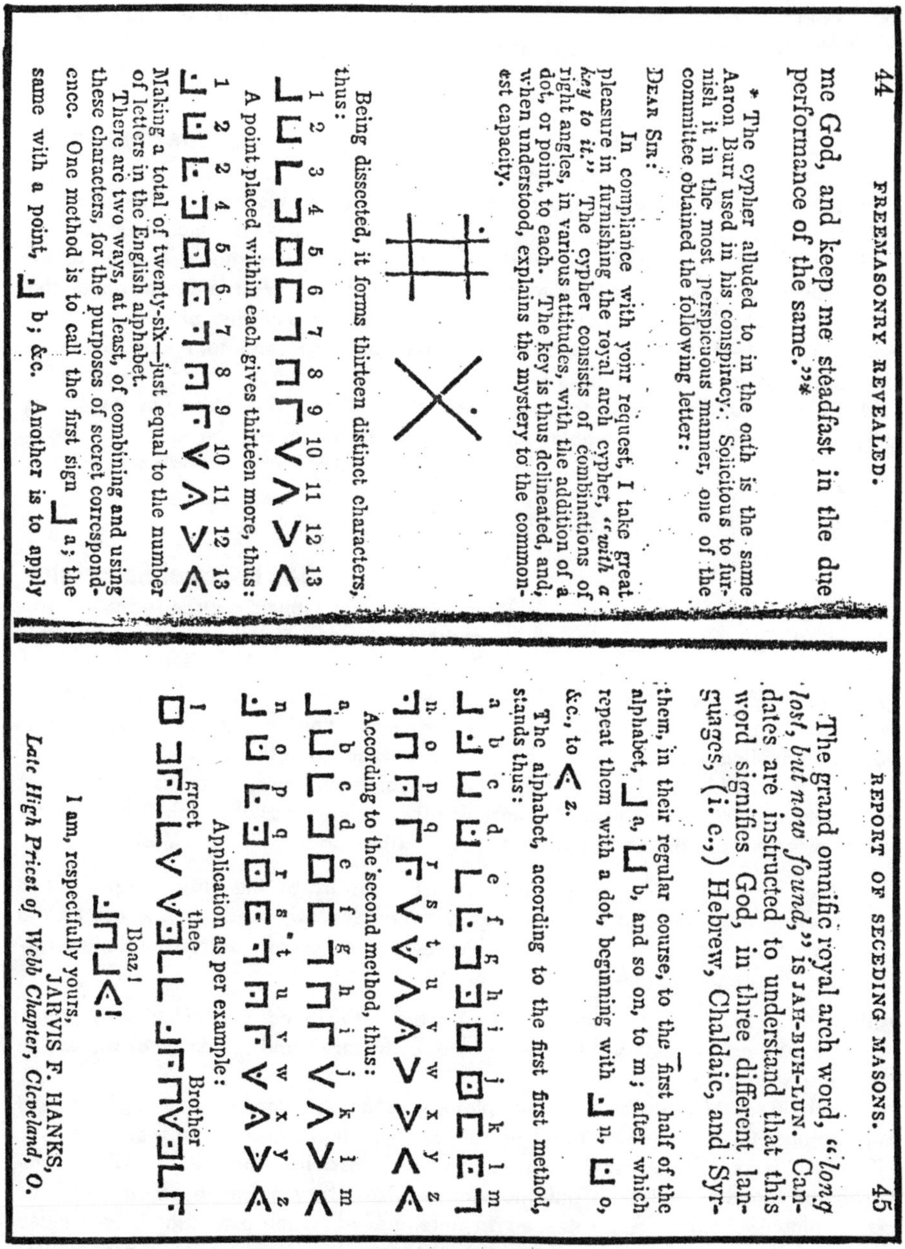

44 FREEMASONRY REVEALED.

me God, and keep me steadfast in the due performance of the same."*

* The cypher alluded to, in the oath is the same Aaron Burr used in his conspiracy. Solicitous to furnish it in the most perspicuous manner, one of the committee obtained the following letter:

DEAR SIR:

In compliance with your request, I take great pleasure in furnishing the royal arch cypher, "*with a key to it.*" The cypher consists of combinations of right angles, in various attitudes, with the addition of a dot, or point, to each. The key is thus delineated, and, when understood, explains the mystery to the common-est capacity.

[cipher key grid figure]

Being dissected, it forms thirteen distinct characters, thus:

1 2 3 4 5 6 7 8 9 10 11 12 13

A point placed within each gives thirteen more, thus:

1 2 3 4 5 6 7 8 9 10 11 12 13

Making a total of twenty-six—just equal to the number of letters in the English alphabet.

There are two ways, at least, of combining and using these characters, for the purposes of secret correspond-ence. One method is to call the first sign ⌐ a; the same with a point, ⌐ b; &c. Another is to apply

REPORT OF SECEDING MASONS. 45

The grand omnific royal arch word, "*long lost, but now found,*" IS JAH-BUH-LUN. Candidates are instructed to understand that this word signifies God, in three different languages, (i. c.,) Hebrew, Chaldaic, and Syr-

them, in their regular course, to the first half of the alphabet, [sign] a, [sign] b, and so on, to m; after which repeat them with a dot, beginning with [sign] n, [sign] o, &c., to [sign] z.

The alphabet, according to the first first method, stands thus:

a b c d e f g h i j k l m
[cipher characters]

According to the second method, thus:

a b c d e f g h i j k l m
[cipher characters]

Application as per example:

erect   thee
[cipher characters]

Boaz!
[cipher characters]

Brother
[cipher characters]

I am, respectfully yours,
JARVIS F. HANKS,
Late High Priest of Webb Chapter, Cleveland, O.

THE ROYAL ARCH KEY
From the "Report of Seceding Freemasons, or, A Summary of Freemasonry," *The Proceedings of the United States Anti-Masonic Convention, Held at Philadelphia, September 11, 1830* (New York: The Proceedings of the United States Anti-Masonic Convention, Held at Philadelphia, September 11, 1830 (New York: Skinner and Dewey, 1830), pp. 44-45.

had given it to them, they also would not prosper when they ignored spiritual matters
(Al 37:44; cf. 45-47).

The Breastplate

The Royal Arch Degree provided for the installation of the Grand Council, whose
principals following the return from Babylon were Joshua, Haggai, and Zerubbabel,
and whose priestly, prophetic and kingly offices continued the Masonic Lodge. During
the installation of the Joshua-elect, the candidate kneels before the chair of his office
while biblical passages are read. They refer to the Levitical or Aaronic priesthood, and
the Leviticus reading describes Moses' institution of the Aaronic priesthood. Over
Aaron's robe Moses bound an ephod over which he put a breastplate. He put the Urim
and Thummim in the breastplate and then put a turban upon Aaron's head and a
golden plate upon the turban to make a holy crown (Lev. 8:7-8). Many of the stories
about Smith's translating the golden plates repeat his claim that he wore the breastplate with the spectacles (Urim and Thummim) attached when he translated.[74]

The Relics of Succession

The breastplate and Urim and Thummim have a biblical source, although the
biblical articles were not spectacles. The spectacles, the Sword of Laban, and the ball-
compass signal that the biblical was mediated to Smith through the Enoch Legend of
the Royal Arch. The latter two relics are non-biblical but have direct antecedents in
the Enoch Legend, whereas the former two relics had been badges of proper succession to the biblical Aaronic priesthood, which was recalled in the ritual.

The Most Excellent High Priest of the Royal Arch wore "a breastplate of cut
glass, consisting of twelve pieces to represent the twelve tribes of Israel."[75] In fact, the
tenth objection that the Saratoga Baptist Association had against the Masons was

> their wearing garments in similation of those worn by the Jewish High Priests;
> making and carrying in procession a mimic representation of the ark of the
> covenant; making and wearing similar representation of the breastplate; inscrib-
> ing on mitres, "Holiness to the Lord."[76]

Although the Masonic ritual recalled the Aaronic priesthood, the Melchizedek priesthood was the only priesthood the ritual actually fostered and the relics of succession
applied to that order.

In the Book of Mormon the breastplate, spectacles, Sword of Laban, plates, and
ball-compass were succession relics passed along to those men whom God chose for
His special work.[77] The relics established proper succession to the priestly office of the
"order of the Son of God," but they were a transitory phase in Smith's work of
establishing the authority he needed to defend God. Once established, he needed
them no longer. This is seen by the fact that long before the translation process was
completed, Smith had substituted the peep-stone for the spectacles and it performed
exactly the same function. Clearly the relics were a veneer. This conclusion finds
further support in the angel's reclamation of the spectacles and plates after the
translation process was completed at the end of June, 1829. But Smith kept the stone.

The Melchizedek Priesthood

In the observances on the Order of High Priest in the Royal Arch, Bible passages that dealt with the priesthood of Melchizedek were read.[78] The Aaronic priesthood came by heredity, but that of Melchizedek by special dispensation from God. In July, 1828 an article designed "to show that Masonry is a religious institution" listed as one of its points that "its priests are consecrated High Priests forever, after the order of Melchizedek."[79] This is based on the New Testament interpretation of the Old Testament account of Melchizedek, but is also a misinterpretation of it. The New Testament book of Hebrews sees Christ as the one and only successor to this special priesthood. There we find no succession of Melchizedek priests.

Joseph Smith and Oliver Cowdery received the Aaronic priesthood May 15, 1829 when they were baptized at the hands of John the Baptist, who was acting on the orders of the Grand Council of three—Peter, James and John, who held a higher priesthood.[80] As Smith completed the translation process it was culminated with his receipt of the Melchizedek priesthood.[81] Carrying the mantle of a dual priesthood, possessing the relics of succession, and having in hand the translation of the golden plates, Smith was now in position properly to defend God.[82]

Smith established his own claim to the Melchizedek priesthood in Alma 13, maintaining the "Lord God ordaineth priests after his holy order, which was after the order of his Son." A person who exercised "exceeding faith and good works" was "called with a holy calling" and could be "ordained unto the high priesthood of the holy order of God."

> This high priesthood being after the order of his Son, which order was from the foundation of the world; or in other words, being without beginning of days or end of years, being prepared from eternity to all eternity, according to his foreknowledge of all things—(vs. 7).

Melchizedek "was also a high priest after this same order . . . who also took upon him the high priesthood forever." And in Moses 6 Adam, Abel, Seth, and Enos had the same priesthood, as did Enoch.[83] They all had had the spectacles, which made them "seers," and all had also been prophets—a select company for Smith to join.

It should be noted that in 1829 and still in 1830 the Melchizedek priesthood for Smith was a symbol of authority and nothing more. Not until June, 1831 does Smith induct others into this higher priesthood and begin to make of this order the administrative hierarchy it was later to become.[84] David Whitmer supports this observation in his comment that early Mormonism had no Melchizedek priesthood.[85]

Masonry and Temples

The Masonic allegory of the secret and sacred name of God concealed in an underground temple is based on the biblical accounts which relate that God revealed a new, divine name (YAHWEH) to Moses (Exodus 6:3) and made that name to dwell in a temple to manifest His presence.[86] Masonic ritual incorporated the Judaic tradition of a prohibition against pronouncing YAHWEH, combined it with the account of the lost "book of the law" discovered at Josiah's time, and, contrary to biblical evidence, inferred that God's name was also lost. The ritual mixes this view with other legends and memories of the trade of masonry to provide a quasi-history from antiquity, particularly concerned with the building of the Solomonic and post-exilic temples.

In 2 Nephi 5:12-17 Nephi has in hand the temple treasure. Using Laban's sword as a model, he produced swords to arm his people so that the could protect themselves from hostile Lamanites while building a temple. With tools in one hand and swords in another, Nephi's workmen built a temple like Solomon's, though less imposing. This is inspired by the account of the building of the post-exilic temple, but the Sword of Laban is the tip-off that Joseph Smith had Masonic ritual in mind when he used the episode.[87]

Smith as Enoch

In March, 1832 Smith revealed that he was Enoch (DC 78:1, 9), but he had been saying it before. The Masonic Enoch foresaw that an Israelite would discover the buried treasure after the Flood, which he also foresaw. Smith made himself an Israelite, a descendant of the biblical Joseph (2 Ne 3:6-7, 15) and a seer (Mos 8:13; 28:11-16). From June to December, 1830 he dictated a vision in which Enoch, high on a mountain, saw a vision of the Flood, Noah building the ark (Moses 7:3, 38-43), and after the Flood Enoch saw truth come out of the ground (Moses 7:69). Enoch was also a seer (Moses 6:35-36) and all signs indicated that the descendant he saw in vision was the seer of 2 Nephi 3:6-7 and Mosiah 8:13, namely, Joseph Smith Jr. Again, the source is the non-biblical Masonic Enoch Legend and Smith was laying claim to Enoch's mantle, later to carry that identification into his death.[88]

The Egyptian Factor

Before his Canandaigua trial in January, 1828, John Sheldon (it was thought) wrote a letter in Masonic hieroglyphics to General Solomon Van Rensselaer, the Revolutionary War hero, and it was published in Sheldon's name.[89] At the time it sensationally underlined the claim of the Explanation of the First Degree Tracing Board:

> the usages and customs of Masons have ever corresponded with those of the Egyptian philosophers, to which they bear a near affinity. . . . they concealed their particular tenets . . . under hieroglyphical figures.[90]

The Saratoga Baptist Association at Milton, N. Y. in 1828 took that claim seriously, charging in the second of its 15 point indictment that Masonic rites "correspond with the Egyptian."[91] The Egyptian obelisks upon which Champollion and Seyffarth had turned public attention were said to have been inscribed with *Masonic* hieroglyphics![92] Smith combined the Egyptian on the marble pillar fragments that Solomon could not translate with the unknown script in which God's name was written on the gold plate in the Royal Arch and came up with "reformed Egyptian" that could only be translated with a key that worked by revelation. Like Solomon, he received revelation as good as any Masonic priest.

MASONIC LORE IN DEFENSE OF GOD

Joseph Smith condemned current expressions of Masonry, but accepted it as a truly ancient form of God's way of maintaining relationships from Adam onward. He used aspects of Masonic ritual and lore in the Book of Mormon and in his stories about his discovery of the stone chest and its contents. By translating the brass plates of Jared's time and the plates of Nephi, Smith pointed to himself as the rightful successor to Masonic tradition and the one upon whom priesthood rightfully rested.

The Indians' Lost Book of God, the Two Sticks of Ezekiel 37:16, the buried voice (book) speaking from the ground in Isaiah 29:4, the sealed book of Isaiah 29:11-12, and Masonic ritual and lore all provided many elements that supported each other as Smith "grabbed on" to a rich lode from which to construct his American scripture. He offered alternatives to the churches and Masonic Lodge of his day: a restored Church and a restored Masonry that were unencumbered by the corruptions and heresies of the lodges and churches in western New York.[92] That is borne out by the high percentage of ex-Masons among Smith's early converts in the 1830s when the anti-Masonic conflict was still fresh. The Mormon development in the 1830s and 1840s that Durham has shown is firm evidence that Smith had not simply been condemning the Masonic Lodge in the Book of Mormon, but transforming it for his own immediate and later use.

FOOTNOTES

1. Lapham, p. 307.

2. S. H. Goodwin, *Additional Studies in Mormonism and Masonry* (Salt Lake City: Grand Lodge of F. & A. M. of Utah, c. 1932), pp. 15-16. A notice that a Baptist clergyman in Illinois had been dismissed because he was a Freemason   was captioned as "Bigotry." WS, July 12, 1825.

3. Alphonse Cerza, *Anti-Masonry* (Fulton, Mo.: The Ovid Bell Press, Inc.; Missouri Lodge of Research, c. 1962), p. 35.

4. Cf. John Robison, *Proofs of A Conspiracy Against All the Religions and Governments of Europe, Carried on in the Secret Meetings of Free Masons, Illuminate, and Reading Societies: Collected from Good Authorities* (Philadelphia: T. Dobson, 1798), 3rd ed. Abbe Barruel, *The Anti-Christian and Antisocial Conspiracy* (Lancaster, Pa.: Joseph Ehrenfried, 1812).

5. PR, March 19, 1819, in a colum entitled "The Moralist."

6. Henry Wilson Coil, *Masonic Encyclopedia* (New York: Macoy Publishing & Supply Company, Inc., c. 1961), p. 58.

7. James C. Odierne, *Opinions on Speculative Masonry* (Boston: Perkins & Marvin, 1830), p. 198.

8. WS, April 13, 1827.

9. WS, December 22, 1826, "Monroe County Meetings."

10. WS, April 6, 1827.

11. WS, February 2, 1827 carried the following advertisement just two weeks after the Canandaigua trial ended:

Trial of the Conspirators:
"an account of the Trial of the Conspirators, on an indictment for carrying away WILLIAM MORGAN, from the jail of Ontario county, on the evening of the 12th of Sept. 1826; together with Throop's Address. Jan. 19."

12. Goodwin, p. 17.

13. WS, March 14, 1828 carried the notice that an anti-Masonic paper called *The Palmyra Freeman* would start publication soon.

14. Rob Morris, *William Morgan: or Political Anti-Masonry, its Rise, Growth and Decadence* (New York: Rober Macoy, 1883), pp. 183-84. Cf. pp. 347-48 where the sequence is listed: Bloomfield, December 11, 1826; Seneca, January 13, 1827; Lewiston, January 25, 1827; Canandaigua, January 31 and February 16; West Bloomfield, February 27; Vienna, March 12; Manchester, March 15; Farmington, March 16; Victor, August 2; and Canandaigua, September 19.

15. Richard L. Anderson, "Martin Harris, the Honorable New York Farmer," IE, Vol. 72 (1969), p. 20.

16. WS, October 5, 1827.

17. Cf. "Marks of Masonry," WS, December 8, 1826.

18. WS, November 10, 1826. Cf. "The Batavia Affair," December 22, 1826 for an editorial typical of the period. It is restrained and not anti-Masonic, but calls for Morgan's release.

19. WS, November 24, 1826. The text follows:

Whereas, much excitement has been caused throughout the community, on the subject of certain imputed, improper and illegal conduct, by certain individuals said to be connected with this ancient Fraternity, towards a man called "Morgan"—
Therefore,

Resolved unanimously, That this Lodge, impressed with emotions of deep regret, that any imputations again the conduct of persons connected with us in the solemn ties of Masonic Brotherhood, should have been made, which can be by any possible implication regarded as a violation of the laws of the government under which we so happily live, and to support which is one of the principal tenets of our order, do cordially agree with and approve of the resolution adopted by "The Ontario Masters' Lodge, No. 23."

20. Charles F. Milliken, A History of Ontario County, New York and Its People (2 vols.; New York: Lewis Historical Publishing Company, 1911, I, p. 414.

21. WS, March 27, 1829.

22. Coil, p. 58.

23. Morris, p. 289. Morris may be mistaken about the date. David Bernard identifies the meeting as that of the Saratoga Baptist Association, prints the 15 resolutions in full, and gives the date as September 12-15. Light on Masonry, pp. 361-66.

24. WS, January 25, 1828.

25. Goodwin, p. 18; cf. n. 2, above.

26. The Palmyra Reflector, December 2, 1829 notes that the Rev. Henry Davis, anti-Masonic pastor of the Baptist Church in Macedon, was leaving a congregation suffering from internal strife. January 22 and 30, 1830, the Reflector states that the local Baptist Church was anti-Masonic.

27. WS, May 4, 1827.

28. WS, October 13, 1826. The letter was signed by a committee of ten men, one of whom signed himself "Ja's Smith," but the letter was reproduced in many papers and in some it was signed simply as "J. Smith.' On this basis Reed C. Durham, Jr., "Is There No Help for the Widow's Son," mistakenly identified the signatory as the Mormon prophet. The committee was formed of citizens from Batavia, however. The letter is found in many forms and publications. Cf. John E. Becker, A History of Freemasonry in Waterloo, New York, 1817-1942 (Waterloo, N. Y.: Seneca Lodge No. 113, F. & A. M., c. 1942), pp. 22-23.

29. WS, May 4, 1827.

30. He warned against "all combinations and associations . . . with the real design to direct, control, counteract, or awe the regular deliberation and action of the constituted authorities," because they destroyed the democratic process; "Farewell Address," pp. 252-53. "Combinations became synonymous with Freemasonry. Cf. Goodwin, pp. 27-29. Freemasonry was called a combination in WS, July 18, 1828; and a "secret combination," PF, November 10, 1829.

31. Secret oaths, secret plans, secret words, secret combinations, secret signs, secret abominations, secret band, secret work, secrets—all were anti-Masonic terms of the time. The Albany Daily Advertiser ran a column debating the use of the term "secret societies" giving the flavor of the rhetoric:

whether Washington meant secret societies or political parties, in the words "all combinations and associations, under whatever plausible character, is of little consequemce; . . . the sentence— Beware of secret societies, is unexceptional—and will last for a freeman's motto, as long as a freeman's blood stains freemasonry.

Reprinted in the Ontario Phoenix, March 31, 1830. Masonry was called a secret society in WS, July 18, 1828 and PF, December 2, 1828. Cf. PF, November 10, 1829.

32. The oaths to the first three degrees all involved the candidate's vowing never to reveal in any verbal or written way the Masonic secrets,

under no less penalty than to have my throat cut across, my tongue torn out by the roots, and my body buried in the rough sands of the sea at low water-mark, where the tide ebbs and flows twice in twenty-four hours.

This is the oath taken in the Entered Apprentice, or first degree, from William Morgan, *Illustrations of Masonry*, reprinted as *Morgan's Freemasonry Exposed and Explained* (New York: L. Fitzgerald, 1882), p. 19. The oath was also printed in WS, November 10, 1826. WS, March 14, 1828 has the obligations and penalties of the Mark Masters through the Knight's Templar degrees.

In Smith's 1830 Book of Moses, 5:29-32, Satan and Cain enter into an oath-bound pact to kill Abel. Cain says: "Truly I am Mahan, the master of the great secret, that I may murder and get gain. Wherefore Cain was called Master Mahan, and he gloried in his wickedness." Cain's descendant, Lamech, also entered into a covenant with Satan and became a Master Mahan. Here Smith injects the Morgan episode and his alleged murder:

> Irad, the son of Enoch, having known their secret, began to reveal it unto the sons of Adam; Wherefore Lamech, being angry, slew him, not like unto Cain, his brother Abel, for the sake of getting gain, but he slew him for the oath's sake. (Moses 5:49-50)

33. The Knight's Templar candidate swore "to advance my brother's best interest by always supporting his military fame, political preference in opposition to another," WS, March 14, 1828. In the same issue the Royal Arch obligation for the candidate for for the degree is printed: "Furthermore do I promise and swear, that I will vote for a companion Royal Arch mason before any other person of equal qualifications." Again, the candidate swore

> that a companion Royal Arch mason's secret given me in charge as such, and I knowing him to be such, shall remain as secret and inviolate in my breast as in his own, when he communicated it to me, *Murder and Treason not excepted.*

William L. Stone, *Letters on Masonry and Anti-Masonry, Addressed to The Hon. John Quincy Adams* (New York: O. Halsted, 1832), p. 75, wrote that the pledge in favor of political preferment and the word "not" in italics were interpolations, but that this was the way the obligation was given in western New York.

The New York county sheriffs had the power to select and summon grand juries for courts in their jurisdiction. In those counties where the Morgan incident took place and in which there were trials, the sheriffs were all Masons, possibly all Royal Arch Masons. The Genessee county grand jury met in February, 1827, where the foreman was a Knight Templar and a good portion of the jury Masons. In Niagara County, where Eli Bruce was sheriff, 16 Masons and several friendly to the Lodge were summoned for jury selection in January, 1827. In April Bruce summoned the grand jurors—of 21 members present several were friendly to the Lodge and 16 were Masons—to the Niagara County court of Oyer and Terminer. Two of the jurors were themselves later indicted for the Morgan conspiracy. A majority of Masons were on the jury at the May session and half of the September session jurors were Masons.

34. Cf. Goodwin's documentation of the charge p. 34. Cf. also WS, November 9, 1827; March 14, 1828; July 18, 1828.

35. Goodwin, pp. 34-35. Cf. WS, March 23, 1827; March 7, 1828; July 18, 1828; September 26, 1828; and PF, December 1, 1828.

36. Some of the passages that deal with the topics are: combinations, 2 Ne 9:9; 26:22; Al 37:21-32. Secret oaths and covenants: 2 Ne 26:22-23 (cf. the contrast that Smith draws with God, who opens His courts to all, 24-33); Al 37:27, 29; Hel 6:25; 4 Ne 42. Masonic secrets already revealed and known: Al 37:23-26; Eth 8:20; 2 Ne 30:17; Mos 8:17, 19. Masonry out to take over and destroy the government and all freedoms: Al 10:27; Hel 6:39; Eth 8:9-25; 9:1, 5-6, 26; 10:33; 11:7; 3 Ne 6:21-30. Masonic judges control the courts: Al 11:20; Hel 6:21, 23; Mos 29:28-32; 3 Ne 6:21-30. Masons claim the right to punish their member according to their own laws and not the laws of the land: Hel 6:21-24.

37. Hel 1:27, 29; 6:25-30, 38; Eth 8:20.

38. 2 Ne 9:9; 26:22; Al 37:30-31; Hel 3:23; 6:21; 3 Ne 7:6, 9; Morm 8:27; Eth 8:18, 22, 24, 25; 9:1, 6; 11:15, 22; 13:18. In 3 Ne 6:10-30 Satan caused class divisions within the church over the educational, financial and professional differences. He used the upper class desire to get ahead as a temptation to gain power and thereby managed to get the lodge started in and among church members. Cf. Moses 5:29-50 and n. 32 above.

39. WS, February 16, 1825.

40. *Ibid.*

41. E. G. Squier, "Report upon the Aboriginal Monuments of Western New York," *Proceedings of the New York Historical Society* (New York: William Van Norden, 1849), p. 54. Cf. "Money Digger," PH, July 24, 1822, which was reprinted from the Montpelier, Vt. *Watchman.* The article reported that

> digging for money hid in the earth is a very common thing; and in this state it is even considered an

honorable and profitable employment. We could name, if we pleased, at least five hundred respectable men, who do, in the simplicity and sincerity of their hearts, verily believe, that immense treasures lie concealed upon our Green Mountains; many of whom have been for a number of years, most industriously and perserveringly engaged in digging it up.

42. Cf. Jerald and Sandra Tanner, *Joseph Smith and Money-Digging* (Salt Lake City: Modern Microfilm Company, 1970) and Wesley P. Walters, "From Occult to Cult with Joseph Smith, Jr.," *Journal of Pastoral Practice*, Vol. I, No. I, pp. 121-37.

43. Arthur Deming, *Naked Truths about Mormonism*, Vol. I, No. I (January, 1888), p. 2.

44. Lucy Mack Smith, Martha Coray manuscript, xerox copy, p. 77, in the LDS Church Archives, Historical Department, Salt Lake City.

45. Reed C. Durham, Jr., "Is There No Help for the Widow's Son," gives detailed information about a talisman found on Joseph Smith by his family when they prepared him for burial in 1844. The inscriptions on the amulet could be either magical or Masonic, or both. But it is not known when Smith acquired this amulet.

46. James Hardie, *The New Free-Mason's Monitor* (New York: George Long, 1818), p. 203. Henry Dana Ward, *Free Masonry. Its Pretensions Exposed in Faithful Extracts of Its Standard Authors* (New York: By the Author, 1828), pp. 104-05 ridiculed the details of the Hiram Abiff allegory. "This is truly Free Masonry; the art of finding new arts, and the way of winning the faculty of Abrac." Ward's comment upon the way Hiram Abiff met his death at the hands of the assassins:

> What a wonder! The Master of "the art of foresaying things," did not foresee his danger; the master of "the art of wonder-working," did not even draw a magic circle; the master of "the way of winning the faculty of Abrac," did not utter a syllable of magic, did not spit out one mouthful of fire, did not make the slightest attempt to conjure a spirit to his rescue; but alas! forgetful of all his masonic defenses, he died; he basely died!

47. Mervin B. Hogan, "The Founding Minutes of Nauvoo Lodge," *Further Light in Masonry* (Des Moines: Research Lodge No. 2), p. 8, shows that Hyrum Smith was transferred into the Nauvoo Lodge from Mount Moriah, No. 112, N. Y.

48. Joseph Capron met Smith's father in 1827. Joseph, Jr. had a stone by which he located a chest of gold watches near Capron's house. The chest was in possession of an evil spirit. Joseph, Jr., therefore, got a polished sword and marched around the treasure site with Samuel Lawrence to fend off satanic assaults. Howe, pp. 258-60.

49. As early as June, 1827, Joseph Smith, Sr. told Willard Chase that Joseph, Jr. had had a vision of the plates a few years earlier. Chase's statement is found in Howe, pp. 240-48. Martin Harris said that Smith discovered the site by using his stone; Tiffany, pp. 163, 169. The Smith family told him the same thing.

50. Peter Ingersoll said that he was hired by Smith in August, 1827 to take him to Harmony, Pa. to pick up Emma's furniture. Isaac Hale remonstrated with Smith to give up his money-digging and pretending to see in a stone, and Smith promised to do so. But on the return trip to Palmyra Smith told Ingersoll that would be hard to do, since others would pressure him to use the stone. Howe, pp. 232-37. Isaac Hale also stated that Smith told him he "had given up what he called 'glass looking.'" *The Susquehanna Register*, May 1, 1834. By the time that Smith told Harris about this decision, the reason he gave for quitting the money-digging business was that an angel told him to; Tiffany p. 169.

51. Oliver Cowdery, Letters to W. W. Phelps, VIII, MA, March, 1835, p. 197.

52. *Ibid.*, pp. 196-97.

53. Lucy Mack Smith, Martha Coray manuscript, p. 78.

54. MA, March, 1835, pp. 196-97. If one objects that Cowdery's record is from the mid-1830s and is projecting back into the 1820s—and that is a valid objection—then there are the other sources that mention the stone chest relics. Willard Chase, Joshua M'Kune and Abigail Harris refer to Smith and Martin Harris talking about the breastplate, Sword of Laban, the ball-compass and the spectacles; Howe, pp. 240-48, 253, 267. Although Chase dated the time he heard of the breastplate, sword and plates as 1829, the fact that he said Emma Smith was to give birth in June dates the time as 1828 when she did give birth. M'Kune lived in Susquehanna County, Pa. and claimed to have known Harris and Smith when they were in Harmony—and that was from April to June, 1828. Abigail Harris's altercation with her husband, Martin, over his involvement with Smith also took place in 1828. Joseph Smith, Sr. told Fayette Lapham in 1830 that his son had found a gold hilt and chain of a large sword, a gold ball with two pointers, the spectacles and plates. Lapham, p. 307. Finally, Smith listed the relics in June, 1829 (DC 17).

55. Hannah, p. 111.

56. *Ibid.*, pp. 125, 127.

57. The Legend is found in Thomas S. Webb, *The Freemason's Monitor; or Illustrations of Masonry* (New York: Southwick and Crooker, 1802), pp. 246-60. Henry Dana Ward's *Freemasonry* extracted many parts of the Enoch Legend from Webb. The *Wayne Sentinel* bookstore ran ads for Webb's *Monitor*, November 24, 1826 and for Dana's book, September 4, 1829. Another popular work, Jeremy Cross, *The True Masonic Chart, Or Hieroglyphic Monitor* was advertised February 14, 1826.

Albert G. Mackey, *The History of Freemasonry: Its Legends and Traditions; Its Chronological History* (7 vols.; New York: The Masonic History Company, c. 1905), I, traces the legend of the pillars from the writings of Josephus as it was transformed into the Masonic legend in the middle ages. Josephus attributed the pillars to the sons of Seth, who wanted to leave the world some memory of their learning and inventions when they pondered Adam's prediction that at one time the world would be destroyed by fire, at another by water. Therefore,

> they made two pillars; the one of brick, the other of stone: they inscribed their discoveries on them both, that in case the pillar of brick should be destroyed by the flood, the pillar of stone might remain, and exhibit those discoveries to mankind; and also inform them that there was another pillar of brick erected by them. Now this remains in the land of Siriad to this day.

Josephus, "Antiquities of the Jews," Bk. I. Chap. ii, in *The Life and Works of Flavius Josephus,* translated by William Whiston (Philadelphia: The John C. Winston Company, n. d. d.), p. 36.

58. Stone, pp. 44-46, gives the gist of the Royal Arch teaching about the "book of the law" discussed in 2 Chronicles 34 and 2 Kings 22, which was the "book of the law of the LORD given through Moses" (2 Chronicles 34:14). Hilkiah, the priest found the book during temple repairs. When it was read to Josiah, the righteous king, it sent him into despair because he had never heard it before and recognized that he and his people were culpable. It was the basis of Josiah's reform.

According to Stone, where the Bible is silent about the "book of the law" at certain periods, rabbinical and Masonic tradition preserved the Pentateuch for the world. It had been lost from the reign of Manasseh to Josiah's time because of Solomon's foresight. He had built a secret vault beneath his temple to keep the sacred treasure safe during the reigns of idolatrous kings, and only Masons knew it. (In variant rituals only Hiram Abiff knew of the vault—not even Solomon.) After Josiah's time the book was hidden again in the secret vault and survived the destruction of the temple at the hands of the Babylonians. After the remnant Jews returned to Jerusalem with Cyrus's permission to rebuild the temple, Ezra and Zerubbabel cleared the ruins for the new temple and rediscovered the vault and the book. Then Ezra, the priestly scribe, "corrected, revised, and re-wrote some of the sacred books" of the Pentateuch (p. 45). Stone gives this as a variant tradition of the Royal Arch.

The Royal Arch tradition was unbiblical, since Ezra returned to Jerusalem from Babylon carrying in his hand "the law of Moses which the LORD the God of Israel had given," Ezra 7:6, 10 14. In fact, the Royal Arch seems to have gotten its tradition from the Apocrypha. According to 2 Esdras 14:18-48, Ezra completed the scriptural restoration 30 years after the temple and part of the scriptures were destroyed in 587 B. C. During a 40 day period, Ezra, inspired by God, dictated 94 books to his assistants and was told to publish the first 24 but to save the rest for "the Sages."

When Joseph Smith translated the golden plates he translated a portion, but was forbidden to translate the "sealed" portion. His Nephite scribes also corrected, revised and re-wrote the records that had come to them.

According to a notice, WS, March 3, 1826, the General Committee of the London Bible Society had resolved a long standing controversy over the Apocrypha by deciding to cease publishing it along with their edition of the Bible. WS, June 2, 1826 contained an informative article about the Apocrypha. Finally, WS, June 6, 1828, the American Bible Society decided no longer to publish the Apocrypha. Before this the Apocrypha was found in American Bibles. Smith used the book of 2 Esdras 13:40-42 in Eth 2:4, revealing his familiarity with, or at least his access to, the Apocrypha. Cf. chap. 5, n. 47.

59. Webb, p. 247.

60. Durham's source shows some variations from Webb, but there were many variations in Masonic ritual in the United States.

61. Webb, pp. 259-60. Cf. Mos 8:11-13.

62. Cf. chap. 6, pp. above.

63. 1 Ne 3:12, 19-20, 24; 4:24, 38; 5:10-22; 13:23; 19:22; 1 Ne 4:2; 5:12; Mos 1:3-4; 28:20; Al 37:3-12; 63:1, 11-14; 3 Ne 1:2.

64. Stone, pp. 45ff. Cf. also Bernard, pp. 142-43. Cf. chap. 7, "Evolution of the Official Version" and notes, as well as the illustration "Royal Arch Key" to the characters, where the language of the long lost word is really three languages: Hebrew, Chaldaic and Syriac. Cf. also Bernard, pp. 138-39. Smith called the spectacles a "key" according to his mother, *Biographical Sketches*, pp. 101-06. Cf. further chap. 2 above, n. 11.

Smith may have combined Masonic lore with his   peep-stone   story.   In the "Report of Seceding Masons," we find the following:

> In the ceremony of the Mark master degree in masonry, the candidate is instructed respecting the curious *white key-stone*, prepared by Hiram Abiff, and the passage from the Apocalypse is made to apply to this circumstance, as a promised reward to the faithful masonic brethren. "To him that overcometh will I give to eat of the hidden manna, and will give him a white stone, and in the stone a new name written, which no man knoweth saving him that receiveth it;" and the lecture continues, representing this *key-stone*, covered with hieroglyphics, as the very stone alluded to in *Holy Writ!*

In the Whitmer-Harris-Knight version of the translation process, Smith read the English translation of the plates as it appeared on the stone in his hat.

65. Webb, p. 259.

66. The episode is non-biblical, but is Masonic.

67. Howe, p. 248.

68. *Ibid.*, p. 267.

69. Lapham, p. 307. The Sword of Laban is also found in 2 Ne 5:14; Jac 1:10; W. Morm 13.

70. *Kansas City Daily Journal,* June 5, 1881.

71. Abbe Barruel, pp. 111-14. The Royal Arch penalty for breaking secrecy was "to have my skull struck off, and my brains exposed." The Knight Templar bound himself, with the penalty that of having "my head struck off and placed on the highest spire in Christendom." WS, March 14, 1828.

72. Durham, "Is There No Help for the Widow's Son?" Webb, p. 56, said that the metal globe was able to improve the mind and to give it "the most distinct idea of any problem or proposition." Another good study of the Enoch Legend's relationship to Mormon origins is that of J. N. Adamson, "The Treasure of the Widow's Son," typescript, n. d. It was published in *Mormon Miscellaneous,* Vol. I, No. 1 (October, 1975), David Martin editor, The New Nauvoo Neighbor Press, Nauvoo, Ill.

73. 2 Kings 4:1, 5-6; 5:17-18; 8:13-14; Deuteronomy 31:24-26; Exodus 16:33-34; Numbers 17:10; 7:89.

74. Cf. n. 54 above.

75. Bernard, p. 141.

76. *Ibid.,* p. 363.

77. 2 Ne 5:12; Jac 7:27; Jar 1, 15; Om 1, 9; Mos 1:15-16; 8:11-18; 28:10-20; Al 37:1-4, 14, 16-18; 63:1, 11-13. These men all held the Melchizedek Priesthood..

78. Webb, 197-99. He lists the passages read: Numbers 6:22-26; Genesis 14:12-24; Hebrews 7:1-5.

79. *Ontario Phoenix*, March 31, 1830, Canandaigua, N. Y.

80. Although this date is well established in Mormon literature, it was not in the 1833 Book of Commandments. Oliver Cowdery referred to it in "Letters to W. W. Phelps," I, MA, September, 1834, pp. 15-16. DC 13 appeared in the 1835 edition of the Doctrine and Covenants and deals with it specifically. Cf. also Smith's description, DHC, I, 39-41.

81. The exact date is not clear, but several statements by Smith, Cowdery and others pinpoint the time between May 15 and June, 1829. Cf. Porter, pp. 157-64 for a discussion and documentation. It would have been the natural completion of the chain of events leading to Smith's having the proper credentials to defend God: he would have had the authority to do it.

82. Brodie, p. 111, n., suggests that Smith may have gotten the notion of the dual priesthood from James Gray's *Dissertation on the Coincidence between the Priesthood of Jesus Christ and Melchisedek,* published in 1810. She supports this with the fact that the Archives of the Reorganized Church of Jesus Christ of Latter Day Saints in Independence, Mo. has Smith's signed copy of Gray's 1821 work, *The Mediatorial Reign of the Son of God.*

83. Smith seems to have been expounding the book of Hebrews in Alma 13 and extended it in the Book of Moses. The following context of Alma reflects touches of Hebrews: Al 12:7—Hebrews 4:12; Al 12:27—Hebrews 9:27; Al 12:34-35—Hebrews 3:4-4:9; Al 13:14—Hebrews 7:1-4; Al 13:7, 9—Hebrews 7:3.

84. For a time only Smith, and possibly Cowdery, had it. No one else was involved with it in this early period.

85. David Whitmer said that the first high priests were ordained at Kirtland, Ohio in June, 1831; "To Believers in the Book of Mormon," Part II, Chap. 3, *An Address*, p. 36. Whitmer said that "we had no high priests, etc. in the beginning" until "after we had preached almost two years, and had baptized and confirmed about 2000 souls into the Church of Christ," (p. 57). Preaching had begun in August, 1829 (p. 56). David's brother, John, one of the Eight Witnesses, was an early church historian appointed by Smith (DC 47; 69:2-8), March 3, 1831. He recorded that on June 3, 1831 the High priesthood was given to several men at a general church conference, Smith ordained Lyman Wight, who was commanded to ordain several others, including Smith, to the high priesthood, the Order of Melchizedek. *John Whitmer's History* (Salt Lake City: Modern Microfilm Company, n. d.), Chap. VII, p. 5.

86. Deuteronomy 12:5, 21; 14:23-24; I Kings 8:16-20, 29; 2 Chronicles 2:1; 20:8-9; I Chronicles 22:7-8, 10, 19; 28:3; 29:16. Post-exilic Jews took the words of the commandment, "Thou shalt not take the name of the Lord (YAHWEH) in vain," to mean that they should never pronounce it; therefore, they substituted "Adonai." The commandment's intention was to forbid a thoughtless use of God's name and to forestall using it to commit perjury. On the other hand, God gave His name (YAHWEH) to men so that they might call upon Him and remember Him as compassionate to the poor and oppressed as well as judgmental toward the sinner, Psalms 9:10; 25; 41; 70.

87. Temples in the Book of Mormon: Jac 1:17; 2:2, 11; Mos 1:18; 3 Ne 11:1. Durham, "Is There No Help for the Widow's Son?," examines how Smith carried out Masonic themes in the Kirtland and Nauvoo temples.

88. See Durham's address.

89. Stone, pp. 196-97; Morris, pp. 140-41, who noted that Averill was a seceeded Mason.

90. Webb, 1860 ed., p. 39.

91. Morris, p. 289.

92. Stone, p. 90.

93. Smith listed "priestcraft" as one of the evils that people needed to reject: 3 Ne 16:10; 21:19; 30:2. Observers have often noted that his use of the term probably referred to the Roman Catholic priesthood and, less emphatically, to the Protestant clergy.

Smith may also have had the Masonic priesthood in mind. He defined the term and then forbade any to hold the office: "priestcrafts are that men preach and set themselves up for a light unto the world; that they may get gain and praise of the world; but they seek not the welfare of Zion" (2 Ne 26:29). This reflects Masonry's perceived business and judicial collusion for political and financial power. The Masonic ritual often points out that the candidate for a higher degree is seeking "light."

Nehor, an enemy of the church, killed Gideon, a righteous man, and was tried by Alma, who charged that Nehor was trying to enforce priestcraft by the sword. "And thou hast shed the blood of a righteous man . . . and were we to spare thee his blood would come upon us for vengeance" (Al 1:10-15). Nehor taught that all would be saved, won a large financial following and popularity, and wore "very costly apparel." Although that could reflect the vestments of the liturgical church bodies, it also reflects the Lodge. Masonic ritual taught that all Masons, by whatever name they called God, would meet in the Grand Lodge above. Their fees for conferring degrees were substantial and their uniforms expensive and striking. The public had been frustrated in seeing charges against Morgan's abductors and fellow conspirators dismissed or light sentences passed, but Smith could make Nehor bear what the public thought those indicated deserved.

9

A God
of Revelation

The God that others worship is not the God for me;
He has no parts nor body, and cannot hear nor see;
But I've a God that lives above—
A God of power and of Love—
A God of Revelation—oh, that's the God for me!

Old Mormon Hymn

REVELATION & SKEPTICISM

God Does Not Change

Deists had honed to a fine edge the argument that the God of Christianity was capricious and that the lack of modern revelations proved Him so. To convince the Gentiles, Joseph Smith had to demonstrate that God still dealt with man as He had in the past. Smith regarded revelation and charismatic gifts as necessary at all times, and urged his readers to accept them on the basis that God is unchangeable.[1] Smith advanced a typical position through a sermon by Moroni:

> And again I say unto you who deny the revelations of God, and say that they are done away, that there are no revelation nor prophecies, nor gifts, nor healing, nor speaking with tongues, and the interpretation of tongues; behold I say unto you, he that denieth these things knoweth not the gospel of Christ; yea, he has not read the scriptures; if so, he does not understand them. For do we not read that God is the same yesterday, today, and forever, and in him there is no

variableness neither shadow of changing? And now, if ye have imagined up unto yourselves a god who doth vary, and in whom there is a shadow of changing, then have ye imagined up unto yourselves a god who is not a God of miracles. But behold, I will show unto you a God of miracles, even the God of Abraham, and the God of Isaac, and the God of Jacob; and it is that same God who created the heavens and the earth, and all the things that in them are. (Morm 9:7-11)

Christians played into the hands of skeptics, Smith had Nephi argue, when they denied present-day revelation and miracles, or when they said,

behold there is no God today, for the Lord and the Redeemer hath done his work, and he hath given his power unto men; behold, hearken ye unto my precept; if they shall say there is a miracle wrought by the hand of the Lord, believe it not; for this day he is not a God of miracles; he hath done his work. (2 Ne 18:5-6)

For a thousand years Christians gave such an explanation for the cessation of revelation and charismatic gifts, but Smith insisted that they were denying God's power (2 Ne 28:6). In his opinion miracles had not ceased since Christ's ascension, nor had angels ceased appearing to men, nor had God kept from men the power of the Holy Ghost (Moro 7:27, 29-36).

Wherefore, if these things have ceased wo be unto the children of men, for it is because of unbelief, and all is vain . . . if these things have ceased, then has faith ceased also. (Moro 7:37-38)

To keep a continuity in God's dealings with men, Smith held skeptics responsible for any suspension of revelation and miracles. Moroni elaborated this in his farewell sermon to the Lamanites when he enumerated the gifts of the Spirit:

all these gifts of which I have spoken, which are spiritual, never will be done away, even as long as the world shall stand, only according to the unbelief of the children of men . . . if the day cometh that the power and gifts of God shall be done away among you, it shall be because of unbelief. (Moro 10:19, 24)

God would produce the Book of Mormon "that I may prove unto many that I am the same yesterday, today, and forever" (2 Ne 29:9; cf. 6-8). That same constancy in God ensured that He would do it in spite of the loss of the first manuscript that Martin Harris transcribed from Smith's dictation. The portions of the plates not yet translated were to be given back to God, who would "reveal all things unto the children of men" (2 Ne 27:22) "according to their faith," and "show unto the world that I am the same yesterday, today, and forever" (2 Ne 27:23). By having Smith usher the book into the world, God thereby proved

to the world that the holy scriptures are true, and that God does inspire men and call them to his holy work in this age and generation, as well as in generations of old; Thereby showing that he is the same God yesterday, today, and forever. . . . By these things we know that there is a God in heaven, who is infinite and eternal, from everlasting to everlasting the same unchangeable God, the framer of heaven and earth, and all things which are in them. (DC 20:11-12, 17)

Throughout the Book of Mormon there is a steady process of equating the Creator of the world with the God of the Old Testament, and Him, in turn, with Jesus Christ. The emphasis on God's unchanging nature is both an appeal to, and an answer to, the belief of deists that the God of nature is different from the God revealed in the Bible. Smith made it clear that God was not some remote Being unmoved by human experience. In a long prediction of the crucifixion of Jesus, all the forces of nature are pictured in upheaval.

And the rocks of the earth must rend; and . . . many of the kings of the isles of the sea shall be wrought upon by the Spirit of God, to exclaim: The God of nature suffers. (1 Ne 19:12)

No deist could accept that, for it made God a changeable Being. Deism had drawn upon many arguments used against Christian theology by Neo-Platonic, Stoic and Neo-Pythagorean philosophers of the second and third centuries A. D. They, too, were offended by the human characteristics of Jesus, who was identified as God-in-the-flesh. Christian theologians adopted Greek thought categories to explain the faith, and had seemingly met those objections with the doctrines of the Trinity and the two natures of Christ—human and divine.

The Unitarian message denied the Trinity doctrine but still held to special revelation as long as it was reasonable.[2] Joseph Smith adopted the Unitarian point of view of Christ[3] in the Book of Mormon, but promoted what Unitarians and Protestants alike thought unreasonable: present-day revelation. Smith chided Christians who denied present revelation for playing the skeptics' game, for that meant that God had changed, if only in the manner of His relating to people. If "he hath done his work," then "there is no God today" (2 Ne 28:5-6) and the alternative is atheism and nihilism.

Smith shifted the ground for God's self-revelation so that men bore the responsibility for any break in the divine-human encounter. Present unbelief, he held, accounted for the lack of on-going revelation and charismatic gifts within and without the churches. God had always related to man on the basis of his faith, and any other terms would, indeed, make God mutable.[4]

The Issue Allegorized

Smith elaborated his views of the controversy among evangelicals, rationalists, and skeptics in a mixture of vision and allegory. It is highly relevant for Smith's defense of God, and clues for its interpretation are dispersed throughout I Nephi 8-15.

An angel led Nephi out of a dark and dreary wasteland to see a tree laden with fruit. He tasted it and was filled with joy, so he invited his family to eat the fruit. While they ate, Nephi noticed a river near the tree. There was also a straight and narrow path leading to the tree but separated from the river by an iron railing, or rod.

Crowds of people walked the path toward the tree, but many missed their way when a dark mist engulfed them. Others, however, held onto the iron rod and safely reached the tree. Once there, they ate the fruit, but felt only shame because many scoffers were ridiculing them. Hence they fell away and vanished.

Still others abandoned the path and iron rod and made their way across the river into the company of the scoffers, joining them in a huge building high in the air. The river separated the tree from the building. While the skeptics were celebrating in their sky-high building, it suddenly fell into the river, carrying its occupants to their destruction.

The allegory suggests that life is aimless without communion with God. The tree of life represents that communion, for it stands for the love that God showed in reaching out to people in Christ's ministry. To eat of the tree's fruit is to know the joy of fellowship with God. Countless multitudes seek it, but it can be found only by walking the path of life guided by the quality of virtue.

A virtuous life, however, is not enough to bring one to fellowship with God. Many hazards await the seeker: temptation and terrors (the dark mist); a living, existential hell (the river); the approval of the sophisticated, which seems more attractive than the tree (the scoffers in the great building); or an existence lost on the broad roads that lead away from the tree to nowhere.

Only by holding on to the Word of God (the iron rod) can one find communion with God. Yet even some who reach the tree and eat the fruit feel shame when scorned by the skeptics, and join forces with them. Others, however, eat the fruit and ignore the jeers.

The scoffers represent the world which rejects Christianity because of the world's pride in scientific knowledge and human reason. All Jews and Hebrews who reject their Messiah fall into this category, and are divided from God by His justice. In the final showdown between unbelievers and the disciples of a Christianity which accepts on-going revelation and spiritual gifts (the twelve apostles of the Lamb, I Ne 11:36), the worldly-wise will be humiliated and their vaunted intellectual defenses will mock them.

Smith made several points in the allegory and its interpretation. (1) Present-day revelation is an essential ingredient of fellowship with God. He pictured this in the joy that Lehi felt when his sons Nephi and Sam accepted his visions, and in his grief when sons Laman and Lemuel rejected them. (2) A person must let the Bible, the iron rod, guide him or he will lost contact with God or become His active enemy. (3) The history of this continent, from the time of the Tower of Babel until the millennium, is one of conflict between those who accept present-day revelation and spiritual gifts, and those who deny them or deny Christ and God.

Is life with God found through His on-going guidance, by some other means, or not at all? That is the issue throughout the allegory and its interpretation. Smith's position was spoken by Nephi, who wanted the same vision that his father had had and, because God does not change, believed that he would get it.

> For he that diligently seeketh shall find; and the mysteries of God shall be unfolded to them, by the power of the Holy Ghost, as well in these times as in times of old, and as well in times of old as in times to come; wherefore, the course of the Lord is one eternal round. (I Ne 10:19)

Christians who denied Smith's position would find themselves in tune with the anti-clerical skeptics Laman and Lemuel, who sang the deistic song:

> Now, he says that the Lord has talked with him and also that angels have ministered unto him. But behold, we know that he lies unto us . . . and he worketh many things by his cunning arts, that he may deceive our eyes, thinking,

perhaps, that he may lead us away into some strange wilderness; and after he had led us away, he has thought to make himself a king and a ruler over us, that he may do with us according to his will and pleasure. (I Ne 16:38)

REVELATION IN THE BOOK OF MORMON

Smith argued that holy living opens one to revelation through voices, dreams, visions, angelic announcements, theophanies prophecy, and written records. The voice of the Lord may speak forgiveness into the mind (Enos 5, 10). The Divine Presence may appear as a reward for faith and transform it into knowledge (Eth 3:18). In dreams God may speak His commands and warnings (I Ne 2:1-2; 3:2; Eth 9:3). In visions one may see the future portrayed (I Ne 1:6-14).

There is no discernible difference between dreams and visions. The allegory of the tree, river, and iron rod is called both a dream (I Ne 8:4) and a vision (I Ne 8:36). Nephi says of the allegory: "Behold, I have dreamed a dream; or, in other words, I have seen a vision" (Ne 8:2). The allegory is the words of his father's "dream or vision" (I Ne 8:36).

Visions

In the Book of Mormon visions are usually previews of history. When Lehi was carried away he saw the heavens open, Christ and his twelve apostles, Jerusalem's destruction,and the Babylonian Captivity (I Ne 1:6-14). Later he was warned in a vision of Jerusalem's impending disaster (I Ne 5:4) and, although his wife complained that he was a "visionary man," Lehi saw a vision that confirmed the city's destruction (2 Ne 1:4; Hel 8:19-22).

Nephi, Lehi's son, said that God "hath given me knowledge by visions in the nighttime" (2 Ne 4:23). Somewhat like the New Testament Paul, Nephi saw things too great for human beings to see and was forbidden to write them down (2 Ne 4:25). Abish, a Lamanite woman, had been "converted unto the Lord for many years, on account of a remarkable vision of her father" (Al 19:16).

A typical prophetic vision is found in I Nephi 13 where Nephi sees the Virgin Mary in Nazareth whisked away by God's Spirit and returned with the infant Jesus. "And the angel said unto me: Behold the Lamb of God, yea, even the Son of the Eternal Father" (I Ne 11:21). Nephi saw the ministry of Christ; John the Baptist baptizing Christ and the attendant theophany; Jesus' trial and crucifixion for the world's sins; the world drawn up in battle formation against the twelve apostles and the world's defeat.

Angelic Ministrations

Angels are sent to rebuke men's disobedience to divine commands (I Ne 3:29-31), comfort the sorrowing (Al 14-15), instruct men as to what they should do,[5] clarify doctrinal matters (Al 40:11-15), interpret dreams[6] or visions,[7] reveal the future,[8] declare repentance (Al 13:22), convince men of God's power (Mos 27:14), and to warn of impending destruction unless repentance is forthcoming (Hel 13:7).

Seeing an angel or hearing his message motivates men to render obedience. Any other response would be astonishing (1 Ne 7:9ff). If an angel says something, there is no room for doubt.⁹ "Angels speak by the power of the Holy Ghost: wherefore, they speak the words of Christ" (2 Ne 32:2-3)—whether of repentance or glad tidings—"in plain terms, that we may understand, that we cannot err" (Al 13:22). They may speak to men, women and children (Al 32:23).

The disobedient do not know that God deals with men through visions and prophecies (1 Ne 2:11-13), and the same must be said of their knowledge of angels. Cessation of revelation through the visits of angels indicates a spiritual low tide; but the dearth of their visits is due to rampant unbelief and not because revelation is now unnecessary. As Moroni explained,"it is by faith that angels appear and minister unto men" (Moro 7:37).

Signs

An angel may give a sign to confirm a vision (1 Ne 11:7). The Lord may give one by which the readers will know of the impending millennium (3 Ne 21:1-7). More often, a sign is given by a prophet to attest his authenticity (Hel 9:24-41), but especially to help people recognize when a prophecy is about to be fulfilled, or to detect when an event has been prophesied.¹⁰

Signs must be offered by God or His agents. They may not be demanded by the skeptical as proof of God's message or existence. Alma disapproved of such demands:

> yea, there are many who do say: If thou wilt show unto us a sign from heaven, when we shall know of a surety, then we shall believe. Now I ask, is this faith? Behold, I say unto you, Nay; for if a man knoweth a thing he hath no cause to believe, for he knoweth it. . . . Faith is not to have a perfect knowledge of things; therefore, if ye have faith ye hope for things which are not seen, which are true. (Al 32:17-18, 21)

Signs were granted when they were asked for, but with dire results. Sherem demanded a sign of the power of the Holy Ghost and received first a scolding and then an affliction which led to his death (Jac 7:13-20). Korihor asked for a sign to prove God's existence, and was offered the works of creation as proof. Unsatisfied, and at his own insistence Korihor was struck dumb as a sign and finally met an ignominious death (Al 30:43-59).

Records

In contrast to the Bible, no book of the Mormon scripture has an unknown author, for every writer is identified by genealogy. The time of each book's composition is also known, for Smith provided a detailed calendar.¹¹

The most ancient record in the American scripture is found in the book of Ether. It tells of Jared and his family leaving the Tower of Babel with their language, by the Lord's dispensation, unconfounded. Jesus appeared to them and commanded Jared's brother to record what he heard and saw during Christ's prenatal visit. The record and two stones by which it could be translated were to be kept sealed until after Jesus' crucifixion (Eth 3:21-22; 4:1). "And the Lord said unto him: Write these things and seal them up, and I will show them in mine own due time unto the children of men" (Eth 3:27).

Generations later Ether, Jared's descendant, edited the record of Jared's brother (Eth 2:13) and added to it. The Jaredites expelled Ether because of his prophetic ministry, but from hiding he watched their destruction and recorded the fulfillment of the Lord's words against them (Eth 13:13-14). When he finished the record, Ether hid it "in a manner that the people of Limhi did find them" (Eth 15:33).

Centuries later the scene focused upon Jerusalem just before the first Babylonian offensive about 600 B. C. Lehi, a pious citizen, saw in vision the city's destruction, the Messiah's advent, and the world's redemption. He recorded this along with other visions and prophecies (1 Ne 1:16, 19). This was noted by Nephi, Lehi's most loyal son, who declared his intention to abridge his father's account and then to write a record of his own life (1 Ne 1:1-3, 16-17). After Lehi fled Jerusalem, he sent his sons back to secure from Laban the 24 brass plates that contained Lehi's genealogy, the record of the Jews (1 Ne 3:3, 12, 24; 4:38), words spoken by prophets since the world's beginning (1 Ne 3:20), and the law of Moses (1 Ne 4:15).

The most important records in the Book of Mormon for verifying the Bible were Laban's brass plates. They contained what has already been cited, and some prophecies of Jeremiah (1 Ne 5:11-13), Jacob (3 Ne 10:17), and Joseph (2 Ne 4:2). The genealogies of Lehi and Laban went back to biblical Joseph.[12] From the "record of the Jews" there were also the Pentateuch and the Old Testament historical books down to the time of Zedekiah (1 Ne 5:11-13).

Since the Tower of Babel, the plates had been handed down along with the "interpreters." This enabled any future translator to understand the original language, and eventually enabled Joseph Smith to translate (Mos 28:20). The plates informed God's people of His mysteries, records and commandments, without which they would have "suffered in ignorance" (Mos 1:3).

Through future generations the plates would be "preserved by the hand of the Lord until they should go forth unto every nation, kindred, tongue, and people, that they shall know of the mysteries contained thereon" (Al 37:4). For that reason Lehi's family carried the plates to America (1 Ne 5:21-22), and the Nephites often copied its contents into the records that form the Book of Mormon (2 Ne 4:15).

When Nephi wrote his account, he left out his father's genealogy and tried to include only those things pleasing to God and beneficial to men (1 Ne 6:5-6). To help his people remember the Lord (1 Ne 19:18), Nephi made two sets of plates, of which the larger contained the secular history of the Nephites and the smaller recorded their religious history.[13]

Nephite editors and writers preserved and added to Nephi's records through the following centuries. Enos wanted to preserve and bring forth a record to future Lamanites in the event of a total Nephite apostasy from Christ. God agreed (Enos 13-16). Two hundred years later, 121 B. C., a righteous Nephite, King Benjamin, committed the records to his son, Mosiah, who had been taught the contents of the records engraved upon the plates of Lehi and Nephi. Although he wanted the people to have them, Mosiah kept the records from them. Later, the records were updated by King Limhi (Mos 1:1-6, 16).

In 46 B. C. the records were again revised and transmitted to future Nephites as a sign to the Gentiles of God's power (3 Ne 3:3-18; 21:5). When the Savior visited them in 34 A. D., he commanded them to fill in past omissions and to update the records (3 Ne 23).

Mormon was one of the last surviving Nephites, who witnessed and recorded the destruction of almost all his people in 385 A. D. He wanted his son, Moroni, to complete the record. Mormon abridged the Large Plates (secular record) of Nephi and added to them his own, noting the fulfillment of prophecies recorded long before by Nephi, Lehi's son. By making his record available to posterity, Mormon hoped to bring the Lamanites back to the knowledge of God (W. Mormon 1-8).

> And now I, Mormon, proceed to finish out my record, which I take from the plates of Nephi. . . . And I, Mormon, pray to God that they may be preserved from this time henceforth. And I know that they will be preserved; for there are great things written upon them, out of which my people and their brethren shall be judged at the great and last day, according to the word of God which is written. (W. Mormon 9, 11)[14]

Mormon recorded the slaughter of his people and buried the records in the hill, Cumorah, in 385 A. D. to preserve them from his contemporaries for future Lamanite generations.

Moroni finished his father's records (Morm 8) and then edited the material of Ether (Eth 1:1-5), giving only a part of Ether's report of Jesus' visit to the Jaredites. Then, since only hostile Lamanites were left, he concealed the plates in the earth (Eth 4:1-3). There they would stay until the Gentiles repented of their iniquity (Eth 4:5-6). When the Gentiles were ready to accept the work of Moroni, then the reader might know that the word of the Father "was commenced upon all the face of the land" (Eth 4:17).

Moroni wrote of the evil of Jared's day to persuade men to do good (Eth 8:26), but he curtailed his account because of his "weakness" as a chronicler (Eth 12:39-40). Ultimately, he was forbidden to continue with Ether's record of the Jaredites (Eth 13:13). Therefore he left instructions for the future translator with his own words added in the hope that future Lamanites might find them of some use (Moro 1).

The next chapter in the record transmission began with the finding of the Nephite records in Hill Cumorah. Appearing now as an angel in September, 1827, Moroni committed the plates and the "interpreters" to Joseph Smith for translation. By identifying the records as the "Stick of Joseph" of Ezekiel 37:16 and the "sealed book" that cries "out of the dust" of Isaiah 29:4, 11-12, Smith made the discovery of the plates a fulfillment of prophecy.

In the face of skepticism Smith tried to bolster revealed religion in several ways. (1) The genealogy provided for all recorders accurately identified them and their times. This plugged the gap that Paine had criticized in the Bible, that books of testimony could not accurately be placed with their times or authors.[15] (2) By tracing the records back to Jared and asserting that prophecies from Adam's time were also available, it was possible to maintain that man had also kept records as part of his relationship with God. (3) In opposition to Paine,[16] the value of hearsay reports of signs and wonders and historical events for revealed religion was strengthened. (4) The communication of matters previously unknown—via prophecy and visions—met Paine's demand that revelation should communicate only material previously unknown.[18]

(5) Christ's interest in bringing records up to date supported the contention that God reveals Himself through human means; namely, language and writing—points

that Paine had denied.[18] (6) The inclusion of "interpreters" with the plates ensured that God provided for an accurate translation of the records. (7) The Bible could be shown to be a revelation by its comparison with and correction by the newly translated Nephite scriptures. (8) The advantages gained can be kept only by admitting ongoing revelations and spiritual gifts as a real mark of Christianity.

Given his orientation, Joseph Smith regained a great deal of territory from deists and rationalists. Further, he used the speculations of Indian origins then in circulation —a lost race pre-dating the Indians—and the theory that Indians are descendants of the lost tribes of Israel to do it.

PERSONAL REVELATION

Smith's Visions

Moroni's disclosure of the plates was the first news the outside world had of the new scripture.[19] Willard Chase heard of it in June, 1827[20] and Martin Harris in October.[21] Smith said that he "could see the place where the plates were deposited, and that so clearly and distinctly that I knew the place again when I visited it."[22] Moroni commanded Smith

> to go to my father and tell him of the vision and commandment which I had received. I obeyed; I returned to my father in the field, and rehearsed the whole matter to him. He replied to me that it was of God, and told me to go and do as commanded by the messenger.[23]

The vision was repeated after the first one in 1823 each year until Smith got the plates in 1827. This was the foundation upon which he began his drive to produce a scripture and found a church. It was not a unique happening in the Palmyra region,[24] but Smith found a way to "prove" his claim that others had not.

The Three Witnesses

Smith arranged for corroboration to come from three witnesses as early as March, 1829. He received the following revelation: "And the testimony of three witnesses will I send forth of my word" (DC 5:15). In April, Smith dictated the principle of three witnesses into the Book of Mormon when he had Nephi enclose the words of his brother, Jacob, and those of the biblical Isaiah with his own to prove the truth of what he wrote. Nephi reasoned that "by the words of three, God hath said, I will establish my word" (2 Ne 11:3). Within a few weeks, Smith had Nephi predict the words of the book being delivered to the scholar, at which time

> the book shall be hid from the eyes of the world, that the eyes of none shall behold it, by the power of God, besides him to whom the book shall be delivered; and they shall testify to the truth of the book and the things therein. (2 Ne 27:12)

Moroni also granted the future translator permission to show the plates to assistants.

> And unto three shall they be shown by the power of God; wherefore they shall

know of a surety that these things are true. And in the mouth of three witnesses shall those things be established; and the testimony of three, and this work, in the which shall be shown forth the power of God and also his work, of which the Father, and the Son, and the Holy Ghost bear record—and all this shall stand as a testimony against the world at the last day. (Eth 5:3-4)

Getting Them Ready

1828 was an exciting year for Martin Harris. His trip to Pennsylvania to get the characters; his return to Palmyra; his journey to the east to consult the scholars; his return home; all this was climaxed by his return to Pennsylvania to take up duties as Smith's scribe. After three months Harris went back to Palmyra with the 116 page manuscript and lost it God denounced Harris through Smith's revelation, but Harris returned in December, once again to transcribe.

Harris soon needed a further witness that he was not being duped. Smith had the Lord demand that Harris confess his sins, pray, and humble himself; otherwise, he should not view the plates. God foreknew that if Harris failed to practice humility before seeing the plates, he would fall into transgression (DC5:23-28, 32).

Oliver Cowdery came to Palmyra[25] and heard of Smith's vision. At the beginning of April he went to Pennsylvania to see the prophet. Smith surmised Cowdery's sincerity to learn the truth and told him of his "'secret thoughts and all he meditated about going to see him, which no man on earth knew, as he supposed, but himself.'"[26] Two days after his arrival, Cowdery became Smith's scribe.

Soon thereafter Cowdery wanted the power to translate and was promised that he should

receive a knowledge of whatsoever things you shall ask in faith, with an honest heart, believing that you shall receive a knowledge concerning the engravings of old records, which are ancient, which contain those parts of my scripture of which has been spoken by the manifestation of my Spirit. Yea, behold, I will tell you in your mind and in your heart. Now, behold, this is the spirit by which Moses brought the children of Israel through the Red Sea on dry ground. (DC 8:1-3)

His attempt to translate was a failure, but the promise came that he would have another chance. When he tried again, he was told that he should study "out in his mind" his proposed translation. If it were satisfactory his bosom would "burn" within him and he would "feel that it is right" (DC 9:8-9).[27]

Cowdery, therefore, asked for instruction and was told that by his presence as scribe and by what he was learning of the restored gospel he could "know that thou hast been enlightened by the Spirit of truth." He should consider his presence and present duty as "a witness unto thee—that the words of the work which thou hast been writing are true," since only God could have known Cowdery's desire for instruction and the "intents" of his heart (DC 6:14-17). A further witness was the peace and satisfaction he had sought and found about Smith's mission (DC 6:22-23). The question was put to Cowdery: ". . . if I have told you things which no man knoweth have you not received a witness?" (6:24).

The second request for assurance about the plates brought out the meaning of the "spirit of revelation." On condition that Cowdery "ask in faith, with an honest heart, believing that you shall receive a knowledge concerning the engravings of old records" (DC 8:1), the "spirit of revelation" would come upon him and speak in his mind and heart the assurance that he wanted concerning the plates (DC 8:1-3).

On May 15, 1829 Smith and Cowdery received baptism and the conferring of the Aaronic priesthood at the hand of the angel, who identified himself as John the Baptist (DC 13).[28] In spite of the angelic visit, however, Cowdery's faith faltered still a third time. Once again God referred him back to the things he had already written and declared them true. Cowdery should have known this because of the manifestations of the Spirit already given him.

> And if you know that they are true, behold, I give unto you a commandment, that you rely upon the things which are written; For in them are all things written concerning the foundation of my church, my gospel, and my rock. (DC 18:3-4)

David Whitmer took interest in Smith's mission when Smith came to the Whitmer home to finish translating the Book of Mormon. David was told to ask in faith, believing, and he should receive the Holy Ghost and stand "as a witness of the things of which you shall both hear and see" (DC 14:8). Jesus declared that he was speaking in person and said: "thou are David . . . called to assist; which thing if ye do, and are faithful, ye shall be blessed both spiritually and temporally, and great shall be your reward" (DC 14:11)

When the Three Witnesses were chosen and eager to see the plates, they received another communique addressed to them jointly:

> And it is by your faith that you shall obtain a view of them, even by that faith which was had by the prophets of old. And after that you have obtained faith, and have seen them with your eyes, you shall testify of them, by the power of God. . . . And ye shall testify that you have seen them, even as my servant Joseph Smith, Jun., has seen them; for it is by my power that he has seen them, and it is because he had faith. . . . And I, Jesus Christ, your Lord and your God, have spoken it unto you, that I might bring about my righteous purposes unto the children of men. Amen. (DC 17:2-3, 5, 9)

On their way to view the plates the four men prayed for the angel to appear and display them. Sure that his presence was a detriment because of his doubt, Martin Harris withdrew. After the others had seen the plates and the angel, Smith went to Harris and prayed with him. Then Harris, too, saw the vision and gained the conviction that he had seen the angel and—at long last—the plates.[29] Soon after the Three Witnesses signed their testimony:

> . . . we . . . have seen the plates which contain this record, which is a record of the people of Nephi. . . . And we also know that they have been translated by the gift and power of God, for his voice hath declared it unto us; wherefore we know of a surety that the work is true. And we also testify that we have seen the engravings which are upon the plates; and they have been shown unto us by the power of God, and not of man. And we declare . . . that an angel of God came down from heaven, and he brought and laid before our eyes, that we beheld and saw the plates, and the engravings thereon; and we know that it is by the grace of God the Father, and our Lord Jesus Christ, that we beheld and bear record

that these things are true. . . . The voice of the Lord commanded us that we should bear record of it; wherefore . . . we bear testimony of these things.

OLIVER COWDERY
DAVID WHITMER
MARTIN HARRIS

The Affidavit Analyzed

Joseph Smith chose men who had aready accepted the reality of angelic visits. Oliver Cowdery had had visions before he came to New York from Vermont.[30] During the winter of 1828-29 he stayed at the Smith home while teaching at the Palmyra Academy. After Smith had returned to Pennsylvania in December, 1828, Cowdery had another vision. According to the 1832 history of Joseph Smith,

the Lord appeared unto a young man by the name of Oliver Cowdery and showed unto him the plates a vision and also the truth of the work and what the Lord was about to do through me his unworthy servant therefore he was desirous to come and write for me to translate . . .[31]

Earlier in this account he had written of Martin Harris that

he had become convinced of the vision and gave me fifty dollars to bear my expenses and because of this faith and this righteous deed the Lord appeared unto him in a vision and showed unto him his marvelous work which he was about to do and immediately came to Susquehannah and said the Lord had shown him that he must go to New York City with some of the characters . . .[32]

Rev. Diedrich Willers wrote on June 18, 1830 that Smith went to the home of David Whitmer with the purpose of "completing the translation" of the Book of Mormon because Whitmer claimed to have "seen an angel." Then he added that this was the 11th place where Smith had "worked on the translation," that he could work only where others had had a visionary experience.[33]

Thus the Three Witnesses believed that on-going revelation was an essential ingredient of true faith. It led them to expect visions, angelic visits, a sign to confirm faith, and the manifestation of spiritual gifts. Further, before Smith began dictating to Cowdery, God had promised that "whosoever believeth on my words, them will I visit with the manifestation of my Spirit" (DC 5:16).

Smith chose men who were assured that three witnesses were to be chosen, that Christ had spoken to them through Smith's voice, that through his voice and pen Smith was Christ's spokesman to his generation, that they would share in the work of restoring the gospel, that their faith would enable them to see the plates, and that any failures on their part to see them would be due to their unbelief.

Prior to the completion of the translation, Harris knew that he was in need of humility, prayer, recognition of and repentance of his sins. He was anxious lest he fail to see the plates. Cowdery had been referred repeatedly back to himself when he sought assurance. He was told to regard his past feelings of inner assurance as God's witness, or sign, that this was the power of the Holy Ghost working in him. Whitmer had been promised temporal and spiritual blessings for his coming role as a witness, and that was from Jesus Christ himself.

In spite of their printed testimony, the Three Witnesses did not "see" the plates as the language indicates. First, Smith told them that they were to see the plates "by your faith . . . as my servant Joseph Smith, Jr. has seen them; for it is by my power that he has seen them" (DC 17:2, 5). Second, A. Metcalf, John H. Gilbert, Reuben P. Harmon, and Rev. Jesse Townsend all said that the Three Witnesses claimed to have viewed the plates only with their "spiritual eyes."[34] Third, in 1838 Martin Harris publicly stated that the Three Witnesses saw the plates only in their imagination, or in a vision, but not with their natural eyes. Again, he added, "he never saw them only as he saw a city through a mountain."[35] It is possible that Smith showed them some plates, but it is more likely that they saw them for inner, psychological reasons.[36]

Smith challenged each person to receive his own testimony and affirm the reality of present-day revelation. Those who wanted a testimony could hope for one in the future.[37] But those who had not received or could not affirm revelation as a personal experience were at least silenced because their unbelief was all that blocked their receiving a witness.

Alexander Campbell told of the frustration he felt after an imaginary conversation with the Three Witnesses:

> I would ask them how they knew that it was God's voice which they heard—but they would tell me to ask God in faith. *That is, I must believe it first, and then ask God if it is true.*[38]

That is what Smith told them, and Campbell illustrated Smith's intent. If he could not affirm a personal witness, neither could he deny the Three Witnesses theirs.[39]

The Eight Witnesses

As with the Three, Smith appears to have chosen the Eight Witnesses because they were spiritually receptive to a new revelation. Rev. Diedrich Willers pictured the Whitmer family as highly gullible, believing in witches. Four of the Eight were Whitmers, and Willers included Hiram Page in the description.[40] Joseph, Sr., Hyrum, and Samuel Smith had their own family tradition of visions.[41]

The second set of witnesses does not carry the same weight as that of the Three. The Eight Witnesses declared that they saw "hefted" the plates of gold, that Joseph Smith showed them the plates that he had translated, that they saw engravings upon the plates, that the plates and engravings had "the appearance of ancient work, and of curious workmanship," and "that the said Smith has got the plates."

Their testimony claimed no revelation. No "voice" declared to them that the "work is true." No "power of God" showed them the plates, just Joseph Smith. No "angel of God" laid the plates before them. No "voice of the Lord" told them to testify of what they saw. For that reason Eduard Meyer concluded that the testimony of the Eight was written primarily as further evidence that Smith, indeed, had the plates.[42] The Eight did claim revelation, however, in their conversations with others.

When David Marks stopped at the Whitmers on March 29, 1830, the Eight Witnesses "affirmed, that an angel had showed them certain plates of metal, having the appearance of gold that were dug out of the ground by one Joseph Smith."[43] They told

Marks some basic points about the Book of Mormon and its contents, but claimed revelation only in the viewing of the plates.

In 1838 John Whitmer apostatized and was confronted by Theodore Turley, who reminded Whitmer that he had "published to the world that an angel did present those plates to Joseph Smith." Although that is not what the Testimony of the Eight says, Whitmer nevertheless claimed that the plates "were shown to me by a supernatural power." But he could not vouch for the translation because he could not read the engravings upon the plates.[44]

As he did for the Three Witnesses, however, Martin Harris publicly denied that the Eight Witnesses ever saw the plates. That led the Eight to pause before they signed their testimony, and then they signed only after much persuasion.[45] Like the Three, the Eight may have been led to "see" an angel present the plates to them, but unlike the Three, the Eight Witnesses had no revelation to help them vouch for the truth of the translation. Meyer's conjecture, then, is further supported: the main purpose for the Eight's Testimony was to bolster the claim of the Three that Smith had the plates. The idea of having the testimony of two sets of witnesses joined to the testimony of the one who found them may well have come from the Pittsfield Parchment story of Ethan Smith.[46]

Faith's New Foundation

Oliver Cowdery explained the basis for faith in a letter to his brother in 1834. People believed that "Jesus is the Christ" because they believed the apostolic testimony that it is so. But people needed an "assurance" to face the arguments of God's enemies. "The salvation of man is of that importance that he is not left to a mere belief, founded upon the testimony or say so of another man!" That directly counters Paine's critique of the Christian ground of faith as taught then. Jesus told Peter in Matthew 16:15-18 that God the Father had *revealed* to Peter that "Jesus is the Christ."[47]

This "revelation" was the Rock upon which Christ would build his Church, against which "the gates of hell should not prevail." No apostle's testimony could reveal this; "flesh and blood cannot reveal it—it must be the Father"; and if "men *know* that Jesus is the Christ, it must be by revelation." When "the everlasting Father reveals to men, that Jesus is the Son of God, they cannot be overthrown."[48]

The possibility of personal revelation undermined the deists. Paine had written that the accurate prediction of an eclipse or transit of Venus proves that man knows the distance between heavenly bodies and their mass when they most closely approach each other.[49] That is, the fact of accurate prediction proves the existence of true knowledge. But if success proved the theory, then deists were put on the defensive.

The Testimony of the Three Witnesses showed the reality of present-day revelation. It validated the records contained in the Book of Mormon. Deists could run their own experiment and seek their own testimony. If one must use scientific presuppositions to check the findings of science, then one must use spiritual guidelines to check matters of religion. Moroni gave one guideline in his address to all future readers of the Book of Mormon, skeptics included:

Behold, I would exhort you that when ye shall read these things . . . . ye would remember how merciful the Lord hath been unto the children of men, from the creation of Adam even down unto the time that ye shall receive these things. . . . I would exhort you that ye would ask God, the Eternal Father, in the name of Christ, if these things are not true; and if ye shall ask with a sincere heart, with real intent, having faith in Christ, he will manifest the truth of it unto you. . . . by the power of the Holy Ghost, ye may know the truth of all things. (Moro 10:3-5)

If deists cannot muster the interest to examine the records with a believing mind, at least they can no longer rail against the adherents of revealed religion. One could not, after all, expect the unchangeable God, who has always related to man only on the basis of his faith, to change His means of relating just to accommodate skeptical minds.

Thus a step has been taken beyond the stand-off with Alexander Campbell. The situation now is that personal revelation has been proved by those who read with faithful hearts. The skeptics must prove that the believers did not receive a witness, but if they fail to do so, then the believers may be right.[50] If skeptics do not want to test the believers' assumptions, then they show themselves to be unfairly critical and unworthy of a hearing.[51]

When Smith freed his converts from the need to validate the Book of Mormon on the same basis that others validated the Bible—by appealing to miracles, apostolic testimony or some form of biblical inspiration—he also gave them a tool with which to build his movement. They, too, deprecated a faith in Christ based upon hearsay evidence and promoted one established instead, by personal revelation.[52]

After his conversion Sidney Rigdon visited members of his congregation in Kirtland, Ohio to win them over to his newly-found faith. He argued that their faith was based upon the Bible, which came to them only upon "human testimony." They denied it

and gave him reasons which he himself formerly urged against *deists*. He then said the *old* revelation was confirmed by miracles, but the Book of Mormon would never be; it was not designed to be thus confirmed.[53]

Rigdon's reply is borne out in what the Book of Mormon does with miracles. Although it speaks about miracles in general as part of the manifestation of the Spirit, actual mention of miracles specifically performed is rare.[54] Joseph Smith would claim some miracles[55] for his new church, but nowhere does it become the final basis for faith. That was reserved for personally experienced revelation.

Choosing Three Witnesses proved to be a highly successful strategy. They frequently testified before large audiences.[56] And even if later developments were to cloud their testimony, the restored church would ride out the storm. After that, only a relatively few would discover that the testimony might imply something other than what it says.

Deists had rejected the deity of Christ and the reliability of the New Testament Gospels because they were based on human testimony. By prompting each convert to get his own personal revelation that Christ is the Son of God, Smith removed the issue from being a matter of secondary testimony. Now it was a matter of knowledge—knowledge communicated directly to the believer and meeting the criteria for revelation stated by Paine. The development of the Christian Church in the Grecian east and the Roman west led to an interpretation of *Peter* as the Rock of Matthew 16:18. Peter's successors were a visible guarantee that the Church still had the faith delivered by Jesus Christ. The Protestant reformers of the sixteenth century interpreted Peter's *confession* that Jesus was "the Christ, the Son of the living God" as the Rock on which Christ would build his Church. The Roman Catholic claim to apostolic succession and ultimate papal infallibility, and the Protestant claim to a succession of faith based on an infallible, inspired Bible were undermined by the deistic polemic, many felt, because both were based on apostolic testimony, or hearsay evidence. By interpreting *revelation* as the Rock, Smith defended God, the deity of Christ, and the biblical revelation against deism in a way that Protestants and Catholics would not— in a way that seemed to answer deistic objections and give believers a sounder foundation for their faith.

SUMMARY

By equating the God of Christianity with the God of creation and by showing that He operates today as He did in former ages, Joseph Smith tried to stop the inroads of skepticism. Records of past revelation and evidence for on-going revelation are found in the Book of Mormon. Deistic grounds for biblical criticism are countered. Personal revelation had to be upheld. Smith supported it with Three Witnesses to testify to it. God does not change. He still reveals Himself. In his way, Smith proved it.

FOOTNOTES

1. The argument is used for other matters as well. Redemption and salvation have been available since the Fall, "for the Spirit is the same, yesterday, today, and forever" (2 Ne 2:4). Little children need no baptism or repentance, and

> if not so, God is a partial God, and also a changeable God, and a respecter to persons; for how many little children have died without baptism. . . . For I know that God is not a partial God, neither a changeable being; but he is unchangeable from all eternity to all eternity. (Moro 8:11-12, 18)

This refers only to the manner of God's dealing with people, not to His essence. Cf. EMS, I, 9 (February, 1833), p. 97, for a similar argument for the Book of Mormon. It contained the full gospel and proved to the Jews and Gentiles that the Bible is true and that God still inspires men and calls them to do His work. The principle is often stated.

2. William Ellery Channing summed up this point in 1819 in his "Baltimore Sermon." He held to the inspiration of the Bible and set forth the "leading principle in interpreting scripture":

> the Bible is a book written for men, in the language of men, and that its meaning is to be sought in the same manner, as that of other books. . . . that God, when he condescends to speak and writ submits, if we may so say, to the established rules of speaking and writing. How else would the Scriptures avail us more than if communicated in an unknown tongue.

Vergilius Ferm, ed., *Classics of Protestantism* (New York: Philosophical Library, c. 1959), p. 245. Paine would have disowned this position as unworthy of God.

3. Cf. George B. Arbaugh, "Evolution of Mormon Doctrine," CH, IX (1940), in which he traces monistic tendencies in the Book of Mormon through tri-theism and then polytheism late in Smith's life. Cf. chap. 3 above on Unitarianism, Universalism, and the Christian Connection as influences upon Joseph Smith.

4. Smith's concern to keep God unchangeable was to find an ironic development years later when he advanced the position that God progresses in His own development. The unchangeable aspect of God, as Smith and later Utah Mormonism was to proclaim it, was to be found only in His manner of relating to humanity.

5. Al 8:14-15, 20; 10:7-8.

6. I Ne 11:25; 12:16.

7. I Ne 11:35-36; 14:29.

8. Mos 3:2-27; I Ne 11; 13; 2 Ne 6:11; 10:3; 25:19.

9. Mos 27:14-15; I Ne 4:3; Al 10:9; 11:31; 21:5.

10. Specific signs given: Christ's birth from a virgin—2 Ne 17:11, 14 (Isa 7:11, 14); the appearance of a new star and a prolonged day at his birth—Hel 14:2-6; 3 Ne 1:15; Christ's crucifixion to be signaled by a three-day darkness—I Ne 19:10; Hel 14:14.

11. Cf. Appendix No. 9, "Book of Mormon Chronology," *A Dictionary of the Book of Mormon* (Salt Lake City: Philip C. Reynolds, c. 1954), pp. 327-37. First printed in 1892.

12. Al 37:3; I Ne 5:14-16; 2 Ne 4:1-2.

13. I Ne 9:1-5; 19:1-6. The Small Plates comprise the books of I Nephi, 2 Nephi, Jacob, Enos, Jarom and Omni. Cf. Hugh Nibley, *Since Cumorah* (Salt Lake City: Deseret Book Company, c. 1967), pp. 143-52. His account of "The Transmission of the Record" is a comparison of parallels between the efforts of the Nephite editors and those of biblical Isaiah; cf. esp. pp. 146-50.

14. Mormon's abridgement of the Plates of Nephi comprises the section from Mosiah to Mormon, chap. 7. He abridged the portion of the smaller plates (the sacred record) now known as the first six books. The Words of Mormon constitute a bridge between the smaller and larger plates, explaining what preceeded and prefacing what follows up through Mormon, chap. 8.

15. Paine, *Age of Reason*, pp. 91-92.

16. *Ibid.*, pp. 168, 183.

17. *Ibid.*, p. 33.

18. *Ibid.*, pp. 38, 170.

19. Joseph Smith dated this vision as having first appeared in 1823. It is often confused with what is called the First Vision, which he dated in 1820. No one knew about the First Vision at this time, and it was not a factor in winning the first converts of early Mormonism. Cf. Introduction, n. 13 and chap. 4, n. 50. As noted in the Introduction, De Pillis locates Smith's quest for authority in the First Vision, when the Father and Son told Smith not to join any church, that none were right. That conviction, however arrived at, may well have been the impetus for his quest.

Backman, "Awakenings," brought to bear his own research upon Joseph Smith's comment that revivals "became general among all the sects in that region of country." He argued that since several revivals in 1819-20 took place within a 20 mile radius of Palmyra, the "region of country" must include much more than the immediate vicinity of Palmyra. Hill, "Secular or Sectarian History?," pp. 82-83 compared the phrase to Smith's later use of it to designate all the area in Iowa and Illinois in Mormon hands, and cited Charles Finney's use of it to designate the whole burned-over district as reinforcement for Backman. Richard L. Bushman, *Dialogue*, IX, 1 (Spring, 1969), pp. 87-89 in "The First Vision Story Revived," develops Backman's point in response to Walters and reduces the issue to the question, "how near is near and how big is big?" Walters's reply to Bushman further develops his case for the revival having been in Palmyra— and therefore not until 1824, not connected with the First Vision. Cf. the entire three article roundtable.

Walters answered the question "how near is near and how big is big?" on pp. 68-70 and further clarified his point in his response to Bushman, p. 97: the revival was in the immediate vicinity of Smith's home, "among the different religious denominations in the neighborhood where I lived," so close that the daily excitement made him "feel the pressure to join the local Methodist Church, just as members of the family had joined the local Presbyterian Church."

20. Cf. Brodie, p. 437, taken from Howe.

21. Joel Tiffany, "Mormonism—No. II," p. 167.

22. DHC, I, p. 13.

23. *Ibid,*, p. 15.

24. WF, May 16, 1821 has a story of a Methodist preacher who asserted that he was one of the "prophets that was to come in the latter days—that the dawn of the millennium has commenced." The story of Asa Wild, WS, October 22, 1823, is pertinent. He had a vision in which Jehovah

> told me that the Millenium state of the world is about to take place; that in *seven* years literally, there would scarcely a sinner be found on earth. . . . above all, various and dreadful judgments executed immediately by God, through the instrumentality of the Ministers of the Millenial dispensation.

All denominations had become corrupt, guided only by reason, not by revelation as the original church. But God would raise up that "class of persons" mentioned in Revelation 14:6-7, "of an inferior class, and small learning," who would be superior Christians in every way. All denominations constitute the

New Testament Babylon. Wild had tried the Calvinist and Methodist churches but found them wanting. Cf. Brodie, pp. 22-23. Cf. also the visions of Solomon Chamberlain, early convert to Mormonism in Porter, Appendix D, pp. 360-62.

25. Before coming to New York from Middleton, Vt., Cowdery associated with a sect "apparently involving millenial expectations and direct revelation as well as some mysterious treasure hunting," according to Cross, pp. 38-39.

26. From an 1878 letter of David Whitmer to Orson Pratt, MS, XL (1879), 772.

27. Cowdery had asked to translate and had been assured that he could do it (DC 8:9-12, 9:1). But when he failed, Smith put into Christ's mouth a confused explanation for Cowdery's failure and a reason why he should not soon try again. *First,* Cowdery had "feared" and did not continue the translation process as he had begun it (DC 9:5, 11). *Second,* Cowdery failed because he had expected Christ to give him the translation (DC 9:7). *Third,* Cowdery was supposed to think through the translation. Christ would give him an inner burning by which Cowdery would "feel that it is right" (DC 9:8). Without that feeling he would be so confused that he would not even know what he did wrong and would have to wait for Christ to give him the translation   (DC 9:9). But note that in verse 7 Cowdery was waiting for Christ to give him the translation! *Fourth,* Cowdery could have translated if he had known all this (DC 9:10), but no one had told him. For these reasons it was not "expedient" that Cowdery should "translate at this present time" (DC 9:3): "the time is past, and it is not expedient now" (DC 9:11). Therefore Smith has Christ say, "I have taken away this privilege from you" (DC 9:5).

Cowdery could have translated, then, but he did not know the conditions of the process. He did something wrong and it was too late for the present. Smith had used this proceedure before to explain the failure of others to find the treasures they sought by having him look into his peep-stone. When William Stafford let Smith and his father look for treasure, they went through an elaborate ceremony, "but as there was some mistake in the process, it did not have the desired effect." Brodie reprints it from Howe, p. 434. Willard Chase reported that Joseph, Sr. told him how his son had followed the instructions of the angel to get the chest with the plates some years before 1827. He could not get them, according to the angel, because he had not obeyed his "orders," Brodie, p. 435. Smith's father-in-law, Isaac Hale, told of the time when Smith directed some money-diggers, "but when they had arrived in digging to near the place where he [Smith] had stated an immense treasure would be found —he said the enchantment was so powerful that he could not see," Brodie, p. 439.

Mormons have tended to discredit Hale's statement because it appeared in Howe's *Mormonism Unvailed,* but Wesley P. Walters's "Joseph Smith's Bainbridge, N. Y. Court Trials,"WTJ, XXXVI, 2 (Winter, 1974), n. 67, pp. 151-52, shows that the statement was first published independently of Howe or Dr. Philastus Hurlbut (ex-Mormon collaborator with Howe). It appeared first in Hale's local newspaper, *The Susquehannah Register.*

28. Indirectly he did deny it during the years that he was out of favor with the Saints, 1838-48, for during this time he joined the Methodist Church.

29. DHC, I, 54-55.

30. Cf. n. 27.

31. Cf. Cheesman, "Analysis of the Accounts," or Jessee, "The Early Accounts."

32. *Ibid.* Confirmed by Harris; cf. Tiffany, "Mormonism—No. II," p. 163.

33. Willers to Mayer and Young. Cf. Quinn, "The First Months of Mormonism" for a translation.

34. Metcalf, *Ten Years Before the Mast,* pp. 73-74 printed a letter from David Whitmer dated April 2, 1887:

> of course we were in the spirit when we had the view, for no man can behold the face of an angel, except in a spiritual view, but we were in the body also, and everything was as natural to us, as it is at any time. . . . A bright light enveloped us where we were, that filled at noon day, and there *in a vision or in* the *spirit,* we saw and heard just as it is stated in my testimony in the Book of Mormon.

Whitmer was not consistently clear in the many statements he made about the event. Cf. Hill, p. 92, nn. 117, 118; cf. also "Murphy and Mormonism," *The Kingston Times,* December 16, 1887, Caldwell County, Mo., where John Murphy cites an interview with Whitmer, in which Whitmer reportedly said that seeing an angel was like having an impression, like a Quaker or Methodist in meditation; it was "being impressed with the truth and reality of it." But the following week, December 23, Joseph R. Lambert replied in "Murphy and Mormonism, The Other Side," and produced many statements that Whitmer had made over the years, that more clearly supported the Book of Mormon statement.

Jesse Townsend's Letter to Phineas Stiles, dated Palmyra, Wayne County, N. Y., December 24, 1833, spoke of the Book of Mormon translation being done in secret with the threat of immediate death for any unauthorized person seeing the plates. "Poor Martin's faith was apparently strengthened by this pretension, but afterward the 'command' was modified, and he claimed to have seen the plates with 'spiritual eyes.'" Tucker, p. 290.

John H. Gilbert said "nobody but Joe himself ever saw the golden tablets or the far-seeing spectacles," "Joe Smith," *The Post & Tribune*, Detroit, Mich., December 3, 1877, p. 3. Cf. also the citation in Hill, p. 92.

35. Stephen Burnett to Br. [Lyman E. ?] Johnson, April 25, 1838, in Joseph Smith Letter Book, 2, located in the Church Archives, Salt Lake City.

36. Hill, p. 92.

37. When Oliver Cowdery delivered his charge to the Twelve Apostles, he stressed the necessity of their getting a revelation that was more than the seeing of an angel; that was, in fact, a glimpse of the face of God. Cowdery assured them that God would never let such a testimony fail. DHC, II, 195.

38. Alexander Campbell, *Delusions. An Analysis of the Book of Mormon . . . and a Refutation of Its Pretensions to Divine Authority* (Boston: n. p., 1832), p. 15. A debate between Tyler Parsons and Elder Freeman Nickerson shows how a Mormon could apply this in his witnessing, and also how the argument was vulnerable. Nickerson "knew" that the Book of Mormon was a true revelation from God "by the power of God, for his voice had made it known to him, by his obedience to his commands."

Parsons. "Do you know of his [Smith's] digging certain plates out of the earth, in the town of Manchester in the State of New York?"
Nickerson. "I did not see him dig them up."
Parsons. "Then how dare you say in your statement to the audience, that you knew it was all true, for the voice of the Lord had declared it? What do you mean by the voice of the Lord?"
Nickerson. "From hearsay; from those that knew it by the power of God."
Parsons. "Mr. Nickerson, do you suppose Cowdery, Whitmer and Harris, the three witnesses that have testified to seeing these plates, have sworn by the same rules you have stated, viz: hearsay?"
Nickerson. "I do not know."

Mormon Fanaticism Exposed, pp. 5, 44.

39. W. W. Phelps published the following charge in EMS, I, 3 (August, 1832), p. 6:

search the revelations which we publish, and ask your heavenly Father, in the name of his Son Jesus Christ, to manifest the truth unto you, and if you do it with an eye single to his glory, nothing doubting, he will answer you by the power of his Holy Spirit: You will then know for yourselves and not for another: You will not then be dependent on man for the knowledge of God: nor will there be any room for speculation.

40. Page said of his experience in becoming a Mormon, that holy angels "came and showed themselves to me as I was walking through the field, to confirm me in the work of the Lord of the last days—three of whom came to me afterwards and sang a hymn in their own pure language." *The Ensign of Liberty, of The Church of Christ*, I, 3 (December, 1847), p. 63, Hiram Page to William McLellin, May 30, 1847.

41. Lucy Smith, pp. 21-59.

42. Eduard Meyer, *Ursprung und Geschichte*, p. 22.

43. *Life of David Marks*, p. 340. Eight years later, however, Martin Harris denied that the Eight had seen any plates.

44. DHC, III, 307-08.

45. Cf. n. 38 above.

46. Cf. Appendix I below and chap. 5 above.

47. Oliver Cowdery to W. A. Cowdery, MA, I, 2 (November, 1834), p. 26.

48. *Ibid.* Smith identified revelation as the Rock in DHC, V, p. 258. His stress upon faith changing to knowledge through revelation may reflect a personal experience of his own, when he saw how valuable the testimony of such an assured person could be at his 1826 trial in South Bainbridge (now Afton), N. Y. His employer, Josiah Stowell had a nephew, Peter Bridgeman, who was worried about his uncle spending money on the treasure hunting activities and swore out a warrant against Smith as a "disorderly" person. His uncle testified in Smith's behalf.

He [Josiah Stowell] swore that the prisoner possessed all the power he claimed, and declared he could see things fifty feet below the surface of the earth, as plain as the witness could see what was on the Justice's table, and described very many circumstances to confirm his words. Justice Neely soberly looked at the witness and in a solemn, dignified voice, said, "Deacon Stowell, do I understand you as swearing before God, under the solemn oath you have taken, that you *believe* the prisoner can see by the aid of the stone fifty feet below the surface of the earth, as plainly as you can see what is on my table?" Do I *believe* it?" says Deacon Stowell, "do I believe it? No, it is not a matter of belief. I positively know it to be true." . . . It is hardly necessary to say that, as the testimony of Deacon Stowell could not be impeached, the prisoner was discharged, and in a few weeks he left the town.

Account of W. D. Purple in the *Chenango Union* (Norwich, N. Y.), May 2,I 1877. Text in Mulder and Mortensen, *Among the Mormons*, pp. 34-37. Cf. Walters, "Joseph Smith's Trials" for the most thorough discussion, and for his comments on Mormon assessments of both the 1826 and 1830 trials. Smith was tried again in 1830 for money digging. The trial was reported in 1831 by A. W. Benton. Once again Josiah Stowell testified for Smith, and the questioning was reported by Benton:

Did Smith tell you there was money hid in a certain place which he mentioned? Yes. Did he tell you, you could find it by digging? Yes. Did you dig? Yes. Did you find any money? No. Did he not lie to you then and deceive you? No! the money was there, but we did not get quite to it! How do you know it was there? Smith said it was!

Reprinted in Jerald and Sandra Tanner, *Joseph Smith and Money Digging* (Salt Lake City: Modern Microfilm Company, 1970), p. 33. The 1826 trial brought out how, for Stowell, belief had become knowledge. The 1830 trial brought out Stowell's willingness to believe Smith contrary to the evidence, and to rationalize the difficulty.

49. Paine, p. 71.

50. Orson Pratt carried this strategy to its conclusion when he spoke of those who had gotten a witness:

This great cloud of witnesses know with the greatest certainty that the Book of Mormon is true. . . . The nature of their testimony is such that it precludes all possibility of their being deceived themselves. Before mankind can be justified in calling these thousands of witnesses impostors, they must prove that none of them have seen and heard as they boldly testify.

"Divine Authority of the Book of Mormon," *Doctrines of the Gospel* (Salt Lake City: Juvenile Instructor Office, 1884), p.43.

51. Further, they can no longer discount books of testimony in the Bible.

52. Nevertheless, the effect was to strengthen hearsay evidence, since, like a scientific experiment, the hearer could reproduce the conditions of the experiment and come up with the same result.

53. PT, February 15, 1831. The report to the paper came from a person identified only as M. S. C., who said that Rigdon asked for a sign a few days before after talking with Cowdery. It seems to have been the asking of someone who had read and believed the Book of Mormon, and now was asking for confirmation of what he already believed. M. S. C. identified himself as a member of the Church of Christ in Kirtland, perhaps a member of Rigdon's congregation.

54. Hel 16:4, 13 reports a later Nephi performing signs, wonders, and miracles, "that they might know the that the Christ must shortly come." 3 Ne 17:7-10; 26:15 has Jesus performing some healing miracles because peoples' faith was "sufficient." 4 Ne 5 sees Jesus' disciples do "great and marvelous works," "healing, and all manner of miracles." There are a few other references, some of them parallel passages with these, and that is the extent of it. But there is no appeal to them as the basis for believing.

55. The first miracle acknowledged by Smith as coming through the new church was his excorcism of a demon from Newel Knight in the middle of April, 1830; DHC, I, 82-83.

56. Reported by an early apostate, Ezra Booth, to the *Ohio Star*, later appearing in Howe's book and quoted in Kirkham, *A New Witness for God*, I, 458.

10

Prophecy
Proves Revelation

> There are certain events plainly predicted in the Prophets, yet future, which, when fulfilled, will convince all the heathen nations of the true God, and they shall know that He hath spoken and performed it. And all the great and learned men of Christendom, and all societies, who put any other than a *literal* construction on the word of prophecy, shall stand confounded.
>
> **Parley P. Pratt[1]**

Prophecy in the Book of Mormon is a massive response to deistic objections. Smith traced prediction back to the time of Jared, including the note that prophecies from the time of Adam were on the brass plates of Laban (1 Ne 3:20) and, soon after the publication of the Book of Mormon, produced prophecies of Adam himself.[2]

Paine scorned the biblical prophets for giving predictions and then, when no fulfillment was forthcoming, explaining away the failure by supposing that God had "repented."[3] In line with other millennialists of the time, Smith assigned unfulfilled prophecies to the events surrounding and including the millennium. As for the idea that God repented, Smith never let it be said in the Book of Mormon and edited it out of his Inspired Version. Conditional prophecy was an exception, since its purpose was to effect repentance.

No room was allowed for Paine's charge that the prophets were "liars and impostors," for Smith made the gift of prophecy depend upon merit. Prophets were identified by their genealogies, their properly recorded calls from God, their exemplary lives, and their fulfilled predictions.

Smith generally acknowledged the objections that skeptics had toward prophecy. He detailed the case against it as he saw it through the person of Korihor, the archvillain and antichrist of the Book of Mormon. Korihor "began to preach unto the people against the prophecies which had been spoken by the prophets, concerning the coming of Christ (Al 30:6). He asked:

> Why do ye look for a Christ? For no man can know of anything which is to come. Behold, these things which ye call prophecies, which ye say are handed down by holy prophets, behold, they are foolish traditions of your fathers. How do ye know of their surety? Behold, ye cannot know of things which ye do not see; therefore ye cannot know that there shall be a Christ. Ye look forward and say that ye see a remission of sins. But behold, it is the effect of a frenzied mind; and this derangement of your minds comes because of the traditions of your fathers, which lead you away into a belief of things which are not so. (Al 30:13-16)

Asked why he taught the people "that there shall be no Christ," and why he spoke "against all the prophecies of the holy prophets," Korihor replied:

> Because I do not teach the foolish traditions of your fathers and because I do not teach this people to bind themselves down under the foolish ordinances and performances which are laid down by ancient priests, in ignorance, that they may not lift up their hands, but be brought down according to thy words. . . . Ye say that those ancient prophecies are true. Behold, I say that ye do not know that they are true. . . . And ye also say that Christ shall come. Behold, I say that ye do not know that there shall be a Christ. (Al 30:23-26)

Samuel, the Lamanite, also encountered disbelief when he told of specific signs to look for in the coming of the Christ (Hel 13-15). When the signs began to appear, however, the unbelieving Nephites

> began to depend upon their own strength and wisdom, saying; Some things they may have guessed right, among so many; but behold, we know that all these great and marvelous works cannot come to pass, of which has been spoken [referring to signs of the destruction and preservation of the Nephites in their remnant]. (Hel 16:15-16)

Smith has presented the rebuttals to the argument from prophecy, arguments popularized by deists: Bible traditions are foolish and untrustworthy; foreknowledge is impossible; prophecy is a delusion used by corrupt priests to manipulate the people; there is no way of knowing the truth of prophecy, since the law of averages would allow for some correct guesses. In the rest of this chapter Smith's counter-offensive will be examined to see how he preserves prophecy as a proof of revelation and then enlists it for his own cause.

THE HOW AND WHY OF PROPHECY

In his concern to demonstrate God's faithfulness to mankind, Smith dealt with covenants, promises and prophecy as facets of one transaction. The Book of Mormon declares that God will fulfill His covenants in the future"[4] as He has in the past.[5] Promises He made to individuals have been and will be fulfilled.[6] As past prophecies have been fulfilled,[7] those still pending will find fulfillment.[8]

The Book of Mormon discloses the fulfillment of some biblical prophecies and a large number of its own, and identifies those yet to be worked out. Old Testament restoration passages are deemed unfulfilled because of their relation to the millennium. Millennial events will be completed after the prophecies pertaining to the bringing forth of the Book of Mormon are realized. The result of this presentation of prophecy is to assure the reader and believer that God will yet fulfill His covenant to Israel by working out the predictions of the millennial agenda.

Paine considered the Christian view of prophecy useless, for it would pass unnoticed by mankind's vast majority, even if predictions were fulfilled. Smith made his scripture record the giving and fulfilling of prophecy for all to read, nullifying Paine's point and preserving prophecy as a proof of revelation.[9]

Prophecy showed that the principles of faith were known to the first inhabitants of the earth. In response to the doctrine that only faith in Christ saves, believers inquired about the status of those who lived before Christ. The standard response was that they, too, were saved by faith when they looked forward to the coming, the predicted, Messiah. If the Jews did not believe, it was not that they were denied full knowledge of the Messiah. Smith made prophecy prove that what was known of Christ in 1829 A. D. was also known at the time of Adam (DC 20:26-28).

The content of doctrine in all ages was always the same: the knowledge of repentance, baptism, faith, and continuing revelation. If anyone should wonder why this should be so, this reply was meant to satisfy:

> And now I will ease your mind somewhat on this subject. Behold, you marvel why these things should be known so long beforehand. Behold, I say unto you, is not a soul at this time as precious unto God as a soul will be at the time of his coming? [Alma is speaking to his son, Corianton, about 73 B. C.] Is it not as necessary that the plan of redemption should be made known unto this people as well as unto their children? Is it not as easy at this time for the Lord to send his angel to declare these glad tidings unto us as unto our children, or as after the time of his coming? (Al 39:17-19)

So the Book of Mormon verifies and clarifies a matter (that the ancients had full, and not just incipient, doctrinal faith) that had left many interpreters on exegetical thin ice.[10]

Fulfilled prophecy was meant to inspire faith in future fulfillment. By including signs of the coming birth and death of Christ and notice of their accomplishment in the Book of Mormon, Smith pointed that reader who had been looking for such signs to those of the coming millennium. By what the Bible and Book of Mormon describe as signs of the last days, including the discovery of the latter book, the reader was encouraged and challenged to expect the imminent wind-up of this world's affairs and the beginning of the millennium.[11]

PROPHECY IN THE BOOK OF MORMON

With but one exception,[12] Smith made prophecy totally predictive, specific and detailed. The messianic prophecies designate aspects of Jesus' life and ministry, his doctrinal positions, the signs of his birth and death, and give the exact number of years from the time of a prophecy to the date of his birth.

In the Book of Mormon Isaiah 29 minutely describes the Harris-Anthon consultation and the coming forth of the American scripture. The three witnesses are predicted in several places. The one to translate the records was known even to the biblical patriarch Joseph, son of Jacob. He knew and predicted that the translator would be his descendant, and that he and his father would also be named Joseph. These are not equivocal predictions, nor can they fit any circumstances other than those intended.

Smith's attitude toward prophecy was very literalistic,[13] a feature that he shared with the conservative and millennialistic Protestants. This may have been partly a reaction to the deistic urging of an allegorical rather than a literal understanding of prophecy. When Christians agreed to understand a prophecy allegorically, then deists scorned them for their embarrassment over a literal interpretation. Smith's use of prophecy exhibits his disdain for anything other than a literal interpretation. He was later to allow the possibility of the correspondence principle as a proper approach to prophecy,[14] but regardless of how he used the text to insert his own theology, he was always literal.[15]

Conditional prophecy accompanied a call to repentance. Nephite prophets warned their nation to repent or be destroyed (1 Ne 1:4). Abinadi enjoined repentance and warned of the wrath of God in the form of their enemies should they refuse (Mos 11:20-26), explaining later that the wrath would come in the form of bondage (Mos 12:1-8). In Enos' time many prophets were required to proclaim forthcoming doom to keep the people in line. "I say there was nothing short of these things, and exceeding great plainness of speech, would keep them from going down speedily to destruction" (Enos 23).

The indictment and threat were there, but never without the promise of a Messiah in whom the sinners could hope (1 Ne 1:18-19). The Book of Mormon emphatically stresses the destruction of the unrepentant, but balances the message with prospective reprieve for the penitent.[16] Contrary to representing God as capricious, conditional prophecy verifies God's respect for man's freedom. He would not violate man's "free agency," but neither would He deny justice and withhold punishment, for that, too, would show God inconstant.[17]

Dynamics

In the Book of Mormon prophecy comes with spiritual power, and is designated the spirit of prophecy, the spirit of revelation, the spirit of prophecy and revelation (or, revelation and prophecy), the Spirit, the Spirit of the Lord, the Spirit of God, and, the Holy Ghost.

The prophetic gift is bestowed in vision (1 Ne 5:2-4; 10:17) and by an inner testimony of the Spirit (Al 7:26). He who prophesies can perceive the Spirit working within him (Jac 4:15), but he may not know what he should do while being led by the Spirit (1 Ne 4:6). Nevertheless, what the prophet says when led is authoritative (1 Ne 10:17).

Thus the Holy Ghost, or the Spirit of the Lord, is the Father's agent to move man to prophesy. He gives authority to speak (1 Ne 10:22), interprets dreams (1 Ne 5:2-4; 2 Ne 28:1), and gives revelations to those who have enough faith (Jar 4). Conversely, no religious act should be performed without the Spirit's authorization (Mos 21:33-34). The Spirit of revelation and prophecy was needed even to command troops (3 Ne 3:19).

The terms "spirit of prophecy" and "spirit of revelation" are used collectively and individually as an extension of the working of God's Spirit. They are synonymous. Alma knew that the words of the fathers were true because he had the spirit of prophecy (which is the Spirit of God) and the spirit of revelation (which is the Holy Ghost) (Al 5:45-47).[18] The many terms, therefore, cannot be distinguished in the Book of Mormon, although they are in later Mormon usage.

Smith's presentation of the prophetic gift and the means by which it was given was congenial to the similar view held by Protestant enthusiasts in western New York. Only his view that prophecy was to be used in the life of the church was actually noteworthy, and even it was shared by Shakers. His view of prophecy was due as much to his desire to convince the gainsayers as to any other reason.

Main Themes

Messianic Prophecy

Prophecy's fullest expression in the Book of Mormon is messianic. In no other particular was Smith so precise as he was concerning the events and significance of Christ's life, as foreseen by those prior to him. His coming was predicted by a line of Nephite prophets[19] and was known to the very year.[20] His many titles and names were also foreknown: Messiah, Savior, Redeemer, Son of God, "Son" of Righteousness,[21] Only Begotten, Holy One of Israel, Mighty One, Father and Son, Good Shepherd, King of Heaven, and the Eternal Father of heaven and earth.[22]

Prophecy gave signs to look for at Christ's birth and death. A new star (Hel 14:6) and the sun shining for two days and a night (Hel 14:4) would announce his birth. A three-day darkness accompanied by frightful earth convulsions would signal his death and make evident that a prophet had foretold the event (Hel 14:20-27).

Prophets knew that Christ would be born of a virgin (1 Ne 11:18), whose name would be Mary (Mos 3:8). He would be baptized by John (1 Ne 11:27), rejected (2 Ne 25:12), mocked and scourged (Mos 15:5), lifted up on a cross (1 Ne 11:33), would break the bonds of death (Mos 15:8), and rise from the dead (2 Ne 25:13).

Christ's mission and work was also known by prophetic foreknowledge. He would atone for the sins of those who followed Adam (Mos 3:11), would redeem his people (Mos 15:1), and satisfy the demands of justice (Mos 15:9). Christ would be the means of salvation to the Gentiles (2 Ne 33:9), would bring in the resurrection of the dead (Al 5:14), and would judge all mankind (2 Ne 33:7, 11). Such knowledge was known ever since the time of Jared (Eth 4:7) and—as the Book of Moses revealed the next year, 1830—was known even by Adam.

The Jews' Fate

Smith operated with the premillennial conception that considers the conversion of the Jews an indispensable part of the last days. So he made the Jews a part of the House of Israel that should be grafted into an olive tree (1 Ne 10:12-24).

It was the unhappy lot of the Jews to be scattered over the earth (1 Ne 10:12) and persecuted by other nations for many generations by God's permission "until they shall be persuaded to believe in Christ" (2 Ne 25:16). Since the Jews would deny Christ, they would be destined to wander the earth and die unmourned, objects of scorn (1 Ne 19:14). They would deny Christ by turning aside, rejecting "signs and wonders, and the power and glory of the God of Israel," and by crucifying him (1 Ne 19:13).

But God would not forget the Jews. They would be gathered in following centuries of dispersion (2 Ne 10:8) and once again occupy the "land of Jerusalem" (2 Ne 20:29), assisted by the rulers and monarchs of the Gentile world (2 Ne 10:8-9). When the scattered Jews "begin to believe in Christ," they shall begin to gather upon the face of the land" (2 Ne 30:7). They will accept Christ and his atonement and no longer look for another Messiah. They will also believe the Book of Mormon (2 Ne 25:16). A place where God can abide with His people will then be established in the mountain-tops and attract to it all nations. From there God's word will go forth. Jerusalem, along with Zion, will be a world center. Universal peace will prevail.[23]

The Lamanite (Indian) Destiny

The Lamanites would be scattered and smitten by the Gentiles as an expression of God's wrath upon them (1 Ne 12:14). God would take away their land (2 Ne 1:11) and cause them to be afflicted, slain, cast out, hated—to become a "hiss and a by-word" (3 Ne 16:9). But they would survive (2 Ne 3:3; Al 9:16).

Lamanite fortunes would change for the better when they discovered their Israelite origin, learned of the gospel and their Redeemer and how to be saved (1 Ne 15:14). They would know that this knowledge comes from God, would rejoice (2 Ne 30:6) and would come into the "true fold of God" (1 Ne 15:15). The gospel restored to the Lamanites would be "a marvelous work." They would be nourished by the Gentiles as the Gentiles do an about face in their treatment of the Lamanites (1 Ne 22:8). The Indians could look forward to the day in future generations when they would become a "white and delightsome people" (2 Ne 30:6).[24] The Gentiles would share the records of the Jews and the Book of Mormon with them (2 Ne 29:13). Together with the repentant Gentiles, the Lamanites, or Indians, would build the New Jerusalem (3 Ne 20:22; 21:22-23).

Great Hopes for Gentiles

The Book of Mormon foresaw the Gentiles' scattering the Indians, possessing the land of promise, and prospering because of the Spirit of the Lord (1 Ne 13:14-15). God's blessing would make them a mighty nation in this land, "mighty above all" (1 Ne 22:7; 3 Ne 20:27).

God would establish His Church among the Gentiles when they repented and obeyed Him. He would give them much of His gospel "which shall be plain and precious" (1 Ne 13:34; 3 Ne 21:22). In turn, the Gentiles would take the "fulness of the gospel" to the Lamanites (1 Ne 15:13) and to the Jews (3 Ne 16:4), that both groups of Israelites might know their Redeemer.

The restored gospel would divide the Gentiles into two camps: those who accept and those who reject the message (1 Ne 14:6-7). Those who reject it would do so because they already had a Bible; that is, they would expect no other scripture (2 Ne 29:3, 9). When the Gentiles should pridefully consider themselves above all other nations and yet allow fraud, false religion, murder, and secret combinations[25] to go unchecked, then God would remove the "fulness" of His gospel (2 Ne 26:22; 27:1; 3 Ne 16:10). In fact, God would use the Indians to destroy them (3 Ne 21:12-18). Even then, if the Gentiles would repent, they would once again be considered as God's people (3 Ne 16:13).

Book of Mormon Foretold

The Book of Mormon would appear when the Indians and Nephites had "dwindled in unbelief." The Nephites would be gone. The Lamanites would have been smitten by the Gentiles and have lost the Nephite records. They would be under the power of the Gentiles. Gentiles would have many churches, yet would minimize miracles and God's power, would prefer human wisdom, would support secret combinations and keep the poor in poverty (2 Ne 26:14-22). There would be "wars, rumors of wars, and earthquakes in divers places" (Morm 8:26-30; cf. 31-34). At just that time the Gentiles would bring forth the Book of Mormon, the appearance of which would demonstrate God's power (1 Ne 13:35).

Joseph Smith Expected[26]

Biblical Joseph was promised from his posterity a "seer," whose name, as that of his father, would also be Joseph (2 Ne 3:6-7, 15).[27] The seer's work would be of great value for the patriarch's posterity, the Lamanites (2 Ne 3:7) and would be highly esteemed by them. The latter-day seer would win the allegiance of the Lamanites for the Lord's word in the Bible (2 Ne 3:11). He would make his full-time career that of doing the Lord's work (2 Ne 3:8), and would become as great as Moses in the eyes of the Lord (2 Ne 3:8-9; cf. Moses 1:41). The seer would be made strong out of weakness (2 Ne 3:13). Although many would seek his destruction, his persecutors would be confounded as the seer received, instead of death, the Lord's blessing (2 Ne 3:14). Like Moses, the seer would have a spokesman (2 Ne 3:18).

The Millennium

Smith included all aspects of the millennial system in Book of Mormon prophecy, but with those changes that introduced the Mormon peculiarities. The gathering of Israel as pertaining to the Indians; the coming forth of the Book of Mormon; the person and word of Joseph Smith, Jr.; and the conversion and gathering of the Jews— all these cluster about the Mormon millennium. Old Testament restoration passages, particularly those of Isaiah, are referred to the times of tribulation that are followed by millennial peace.[28]

SMITH AS PROPHET

Several references in the Doctrine and Covenants indicated that Smith tried predictive prophecy before the founding of the church, but the majority of them are expressions of confidence in the eventual success of the efforts undertaken. David Whitmer reported one prophecy not recorded in the official edition of Smith's revelations.[29] Its failure may indicate why Smith was cautious during this early period. Smith's role as a predictive prophet was more potential than actual before he left New York for Ohio in 1831.

SUMMARY

Deists tried to put Christianity in a bind by showing its argument from literally fulfilled prophecy to be absurd. Joseph Smith tried to refute their position. He furnished what he thought was abundant proof of literally fulfilled prophecy, thus side-stepping the barbs that deists threw at the "spiritualizers."[30]

Smith's offensive against skeptic scorn for the argument from prophecy was many-sided. He made prophecy synonymous with prediction that was specific, precise, and often conditional. The reception and working of the prophetic gift was in line with the Old Testament as Protestants of that time interpreted it. In affirming the fulfillment of biblical predictions, Smith confirmed the Bible's claim to be special revelation, found sanction for his new scripture, and revealed himself as another fulfillment of prophetic hope as the world stood poised at the brink of the millennium. And by making ancient prophecy deal with matters of nineteenth century concern congenial to his theology, Smith strengthened the claim for the Book of Mormon's being a special revelation.

The how and why of prophecy in Smith's American apologetic was to save prophecy as a proof of revelation and as evidence for the Christian position. Thus he withstood skepticism and put himself in leadership of a church that provided continual revelation.

FOOTNOTES

1. *A Voice of Warning*, p. 20.

2. PGP, Moses 5:10; 6:8, Adam prophesies; Seth, 6:13; Enos, 6:13; Enoch, 7:2, 41-46; Methuselah, 8:3; Noah, 8:16. Written in June-December, 1830.

3. Paine, p. 82.

4. 1 Ne 14:17; 2 Ne 6:12; 3 Ne 16:5; 20:27; 21:7; 29:9.

5. 1 Ne 9:6; 10:13, 17; 18:11; 20:14; 2 Ne 3:14; 5:19;19:17; 31:18; Al 37:16-17; 50:19; 3 Ne 27:18.

6. Morm 5:14; Eth 13:11-12.

7. 1 Ne 20:13-14; 22:20; Morm 1:4, 19; Mos 20:21-22; Al 37:26; 3 Ne 1:13; 10:11-14; 15:6; Eth 15:33.

8. 3 Ne 20:11-12, 22; Moro 8:29; 10:28. Cf. DC 5:20, "Behold, I tell you these things, even as I also told the people of the destruction of Jerusalem; and my word shall be verified at this time as it hath hitherto been verified."

9. 3 Ne 8:2ff; 9:16-17; 10:11-12; 11:10-12; 16:17-20; Morm 1:19; 2:10. A dramatic proof is found in 3 Ne 1:4-22, where men began to taunt those who believed the prophecy of Samuel, the Lamanite: "And the people who believed began to be very sorrowful, lest by any means those things which had been spoken might not come to pass" (vs. 11). The unbelievers appointed a day to put to death the believers in the

prophecy, "those who were about to be destroyed because of their faith in the tradition of their fathers" (vs. 11). But the prophecy was fulfilled and America's earliest skeptics were confounded.

10. Smith explicitly stated that the plan of redemption had to be the same in all ages or else God had made a change in plans. Cf. his editorial in EMS, II, 17-19 (October-December, 1833), 4-24. Also found in DHC, II, 16.

11. In common with other millennialists, Smith thought that human effort could help bring in the millennium. If he could arouse the expectation of the faithful, the Lord would the sooner come to his temple. Prophecy, then became the cause of—rather than the foreseeing of—the event, as in I Ne 10:13; Moro 8:29.

12. Only in Al 8:25 is prophecy found without the predictive factor. In Doctrine and Covenants, only in Section 34:6-10.

13. Especially in portions reproducing texts declared fulfilled by the New Testament. It is also true of those pertaining to the millennial scheme of events and those portraying the circumstances surrounding the emergence of the Book of Mormon.

One important factor about this literalism was Smith's conviction that he could do something to force fulfillment of a prophecy. This lay behind Smith's use of Isaiah 29:11-12. Emily Austin said that Smith was talking about Isaiah 29 in January, 1827, more than a year before Martin Harris went to Charles Anthon. The literalism lent itself to schemes by which man could intentionally fulfill prophecy.

14. Cf. DC 77:2, dealing with the "beasts" of Revelation 4. Paul's "earthly" corresponding to the "heavenly" is touched upon in DC 128. Parley Pratt, Voice of Warning, pp. 6-7, 25, later contrasted the literal prophetic fulfillment with what he called the modern system of "spiritualizing" of which, he felt, the biblical prophets knew nothing.

15. He thought that the four beasts were real, saved from other worlds and now living in heaven with real power over earth's inhabitants; DHC, V, 340-44.

16. Used of individuals: 2 Ne 5:22; Al 5:51. Used of nations and peoples: I Ne 14:5-7; 22:18; 2 Ne 6:12; 28:17, 19; 31:13-14; Jac 3:3; Mos 11:20-25; 29:19-20; Al 8:16, 29; 10:20-23; 13:27, 30. This list is only partial.

17. Cf. Hel 14:29-31.

18. Cf. Al 12:7; 5:46; 17:3; 8:24.

19. By Lehi: I Ne 1:19; 10:17; Hel 8:22. By Nephi, son of Lehi: I Ne 11:16. By Alma: Mos 18:2. By Ammon: Al 18:39. By Aaron: Al 21:7, 9. By Samuel, the Lamanite: Hel 14:2. By Nephi, son of Helaman: 3 Ne 6:16. Also by biblical Moses: 3 Ne 20:23.

20. Six hundred years from Lehi's time, I Ne 16:4; five years from the time of Samuel, the Lamanite's prophecy, Hel 14:2; the very next day after Nephi, son of Helaman, cried out in behalf of those who were to die for believing the prophecy of Samuel, the Lamanite, 3 Ne 1:13.

At Smith's time people were unaware that the modern calendar, which counted 1 A. D. with the Roman year 754 (AUC), was mistaken by more than 4 years, so that Christ's birth must be placed prior to 4 B. C. Wesley P. Walters alerted me to the fact that by counting back exactly 600 years from Christ to Zedekiah, Smith wove a modern chronological error into the Book of Mormon. There are fewer than 593 years between Zedekiah and the birth of Christ.

21. Apparently Smith meant to apply the title "Sun of Righteousness" from Malachi 4:2, which had been applied to Jesus early on in church history. When Cowdery heard the word "sun," he transcribed it "son." Smith used the rest of the verse ("with healing in his wings") to describe Jesus' resurrection from the dead, 2 Ne 25:13.

22. I Ne 19:17; 13:40; 15:14; 2 Ne 25:16; 26:9; Jac 4; I Ne 19:14; 21:26; Mos 15:2; Al 5:38, 50; 11:39. One citation is given for each name or title. All but three occur many times.

23. 2 Ne 12:1-4 (Isa. 2:1-4). Cf. also 2 Ne 21:11-12 (Isa. 11:11-12).

24. Humboldt passed along a report from Little Crook-back, chief of the Miami Indians:

> that the children of the Canada Indians were born as white as Europeans; that the adults are darkened by the sun, and the grease and the juices of herbs with which they rub their skin, and that part of the waist of the females, which is perpetually covered is always white.

New Spain, I, p. 109. On p. 110, n., he says that the chief's account "is partly confirmed by Father Gamilla, who says that the Indians remain white for several days after they are born, with the exception of a small spot, . . . of an obscure colour."

Dark skin as a sign of God's displeasure is taught in I Ne 12:23; 2 Ne 5:21-23; Al 3:6-9; Morm 5:15. The background to this was the biblical account of Noah's curse on his son Ham, Genesis 9:20-25, when Ham mocked his father after discovering him drunk and nude. Noah's curse struck Ham's son, Canaan—

an ancient Semitic convention to cause one's posterity to suffer for one's own misdeeds—with future servitude: "A servant of servants shall he be unto his brethren." The long-time and widely-prevailing interpretation of this passage saw it as the origin of the black, caucasian, and semitic races. It was also used to justify the institution of slavery in America and elsewhere.

Jerald and Sandra Tanner, *Mormonism Like Watergate?* (Salt Lake City: Modern Microfilm Company, 1974), pp. 6-14, printed W. W. Phelps's version of a little-known 1831 revelation of Joseph Smith, in which it is made clear that he envisioned inter-marriage with the Indians as a way of making them "white and delightsome." Verse 4 reads:

> Verily, I say unto you, that the wisdom of man, in his fallen state, knoweth not the purposes and the privileges of my holy priesthood but he shall know when ye receive a fulness by reason of the anointing: For it is my will, that in time, ye should take unto you wives of the Lamanites and Nephites, that their posterity may become white, delightsome and just, for even now their families are more virtuous than the gentiles.

Dr. Leonard Arrington, Church Historian of the Church of Jesus Christ of Latter-day Saints, Salt Lake City, confirmed the existence of the Phelps copy. In a telephone conversation on June 13, 1975, he stated that the revelation may be released for scholarly study sometime in the future, but not yet.

The Tanners demonstrate that Martin Harris, Oliver Cowdery, Brigham Young, Phelps, and apostate Ezra Booth all knew about the revelation, for it was also the first revelation on plural marriage. Following the revelation Phelps wrote:

> About three years after this was given [July 17, 1831], I asked brother Joseph, privately, how "we," that were mentioned in the revelation could take wives from the "natives" as we were all married men? He replied, instantly "In the same manner that Abraham took Hagar and Keturah; and Jacob took Rachel, Bilhah and Zilpah; by revelation—the saints of the Lord are always directed by revelation."

The Tanners also show that many high church leaders and scholars of the past, such as Joseph Fielding Smith and John A. Widtsoe, knew of the revelation. Further, they demonstrate that Brigham Young's attitude toward inter-marriage with the Indians during the Utah years, during which time many Mormon men took Indian wives, carries out the principle established in the revelation.

25. Cf. chap. 8, n. 31.

26. Cf. Smith's role in Isaiah 29 as seen in Appendix II.

27. David Whitmer, one of the Three Witnesses, agreed that Smith was the "man who is not learned" of Isa. 29, but not that he was the Choice Seer. The Seer was to be a descendant of Lehi through the youngest son, Joseph (2 Ne 3), from whom the Indians descended, and the Choice Seer was to come from the Indians. *An Address*, pp. 26-27.

28. Specific application of Isaiah's words to this period is made in 1 Ne 22:13, 15, 23; 2 Ne 6:13-14; 19:5, 19; 22:18; 27:2-3; 30:10; 3 Ne 26:3; Eth 4:9.

29. Hiram Page and Oliver Cowdery were sent to Toronto with the assurance that they would find there a man to buy the copyright to the Book of Mormon to enable its publication. According to David Whitmer, *An Address*, p. 31, the prophecy was written on a piece of paper, but was never printed. That squares with the way the 1831 revelation on mixed marriage with the Indians was delivered; cf. n. 24 above.

30. Rejection of "spiritualizing" was to be an on-going weapon in Mormon polemics against Protestant interpretation of the Bible. Most millennialists agree with this position against mainline Protestant interpretation. Some passages, however, could have both a literal *and* a spiritual fulfillment. Cf. 1 Ne 22:1-3, 6, 27 with Isa. 48-49.

11

Records
of Revelation

Mr. R. with great show of good nature, . . . spoke of the supernatural gifts with which he said Smith was endowed; He said he could translate from any language in which they were now extant, and could lay his finger on every interpolation in the sacred writings, adding, that he had proved him in all these things.

Painesville Telegraph, February 15, 1831

"If time would permit me, I would . . . show you that the Book of Mormon is all true. I know it by the power of God; and it proves the Old and New Testament true, and those books prove the Book of Mormon true."

Elder Freeman Nickerson'

In defense of God, Joseph Smith assailed the natural revelation of deism and the static revelation of traditional Christianity. To enable revealed religion to overcome natural religion, however, he supported the deistic attack upon the view that the present Bible is God's complete and errorless revelation to mankind. Destruction of the traditional view left him free to preserve special revelation by his own means.

If revelation were only a phenomenon of the first century Church; if prophecy died with Christ and a few minor voices of the New Testament; then, deists pointed out, God has changed His manner of relating to humanity. Then it followed that Christendom's closure of the biblical canon made sense. But that premise and action, if granted, confirmed the deist in his belief that the biblical and Christian view of God was inconsistent with God's constancy. To avoid admitting the force of that argument,

Smith disparaged a Christendom that held sacred a book whose contents had been decided, as Paine saw it, by a committee vote.

Smith concurred with Ann Lee in urging on-going revelation as an effective counter, but went beyond the Shakers to couple present-day revelation with a new scripture. Smith's apologetic favored an open canon and continuous revelation, not only in its forms of visions, angelic ministrations and gifts of the Spirit, but also in revelatory records. He could maintain God's special revelation to man only if he could uphold the Bible as a medium of revelation. To defend the Bible, Smith sought the status of revelation for the Book of Mormon.

THE BIBLE - STICK OF JUDAH

Smith's Attitude toward the Bible

Smith began with the Protestant tradition that the biblical books in their original autographs presented a true picture of God's relationship with mankind, and were without error. The Bible first came forth "from the Jews in purity unto the Gentiles, according to the truth which is in God" (1 Ne 13:25)

Deists were scandalized that a special revelation caused so many variant interpretations, so they scuttled the Bible. The Shakers' solution was to seek modern revelation[2] and retain the Bible. The Protestants worked to develop a proper hermeneutic.[3] Smith agreed with the Shakers but believed that the Bible had once been a clearly understood book. Originally it contained the "plainness of the gospel of the Lord" and was "plain unto the understanding of the children of men" (1 Ne 13:24, 29). Still, the Bible was a problem.

Two major defects of the present biblical text, Smith concluded, were caused by accidental and deliberate corruption. References to sources consulted in the writing of biblical books (such as the Book of Jashar, Joshua 10), indicated the canon's incompleteness.[4] Deistic biblical criticism was right![5] And according to the restored gospel, many items important to man's salvation had been lost or deleted from the Bible.[6]

How can one explain the loss of biblical books and the corruption of the biblical text? Smith blamed the Roman Catholic Church, the "great and abominable" church of 1 Nephi 13. That church received the complete, uncorrupted Bible from the Jews, but took away "many parts which are plain and most precious; and also many covenants of the Lord have they taken away" (1 Ne 13:26). The missing portions are those "which were plain unto the children of men, according to the plainness which is in the Lamb of God" (1 Ne 13:29). Herein lies the explanation for conflicting interpretations, textual corruptions, errors, contradictions, closing of the canon, and any further problems otherwise insoluable.

Satan is the head of the "abominable church." He decimated the Bible to pervert the "ways of the Lord" and to lead men astray (1 Ne 13:27). His success was phenomenal! "Because of these things which are taken away out of the gospel of the Lamb, an exceeding great many do stumble, yea, insomuch that Satan hath great power over them" (1 Ne 13:29). As a result the Gentiles are in an "awful state of blindness" and "stumble exceedingly" (1 Ne 13:32-34).

Christ's solution to the incomplete and corrupt Bible was to supply through the Book of Mormon what was missing:

> I will be merciful unto the Gentiles in that day, insomuch that I will bring forth unto them, in mine own power, much of my gospel, which shall be plain and precious, saith the Lamb. (I Ne 13:34)

By making the text so obvious in meaning, Smith would deny skeptics   the argument that the "unclear" words were unworthy of God and therefore could not be special revelation.

The Book of Mormon Reinforces the Bible

By Confirmation

In the face of the deistic critique, Smith's apologetic established Genesis as authentic. The Book of Mormon verifies that man was created in the image of God (Mos 7:27); that Adam and Eve were in the Garden of Eden, took the forbidden fruit and suffered expulsion;[7] that they were kept out of the Garden by a flaming sword and cherubim lest they eat and live forever (Al 12:21). Evidence of the consequences of the Fall are found in Cain's murder of Abel (Hel 6:27), the Flood covering the earth,[8] and God's confusing the languages when He dispersed the people from the Tower of Babel.[9]

The Mormon record also confirms the existence of the patriarchs. Abraham paid tithes to Melchizedek, who is described as king over Salem (Al 13:14-19). Abraham's near sacrifice of Isaac,[10] His further covenanting with Isaac and Jacob, and His subsequent identification as the God of Abraham, Isaac and Jacob[11] are all borne out. Isaac's son, Jacob, finds frequent mention.[12] Joseph's torn coat is recalled (Al 46:23) as well as his brothers' selling him into bondage.[13]

The Book of Mormon confirms events involving Moses that ensued during his leadership, such as that including his rod and spokesman (2 Ne 3:17), the Exodus events of dividing the waters of the Red Sea and the destruction of the Egyptian regiment,[14] and the reception of the Law at Mt. Sinai (specifically the Ten Commandments).[15] Frequent stress is put upon the importance of the Mosaic code.[16] Support is found for the pillar of light leading the Israelites, the brazen serpent incident, the water from the rock, and the manna feedings.[17] To convince the Gentiles, Smith corroborated God's command to destroy the Canaanites,[18] David and Solomon's polygamy and keeping of concubines (Jac 2:23-24), Zedakiah's reign (just before the fall of Jerusalem to the Babylonian Captivity of the Jews,[20]) the careers of Elijah, Jeremiah and Malachi,[21] and both the career and writings of Isaiah.[22]

In the New Testament confirmation was given for John the Baptist's testimony about Jesus, Jesus' baptism by John,[23] Jesus' choosing of John the Apostle, John's writing of the last days (I Ne 14:20-27), and the fourth Gospel's report of the misunderstanding that John the Apostle should tarry until Jesus comes again (3 Ne 7:19).

The Book of Mormon substantiates the events and significance of Christ's life. Mary conceived a child by the Holy Ghost, gave birth, and yet remained a virgin.[24]

Jesus chose his twelve disciples, performed his miracles, endured persecution, suffered for mankind, died by crucifixion, was buried, and rose from the dead on the third day.[25] He preached his Sermon on the Mount again, in America (3 Ne 12-14). By his ministry he fulfilled the Mosaic Law and ended the law of circumcision.[26]

The reservations of Thomas Paine about the historicity of the Old and New Testaments could hardly be taken seriously if there were *two witnesses from antiquity* confirming the reality and significance of the persons and events of the Bible.

By Clarification

A variety of what were considered biblical problems was solved in the Book of Mormon. Smith added, omitted, changed, interpreted, or reinterpreted words and clauses of biblical passages to make them logically or doctrinally more acceptable, particulary those that had seemed unclear or contradictory.[27]

One scientific consideration is the problem of Joshua telling the sun to stand still in Joshua 10:12-14. Smith tried to make the miracle more acceptable by up-dating the Ptolemaic assumption of the biblical text to that of a Copernican outlook:

> Yea, and if he say unto the earth, move, it is moved; yea, if he say unto the earth, thou shalt go back, that it lengthen out the day for many hours, it is done; and thus according to his word, the earth goeth back, and it appeareth unto man that the sun standeth still; yea, and behold, this is so; for sure it is the earth that moveth, and not the sun. (Hel 12:13-15)

In line with Smith's intention to bring doctrinal peace to Christendom (DC 10:44-63), he clarified many issues that were of current interest. In some cases the American scripture lends the weight of antiquity to endorse a doctrinal position; in others, it uses it to repudiate that which is considered a corrupt innovation. The doctrines thus clarified[28] find no final or unique settlement in the Book of Mormon; a majority of them were later modified and developed by Smith and succeeding Mormon church leaders. Two examples will indicate the nature of the doctrinal clarification.

In its treatment of the Trinity the Book of Mormon adopts the early Unitarian view. Smith said, "Christ was the God, the Father of all things" (Mos 7:27), and later gave a theological interpretation:

> And now Abinadi said unto them: I would that ye should understand that God himself shall come down among the children of men, and shall redeem his people. And because he dwelleth in flesh he shall be called the Son of God, and having subjected the flesh to the Father, being the Father and the Son—The Father, because he was conceived by the power of God; and the Son, because of the flesh; thus becoming the Father and the Son—And they are one God, yea, the very Eternal Father of heaven and of earth. (Mos 15:1-4)

Smith affirmed this Unitarian position later in the dictation process: "Behold, I am Jesus Christ. I am the Father and the Son" (Eth 3:14).[29] Later developments were to see his original Unitarian position develop into tritheism and then into polytheism.[30]

One of the questions which millennialists have never settled is the number of resurrections. Revelation 20 speaks of two. In Alma 40:4-21 Smith stressed that whether there shall be one time, or a second time, or a third time, that man shall come forth from the dead, it mattereth not; for God knoweth all these things; and it sufficeth me to know that this is the case—that there is a time appointed that all shall rise from the dead. (Al 40:5)

Whenever resurrection comes, the important thing to notice is that there is an interval between death and resurrection spent in one or more intermediate states. (Al 40:20-21).[31]

THE BOOK OF MORMON— STICK OF JOSEPH

God's Word with A Difference

The Book of Mormon undercut criticisms of the Bible by denying the traditional positions on biblical inspiration, thereby making for itself a necessary place along with the Bible. Following the Reformation, the Protestant churches supported their claim that the Bible was sole authority in matters of doctrine by appealing to biblical inspiration. Deists wondered how such inspiration could explain the historical inaccuracies, contradictions, and errors that they seemed to find in the biblical text.

Smith side-stepped the deistic objections and joined in protest against the orthodox position. The Nephite writers of the American scripture held that their records contained the word of God, but not that every word was God's word. They admitted the possibility of errors, and "if there be fault, it be the mistake of men."[32] They ruled out all inspiration theories as inapplicable to the Book of Mormon.

No one in the first quarter of the nineteenth century would have expected the writers of God's word to select their materials as the Nephite writers of the Book of Mormon did theirs. They wrote "according to my memory" (Eth 5:1), "according to the best of my memory" (Jac 7:26), "according to our knowledge" (Morm 8:1), "as seemeth me good" (Morm 10:1), what they thought was "sacred" (1 Ne 19:16), or "considered to be precious" (Jac 1:2) and, in Mormon's case, what his father had told him (Morm 9:32). They also revealed that their purpose in writing was to persuade to their position.[33]

When Book of Mormon authors used material other than that provided by memory, they edited what they had by abridging, omitting, or adding to their subjects. Christ himself dictated a section of the records that had been omitted (3 Ne 23). This open admission of an incomplete collection of records in the Book of Mormon hit hard at the idea of a closed canon as God's word.

In contrast to the Protestant interpretation of 2 Timothy 3:16-17 ("all scripture is given by inspiration of God"), the Book of Mormon admits on its title page the possibility of mistakes and faults. And a most striking feature of the work is that Nephi and Moroni call attention to their literary incompetencies.

Nephi admitted that his ability to write was far overshadowed by his ability as a public speaker, "for when a man speaketh by the power of the Holy Ghost the power of the Holy Ghost carrieth it unto the hearts of the children of men" (2 Ne 33:1). Resigned to the fact that many harden themselves against the Holy Ghost and "cast many things away which are written and esteem them as things of naught" (2 Ne 33:2), Nephi still believed that his words would "be made strong unto his readers and lead them to Christ"(2 Ne 33:4).

Moroni wrote from the material available to him only a few words "because of my weakness in writing" (Eth 12:40). Although imperfections might be found in his records, he knew of none, but explained that "if there be faults they be the faults of a man" (Morm 8:12, 17). He was "mighty" in speech but not in writing, being hindered by awkward hands in the writing process. Compared to the overwhelming effect of the composition of Jared's brother [no sample is supplied in the Book of Mormon], Moroni knew that his production was lackluster. He confessed that what he had to write was so awe-inspiring

> that we cannot write them; wherefore, when we write we behold our weakness, and stumble because of the placing of our words; and I fear lest the Gentiles shall mock at our words. (Eth 12:15).[34]

In prayer Moroni asked the Lord to let the Gentiles read his words with charity and to accept the truth of his message regardless of inept phrasing and expression. His attitude, and that of Smith, is summed up in these words:

> Condemn me not because of mine imperfection, neither my father, because of his imperfection, neither them who have written before him; but rather give thanks unto God that he hath made manifest unto you our imperfections, that ye may learn to be more wise than we have been. (Morm 9:31)

Besides lack of literary skill, Mormon exposed another route by which imperfections might have crept into the records comprising the Book of Mormon. Any fault, he wrote, could be attributed to his having to use a form of Hebrew altered by contact with the Egyptian language.[35] Had he been able to use pure Hebrew, no such likelihood would have to be considered (Morm 9:32-33).[36]

The Book of Mormon, therefore, appears to be a very human composition. The Nephite authors' anxiety over the proper phrase and their admission of possible errors in spite of the care that an author devotes to his material are not what one would have expected for the revelation of God. Where Christendom was seeking to fortify its apologetic of verbal or plenary inspiration, or both, Smith abandoned it.[37]

Thomas Paine's strictures against changeable language and vulnerable manuscripts applied full force to the Book of Mormon, but this very weakness turns out to be a strength in Smith's American scripture. By deserting the traditional argument for inspiration as a means of maintaining an authoritative revelation, Smith also avoided the areas that deists attacked. He was free to advocate a new basis for accepting the Bible as the word of God, one by which the Book of Mormon would ride in on the Bible's coattails as still another revelation.

Possession of the golden plates made Smith vulnerable; therefore, he shifted attention from the plates to the translated records. Harris's loss of the first manuscript was the immediate cause of the shift, for if Smith's enemies had stolen the manuscript, then comparison between the old and a new translation could turn up embarrassing differences. God revealed (DC 3) that He would still bring forth His record, even without the missing manuscript, but He gave Smith alternate plafes to translate up to the point previously reached on the first attempt. The alternate plates contained the same materials and formed what is now known as 1 and 2 Nephi.

Another impetus for shifting attention from the plates to the record that Smith was dictating came in the interchange with Oliver Cowdery, his scribe. The third time that Cowdery needed assurance that Smith really had the plates, God referred him back to the things he had already transcribed and to his previous assurances. If Cowdery was satisfied that his spiritual manifestations were genuine, then he was commanded to "rely upon the things which are written; For in them are all things written concerning the foundation of my church, my gospel, and my rock" (DC 18:3-4).[38] The message was clear: when not even the spiritual witness is enough, rely upon the Book of Mormon in its English translation.

Perhaps the most pressing reason for shifting attention to the written record rather than the plates was Smith's knowledge that every convert and skeptic would want to examine them. Pre-publication requests to see them, like those made by Harris and Anthon, were forestalled by having the plates revealed only to worthy men. They could be taken away because of unfaithfulness. No one was to use them to "get gain." After the Three Witnesses saw them the angel reclaimed the plates from Smith.[39] The situation was anticipated (that the plates would be gone) and dealt with in advance in Mormon 8. Moroni explained that he was the one "who hideth up this record unto the Lord; the plates thereof are of no worth. . . . But the record thereof is of great worth" (Morm 8:14). With the plates declared unavailable for public view, attention is directed to the record in hand, the Book of Mormon.

Smith adapted a standard Protestant position for his own apologetic. Faced with the lack of the original biblical manuscripts, Protestants developed textual criticism to arrive at an authentic biblical text. Out of necessity and conviction, they held that if there were carefully made copies of the original biblical writings, and if there are reliable translations of the copies, then one has the word of God. Smith simply applied this reasoning to the Book of Mormon. God does not want men to heed the plates for their own sake, for then, like medieval relics, they could be exploited "to get gain" (Morm 8:14). It is the *message* of the plates that mankind must heed; with a reliable translation, then, which Smith supplied through the spectacles and the leading of the Holy Ghost, they need not be concerned about the absence of the plates today.

Smith, therefore, focused upon the translation. At just this point he established the *new foundation* upon which the Book of Mormon could rest as the word of God. The only inspiration claimed for the Book of Mormon was that it was given to Joseph Smith by inspiration; to others, it is confirmed "by the ministering of angels" (DC 20:10). The testimony of the Three Witnesses states that an angel showed them the plates and that the voice of God declared "that they have been translated by the gift and power of God." The men had no basis to judge whether the plates and their engravings were genuine.[40] Their testimony deals with the translation—Cowdery's handwritten transcription of Joseph Smith's dictation—later published as the Book of Mormon.

Personal revelation, then, is the basis for determining any claim to revelation. Smith translated by inspiration, but he translated a book that had been edited, contained possible flaws, and possibly was incomplete. One can have the angel's assurance that the translation is truly faithful to the original on the plates; he can have a "witness," a "testimony," by following Moroni's advice to the seeker of religious certitude (Moro 10:3-5). Based upon that personal assurance, or revelation, the Book of Mormon is placed beyond the power of deistic logic. The claim of the American scripture to be God's word and revelation rests entirely with the readers' desire to accept it as such.

God's Word in Simplicity

After Smith set forth the principle in I Nephi 13 that the Bible was missing many sections "plain and precious," he hammered home the contention that the same could not be said of the Book of Mormon. The Lord's doctrine was given in "plainness, even as plain as word can be" (2 Ne 32:7). Repentance and glad tidings alike were preached "in plain terms, that we may understand, that we cannot err" (Al 13:22), simple enough that even children might understand (Mos 2:40).

When a Nephite prophet hurled denunciations, it was done "according to the plainness of the word of God" (Jac 2:11), for only hard-hitting bluntness could save the people from destruction (Enos 23; Al 5:43). Lucidity in preaching will draw the peoples' hostility toward the preacher (Al 14:2) and they, like the people of the Bible, may despise plain words and kill the prophets (Jac 4:14). But hostility will come forth, at least, for the right reason: they very well understand the message.

"Plainness" in predictive prophecy was God's manner of working among men (2 Ne 32:2-3) and Mormon prophets prophesied

> to the understanding of man; for the Spirit speaketh the truth and lieth not. Wherefore, it speaketh of things as they really are, and of things as they really will be; wherefore, these things are manifested unto us plainly for the salvation of our souls. (Jac 4:13)

Nephi's predictions were so plainly understood that "no man can err . . . man shall know of a surety, at the times when they shall come to pass" (2 Ne 25:7, 20). Forecasting of this quality meant that men could not "misunderstand" the import of the prediction nor the indications of its fulfillment (2 Ne 25:28).

Through such devices of rhetoric Joseph Smith nullified the deists' complaint that predictive prophecy was equivocal. He made prophecy distinct as to its intent and obvious as to its fulfillment. The mysteries of faith in the Book of Mormon are matters of information previously unknown, but susceptible to man's intellect. Paul's estimate of God's judgments as unsearchable and His ways inscrutable (Romans 11:13) is not characteristic of mysteries of faith in the Book of Mormon. Its mysteries have no obscurity or paradox. The Stick of Judah, therefore, needs the Stick of Joseph for its understanding and defense. If one is to reject the Book of Mormon, one cannot defend the Bible against the attacks of deism, skepticism, and unbelief.

A JOINT WITNESS FOR CHRIST

The Lord told Ezekiel to join the stick of Judah with the stick of Joseph and "make them one stick (Ezekiel 37:19). That was Joseph Smith's self-appointed task. By his standard he provided two major witnesses for the proposition that God reveals Himself to man beyond the testimony of nature. He made the Book of Mormon dependent upon the Bible for its source material, and the Bible dependent upon the Book of Mormon for its defense. The reader of the Book of Mormon, therefore, finds himself urged to accept God, the record of Joseph—the Book of Mormon, and, also, the latter-day saint and prophet, Joseph Smith.

FOOTNOTES

1. Tyler Parsons, *Mormon Fanaticism Exposed*, p. 69.

2. Cf. chap. 3 above, section on Shakers.

3. A popular introduction to biblical study incorporated the findings of near-eastern archeology through many editions. Thomas Hartwell Horne, *An Introduction to the Critical Study and Knowledge of the Holy Scriptures* (new ed. from the 8th London ed., corrected and enlarged; 2 vols.; New York: Robert Carter & Brothers, 1856), I, 5-6, wrote in his preface of 1834 the following:

> VOLUME I, contains a CRITICAL INQUIRY into the Genuineness, Authenticity, uncorrupted Preservation and Inspiration of the Holy Scriptures, . . . particularly a *new branch of evidence for their credibility*, which is furnished by coins, medals, inscriptions, and ancient structures. This is followed by a refutation of the very numerous objections which have been urged against the Scriptures in recent deistical publications.

Joseph Smith owned a four volume edition of Horne and wrote in each volume, "Joseph Smith, Jr., Kirtland, Ohio, 1834." Cf. Richard P. Howard, "Latter Day Saint Scriptures and the Doctrine of Propositional Revelation," *Courage*, I, 4 (June, 1971), p. 214. The Smith's personal edition of Horne is in the archives of the Reorganized Church of Jesus Christ of Latter Day Saints in Independence, Mo.

4. The years 1826-28 saw the issue of including the Apocryhpha with the canonical books decided. The *Wayne Sentinel*, March 3, 1826, carried an item on the question, noting that "the General Committee of the Bible Society, in London, have determined henceforward, wholly to exclude the Apocrypha from their edition of the Sacred Scriptures." Three months later it printed an informative article explaining the origin and canonical status of the Apocrypha, *ibid.*, June 2, 1826. Two years later the notice appeared that "The American Bible Society have unanimously resolved, that no books containing the apocrypha, shall hereafter be issued from their depository," *ibid.*, June 6, 1828. The "lost" books, such as the Book of Jashar and other chronicles referred to in the Old Testament, were the subject of conjecture and conversation among the Saints. Smith believed that the apostolic church had some of them, DHC, I, 132.

5. In EMS, July, 1833, 106, an article that had Smith as its authority stated:

> As to the errors in the Bible, any man possessed of common understanding, knows, that both the old and new testaments are filled with errors, obscurities, italics and contradictions, which must be the work of men.

Examples cited are typified by Genesis 6:6, where it is said that the Lord repented.

> "The Lord never said that he repented as it is thus recorded in the present English bible: But it is thus: And it repented Noah, and his heart was pained, that the Lord had made man . . ."

Ibid. Cf. Arbaugh, *Revelation in Mormonism*, pp. 84-85 for Smith's theological presuppositions in revising the Bible.

Examples of Smith's editing of biblical materials to eliminate italics can be seen in Howard's *Restoration Scriptures* p. 165, Facsimile No. 8, which reproduces Isaiah 3 to 5:9 from the Bible Smith bought on October 8, 1829. Isa. 3:18 reads:

> In that day the LORD will take away the bravery of *their* tinkling ornaments *about their feet*, and *their* cauls, and *their* round tires like the moon."

Smith drew lines through the italized words and reproduced it in the 1830 edition of the Book of Mormon in this way:

> In that day the Lord will take away the bravery of tinkling ornaments, and cauls, and round tires like the moon."

The Book of Mormon, 1830 edition, p. 89. The Inspired Version of Isa. 3:18 is identical.

6. He wrote that in 1838, DHC, I, 245.

7. Al 42:2; 2 Ne 2:18-19.

8. *Ibid.*

9. Title Page; Om 22; Mos 28:14; Hel 6:28; Eth 1:3.

10. I Ne 15:18; 22:9; 2 Ne 19:14; 3 Ne 20:25, 27; Morm 5:20; Eth 13:11.

11. Mos 7:19; I Ne 17:40; Al 5:24.

12. Al 46:24; I Ne 5:14; Eth 13:7.

13. Al 10:3; I Ne 5:14; 2 Ne 3:4; 4:1.

14. Hel 8:11; 1 Ne 4:2; 17:26-27.

15. Mos 12:33-36; 13:12-24.

16. Eth 12:11; 1 Ne 4:15-16; 5:11; 2 Ne 3:17; 25:30; 3 Ne 15:4-8; 25:4.

17. 1 Ne 1:28-30, 41; B. H. Roberts, *New Witnesses for God*, II, 47-48, applied this corroboration of the Pentateuch against the inroads of negative higher criticism.

18. 1 Ne 17:28-30. Paine had stressed his outrage at the Bible for making God command wars of destruction. Smith developed a rationale for such commands in the episode of Nephi getting the brass plates from his uncle, Laban, who had tried to kill Nephi and his family, 1 Ne 4:1-8. The Spirit told Nephi:

> Slay him, for the Lord hath delivered him into thy hands; Behold the Lord slayeth the wicked to bring forth his righteous purposes. It is better that one man should perish than that a nation should dwindle in unbelief. (1 Ne 4:11-12)

Nephi thought that his posterity could keep God's commandments in the land of promise, America, only if they had the commandments that were engraved on Laban's brass plates. The parallel this provides to Israel entering the promised land to live in a covenant relationship with God is clear. Their wars of destruction wiped out the local population to enable the people of Israel to keep the law by eliminating possible sources of spiritual contamination. This was a widely used explanation.

19. Om 15; 1 Ne 1:4; 5:12-13.

20. 1 Ne 1:13; 10:3; 17:43; 20:14, 20; 2 Ne 6:8-9; 25:10-11.

21. Hel 8:20; 1 Ne 5:13; 7:14; 3 Ne 24:1; 25:5.

22. 1 Ne 20-21; 2 Ne 7-8; 12-24.

23. 1 Ne 10:7-10; 11:27; 2 Ne 31:4-8.

24. Al 7:10; 1 Ne 11:13-20.

25. Mos 3:5-7; 1 Ne 11:28-36; 12:9; 13:24, 26,39-41; 3 Ne 17:7-8; 28:21-22; Mos 3:7.

26. Moro 8:8; 3 Ne 15:5-8. Cf. n. 28 below.

27. 2 Ne 12:1-2 corrects Isaiah 2:2-4; 2 Ne 23:11—Isa. 3:17; 2 Ne 17:19—Isa. 8:19; 2 Ne 29:3—Isa. 9:2; Mos 5:7, 14:10-13, 15:10-13—Isa. 53:10; 3 Ne 12:13-Matt. 5:3; 3 Ne 12:6—Matt. 5:6; 3 Ne 13:24-25 —Matt. 6:25; 3 Ne 13:30— Matt. 6:30; 3 Ne 13:32—Matt. 6:32; 3 Ne 13:34—Matt. 6:34; 3 Ne 15:16-24 —John 10:16; 3 Ne 28:3-9, 12-15, DC 7:6 (cf. 7:1-8)—John 21:21-23; Al 21:37—Genesis 3:24. This is a partial list.

28. As De Pillis, "The Quest," p. 79, pointed out, the famous quote from Alexander Campbell, *An Analysis*, p. 13, that Smith had definitively answered every current theological question is an overstatement. Ross Warner, "The Fulfillment of Book of Mormon Prophecies: A Study of Problems Relative to the Fulfillment of Selected Prophecie in the Book of Mormon, with Particular Reference to the Prophetic View from 1830 Onward" (unpublished Master's thesis, Brigham Young University, 1961), p. 52, lists the doctrines that are clarified in the Book of Mormon: the nature and personality of God, the fall of man, the atonement, free will, the nature of the gospel, faith, repentance, baptism, the work of the Holy Ghost, the Lord's Supper, the judgment, the resurrection, the reality of the devil. He cites proof texts for each. They may also be found in the index of modern editions of the Book of Mormon. Warner, pp. 45-49, also deals with Christ's fulfillment of Mosaic law.

29. Later Mormons took the Book of Mormon position that Christ was both the Son and the Father and explained that, since Christ is also the father of the spirits in this world (a teaching Smith did not have when he produced the Book of Mormon), he is *therefore* both the Father and the Son. Still another explanation later derived from the teaching that each man will be a god on his own planet: The Father of Christ has appointed Christ to be God to the people on earth. He is the only God we know and the Father of all spirits on Earth; therefore, he is the Father, but still the Son.

30. That evolution is traced by Arbaugh, "Evolution of Mormon Doctrine." Cf. also Smith's redefinition of "eternal damnation" and "endless torment" in DC 19, given in March, 1830. The interpretation is Universalistic.

31. This debate between the pre-millennial and a-millennial positions is centuries old.

32. Title Page, Book of Mormon. Cf. also 1 Ne 19:6 and chap. 2, n. 30.

33. Cf. "Smith's Goals for the Book of Mormon," chap. 1.

34. Cf. n. 30, chap. 1.

35. The best Mormon studies of the "reformed Egyptian" upon the plates are those of Ariel Crowley, IE, (January, February, April, 1942; September, December, 1944). He tried to match the "Caractors" of the Anthon Transcript with Egyptian counterparts or with Serabit inscriptions from the Sinai wilderness. Sidney B. Sperry, *Book of Mormon Compendium* (Salt Lake City: Bookcraft, Inc., 1968), p. 39, cites an

Aramaic religious text in Demotic script translated, in part, by a scholar at the University of Chicago. Contra, cf. Wesley P. Walters, "Joseph Smith Among the Egyptians," *The Journal of The Evangelical Society*, XIV, 1 (Winter, 1973), 25-45. The "reformed Egyptian" is referred to elsewhere in the Book of Mormon in 1 Ne 1:2; 3:19; Mos 1:4.

36. Inevitably Smith's attitude that the Bible was full of errors came full circle. He had to concede the possibility for the Book of Mormon, but it was supposedly more reliable because it was translated by someone with the "gift of translation." How could Mormons explain a phenomenon in the Book of Mormon that Smith had criticized in the Bible? They adapted an argument from Protestant apologetics: the many editorial changes have not altered the meaning of even one passage. Cf. Hugh Nibley, *Since Cumorah*, p. 6.

But Nibley is wrong. A case in point is *1 Ne 11:18*. After Smith dictated the manuscript of the Book of Mormon, Cowdery and others emended it for the press. This version is designated E MS (1829). Both it and the 1830 edition have "the virgin which thou seest, is the mother of God." After 1830 the E MS was revised still further. The post-1830 revision and the 1837 edition have what appears in the present version: "the virgin whom thou seest, is the mother of the Son of God."

1 Ne 11:21 in the 1829 E MS and the 1830 edition have "behold the Lamb of God yea, even the Eternal Father!" The 1837 edition and present editions have "the Son of the Eternal Father!"

1 Ne 11:32 in the E MS (1829) and the 1830 edition have "the Lamb of God is the eternal Father," referring to Christ. The 1837 and present edition have "the Son of the everlasting God."

1 Ne 13:40 in E MS (1829) and the 1830 edition have "the Lamb of God is the Son of the Eternal Father." The 1837 and present edition have "the Lamb of God is the Son of the Eternal Father."

Cf. Howard, *Restoration Scriptures*, pp. 47-48, who notes that these changes correspond to Smith's developing ideas of God as found in the 1835 edition of the Doctrine and Covenants in Smith's "Lectures on Faith," p. 55; *ibid.*, p. 49.

37. Cf. n. 24, p. 29 above. It has been argued that since Smith was dictating and not writing the Book of Mormon manuscript, mistakes are those of his scribes and not his own. That would be true for mistakes of spelling and punctuation. But theological alterations as extensive as those noted in the previous footnote are not due to the scribe missing a word here and there.

38. Cf. discussion in chap. 9, "Preparing the Witnesses."

39. Smith said, "When, according to arrangements, the messenger called for them, I delivered them up to him; and he has them in his charge until this day . . ." DHC, I, 19.

A patriarchal blessing given to Newel K. Whitney, however, may indicate that the spectacles were still being used. The introduction to the blessing states that Joseph Smith, Jr. gave it "through the Urim and Thummim" on October 7, 1835, and that the blessing was written by Frederick G. Williams. It was in the Patriarchal Blessing Book of Joseph Smith, Sr., now in the LDS Church Archives. It was "recorded by Oliver Cowdery, Jan. 22, 1836;" *The Contributor*, VI, 4 (January, 1885), p. 129. The article on Whitney runs from pp. 123-32. We know that Cowdery copied some blessings on that date, since he put down in his Sketch Book for that date, "Copied blessings." BYUS, XII, 4 (Summer, 1972), p. 419.

James Lancaster's suggestion that "Urim and Thummim" were used both of the spectacles and the peep-stone could account for this usage; cf. chap. 2, n. 11 above. But it could also indicate that Smith had forgotten that he had already delivered the plates to the angel, just as he forgot what he had said about the characters when he dictated the Official Version of the Harris-Anthon consultation.

40. Apostate John Whitmer, one of the Eight Witnesses, said just that in his exchange with Theodore Turley in 1839; DHC, III, 308.

12

An American Prophet

"Once in the world's history we were to have a Yankee prophet, and we have had him in Joe Smith. For good or for evil, he has left his track on the great pathway of life; or, to use the words of Horne, 'knocked out for himself a window in the wall of the nineteenth century,' whence his rude, bold, good-humored face will peer out upom the generations to come."

John Greenleaf Whittier[1]

Joseph Smith once declared in a funeral sermon, "No man knows my history," but his achievement, his claims, and the movement he bequeathed posterity demand that we not dismiss it, that we hear him as fairly as we can.

Of all the titles and offices that he assumed, that of prophet is best known. He assumed the role by criticizing his society for creating a climate in which unbelief and immorality could flourish; by calling respectable religionists to account for their failure to carry out what he saw as the implications of their profession; by standing outside the accepted religious groupings, while regarding himself as God's standard bearer.

All facets of his career proclaim him distinctly American in his concerns and aspirations, American in his theology with its New England roots intergrown with the political doctrines of the previous 50 years.

ACCENT ON AMERICA

Beware of Apostasy

Subversive international forces were suspected at work behind the scenes when

William Morgan disappeared in 1826, and the resultant anti-masonic furor was, in part, a reaction against foreign entanglements. Smith donned the prophet's mantle against this backdrop to warn America against apostasy from God. His jeremiads against unbelief single it out as the precursor of unhappiness, degradation, and eventual personal and national disaster.[2] The loss of belief in personal and present-day revelation, the disregard for gifts of the Spirit, and the dearth of angelic ministrations strip a would-be Christian nation of its pretensions, revealing how far America had fallen. Affiliation with the Freemasons was unthinkable, then, because it smacked of French deism and atheism. The watchman of Israel was sounding the alarm.

Smith held that a nation can advance only so far in infidelity before God chastens it with wars and suffering to call it back. Ultimately, He may let it be destroyed as were the earlier American civilizations of the Nephites and Jaredites. Smith pointed to the American Indians as living examples of God's displeasure. Their dark skins, lack of civilized arts, and traces of pure religion corrupted in the past should warn America to repent of its skepticism and immorality, its religiosity and philosophy, and to return to Christ in humble faith. In this particular Smith showed a view of repentance that came from the post-Revolutionary War period. Perry Miller demonstrated that repentance during this time came to be motivation.

> Out of the years between the Stamp Act and the Treaty of Paris emerged a formidable, exhaustive (in general, a repetitious) enunciation of the unique necessity for America to win her way by reiterated acts of repentance.[3]

What moved the rank-and-file Americans to victory in the War for Independence was not the use of political terms, but

> the universal persuasion that they, by administering to themselves a spiritual purge, acquired the energies God had always, in the manner of the Old Testament, been willing to impart to His repentant children. Their first responsibility was not to shoot red coats but to cleanse themselves, only thereafter to take aim.[4]

Repentance was not "a failure of the will, but a dynamo for generating action." It was "Protestant self-distrust with confidence in divine aid."[5] As Smith urged it in the Book of Mormon, repentance was a call to action.

Smith coupled that call with the warning to persevere[6] in obedience to God's commandments.[7] Here, too, he could rely upon the fusion of religious and patriotic motifs. "What kept them going," to apply Miller, "was an assurance that by exerting themselves they were fighting for a victory thus providentially predestined."[8] The rise of the lodge and the rampant skepticism showed that America was on the verge of apostasy, but the nation could do something about it. By repenting and holding the line it could receive God's approval once again.

God Bless America

The story that Smith wrote into the Book of Mormon is another exodus theme to which, as a prophet, he returned time after time to recall a nation to its former greatness. In prehistoric times God preserved for the Jaredites a wilderness, a land for "a righteous people," the "quarter where there never had man been" (Eth 2:4, 7). He led them into America with the promise that they would be the greatest nation on earth (Eth 1:42-43).

God brought to America only those people He wanted here (2 Ne 1:6). He withheld knowledge of the New World from many nations for the sake of the patriarch Joseph's descendants (2 Ne 3:2). God planted that broken-off branch "in a good spot of ground . . . choice unto me above all other parts of the land of my vineyard," specifically, in the United States (Jac 5:43). He consecrated the best of lands for the Nephites and Lamanites (2 Ne 10:19), a land that is "most precious, "holy," "delight-some," "choice," "choice above all other lands," the "land of promise," the "land of liberty," the "promised land."

America will be a Christian land for God consecrated it unto the Christ He was to send (2 Ne 1:7). Christ, in turn, was to give the land to the Nephites for their inheritance (3 Ne 16:16). This land would be the New Jerusalem (3 Ne 20:22), and its inhabitants would be considered blessed among the nations of the world (3 Ne 24:12).

Land of the Pilgrim's Pride

America is God's reward for fidelity (Eth 1:38) and those who receive it will prosper (1 Ne 2:20). Biblical Joseph's posterity shall keep America forever (2 Ne 3:2), "and there shall be none to molest them, nor to take away the land of their inheritance; and they shall dwell safely forever" (2 Ne 1:9).

Faithfulness to God's commandments ensures freedom from bondage to other nations. When the Gentiles would come into the land and receive the restored gospel, America would be a land of liberty and blessing. During their stay no kings should rule,' for God would protect the Gentiles by His might against kings and outside tyranny. Those who fight against this nation, against Zion, shall perish (2 Ne 10:10-13), but by their willing obedience the Gentiles shall be adopted as Nephites (1 Ne 14:2). God will raise them up as a mighty nation upon the "face of this land" to scatter the seed of Nephi—the Indians (1 Ne 22:7-8).

Like the Jaredites, Nephites and Lamanites before them, the Gentiles would be guided by the hand of God to America. His Spirit would impel Christopher Columbus go "forth upon the mighty waters" to "the promised land"(1 Ne 13:12), just as the inhabitants of colonial America were led here to "prosper and obtain the land for their inheritance" (1 Ne 13:12).

Prophet Smith brings his reader to the present by drawing the parallel between ancient and modern times. The calamitous end of the Nephite and Jaredite civilizations indicates that if the inhabitants of America are to realize God's promise for this land, they must fulfill the condition laid upon all who live here. Those who possess America "should possess it unto the Lord" (Eth 9:20) and be faithful to him (1 Ne 7:13). As from the earliest times, that means serving the only true God, "the God of the land, who is Jesus Christ" (Eth 2:8, 12) by worshipping God (2 Ne 10:19) and keeping His commandments (1 Ne 2:2).

Moroni sums up the condition and the consequences that come from ignoring it:

> this is a land which is choice above all other lands; wherefore he that doth possess it shall serve God or shall be swept off for it is the everlasting decree of God. And it is not until the fulness of iniquity among the children of the land, that they are swept off. And this cometh unto you, O ye Gentiles, that ye may know the decrees of God—that ye may repent, and not continue in your iniquities until the fulness come, that ye may not bring down the fulness of the wrath of God upon you as the inhabitants of the land have hitherto done. Behold, this is a choice land, and whatsoever nation shall possess it shall be free from bondage, and from captivity, and from all other nations under heaven, if they will but serve the God of the land, who is Jesus Christ, who hath been manifested by the things which we have written. (Eth 2:10-12)

Smith made sure that the reader of the Book of Mormon would take the message as meant for him by having his Nephite prophets moralize for the benefit of the future Gentiles. Rebellion and iniquity bring a curse upon the land. Transgressors are brought down with sorrow (Enos 10). The people may be taken into captivity (2 Ne 1:7). When those who possess the land are "ripened in iniquity," they will be "swept off" and "destroyed" by the "fulness of his wrath" (Eth 2:8-9; 9:20). Thus Smith urges America to make or renew the covenants that previous generations and civilizations had had with God.

Smith's subsequent persecution at the hands of American religionists; his church's pilgrimmage to Kirtland, O., from there to Independence, Mo., and then to Commerce (Nauvoo), Ill.; his imprisonments; and the church's suffering only illustrated how close America was to judgment. The shabby treatment given his church by the Missouri judiciary did not lessen Smith's faith in the principles upon which the country had been founded. His attitude toward the U. S. Constitution was such that Mormons now consider it an inspired document—proof of God's hand in founding the country. Ultimately, Smith was to seek redress for the losses sustained by his people while in Missouri by running for the nation's highest office. Such was his faith in America.

The Church Restored

To the seekers and dissenters of his time Joseph Smith brought the answer to their need—the true Church of Christ restored to earth.[10] The Book of Mormon clearly showed that Christ had once established his Church in America with a full complement of offices and spiritual gifts. Following the death of its apostles the American church—like the European and Asian churches before it—lost its apostolic fervor, faith, and validity. The Protestant polemic which identified the Great Apostasy with the rise of the Roman Catholic Church was applied to the American scene to explain the loss of the American Church. The apostasy of the Church in the eastern and western hemispheres showed the need for a restoration.

Churches in the burned-over district were clearly apostate, bereft of spiritual gifts, denying the principle of on-going revelation, served by self-seeking ministers, doctrinally contentious, and without apostolic church organization, Smith maintained. But his new scripture; his restored Aaronic and Melchizedek priesthoods bestowed by the hands of John the Baptist, Peter, James, and John the Apostle; and the full restoration of the complement of church officers as in apostolic times cemented Smith's claim to have effected the displacement of the false churches by the true Church. Church polity and practice had already been introduced in the Book of Moroni, and was further explicated for several years in the Book of Commandments and the Doctrine and Covenants.

Certain that Satan was the cause of doctinal strife,[11] Smith cleared away the clutter of religious controversy and enabled the restored church to get on with preparations for the millennium. Other religious organizations were thereby denied any authority to engage in ministry, argue doctrine, or challenge Smith's church. Nor could the corruption of the clergy, the decimation of the Bible, or the doctrinal aberrations and historic scandals that weakened Christendom's witness to Christ be charged to the restored Church of Christ.

SMITH IN LATER YEARS

Preparing the Lord's Way

Joseph Smith thought that the millennium might dawn with the turn of the century and anticipated seeing Christ at his Second Coming.[12] He promised others that they, too, would see Christ.[13] Oliver Cowdery headed the 1830 mission to Missouri with the same enthusiasm. He was reported by an Ohio newspaper to have predicted the world's end within a few years.[14] Sidney Rigdon proclaimed that the world would be destroyed within two to three years.[15] Rigdon had a ten hour conversation with W. W. Phelps of Canandaigua about the new faith and "declared it was true, and he knew it by the power of the Holy Ghost, which was again given to man in preparation for the millenium."[16] Four months after Cowdery's visit the same newspaper reported Martin Harris's declaration that the Saints would see Christ before the end of 1846.[17]

The time setting aspect of millennialism did not persist in Smith's millennial hope.[18] He focused instead upon gathering a people from the nations to meet the Lord. This was more consistent with western New York's belief that the efforts of the faithful in evangelism, education, or missions would ring in the Day of the Lord. "It might even be the case that the Mormons," wrote Klaus Hansen,

> by assigning to man the primary responsibility for creating the millennium, interjected into the optimistic doctrine an insurance clause against a remote possibility that the Lord, perhaps, might fail to appear.[19]

Smith sent his missionaries to recruit converts to help build the city of God. Cowdery traveled to Missouri to found a City of Refuge.[20] Rigdon followed him in 1831 to consecrate the land to the west of Independence as "Zion." Here the Indians could gather as the tribes of Joseph were increasingly displaced by the U. S. government's removal policy.

At the dedication of the temple in Kirtland, Ohio in 1836, Smith and Cowdery saw the heavens opened. Moses appeared to give them "the keys of the gathering of Israel from the four parts of the earth" (DC 110:11; cf. 12-16). The time was near. In 1837 the English mission field was opened to yield 2500 converts who set sail to join the prophet before his death.[21] Thousands more were to follow from Scandanavia in the 1850s.[22]

Thus one of the goals of the Book of Mormon began to find fulfillment. Zion was being formed in the United States, the Indians had the restored gospel preached to them, and within a few years Orson Hyde consecrated the Holy City of Jerusalem as the gathering place of the Jews.[23] All was being readied for Christ's coming.

Latter-Day Revelation

Fifteen hundred years of church history had encrusted revelation with the weight of tradition and institutional inertia, so much so that in spite of Protestant efforts to let God speak through the Bible, some perceived Him as more remote than ever.

Deism accepted a remote God who could communicate through nature, but rejected special revelation. Orthodoxy reacted by developing its science of textual criticism and by relying upon its doctrine of biblical inspiration to assure contact with God. Catholicism guaranteed the institution as the assurance. Pietism looked within man.

Joseph Smith sided with Pietism in rejecting orthodox Protestantism's doctrine of biblical inspiration in favor of his own inner assurance. By making revelation personally available Smith tried to win for himself, and thus for others, the privilege of writing his own commentary on the significance of encountering God. But after he won the changes and freedom he wanted and in order to conserve what he had won, Smith set in motion the very forces he once had decried in the churches of his day.

The principle of personal revelation led to power struggles within the infant latter day church until Smith received revelations allowing only himself to get instruction, teaching, or revelation for the church (DC28:11; 43:3-6). He followed the dictum that no one could receive revelation for someone of higher authority.[24] Secure from attack upon his status from within the church, Smith was able to lead the church as Prophet, Seer, and Revelator.

Revelation continued in the form of books of ancient patriarchs, written instructions for the problems of restoring the church, many revelations that were not officially recorded, and the inspiration to revise the Bible. The written revelations were published in 1833 and, revised and enlarged, again in 1835. These were to be the most influential of the Mormon scriptures, the factor differentiating Mormonism from dissenting Protestantism. Arbaugh's study traces the further development of "revelation in Mormonism."

Approximately 65 per cent of Smith's revelations came in the first four years of his public activity, 1828-33; from 1834-39, 18 per cent; none in 1840; and 8 per cent in 1841-45. Following Smith's death, revelation for the church effectively ceased. Arbaugh compared Mormon revelation after Smith to the dogma of papal infallibility: it lent a "certain spiritual potentiality."[25]

SMITH IN PERSPECTIVE

R. W. B. Lewis characterized post-revolutionary American optimism according to the literary figure of the American Adam, using Emerson's categories of the Party of Memory and the Party of Hope to analyse American intellectual thought from 1820-1860. It provides a helpful way to view Joseph Smith.[26]

Huddled along the eastern edge of a vast continent, many looked back in Memory to the Old World and its traditions. Others faced west in Hope to heed the call of the west. With them, Joseph Smith breathed the optimistic air flowing in from the Rockies. Fearful that the call was a summons to barbarism, American Christendom launched the Second Great Awakening to stem the tide. Perry Miller showed that the battle of the churches against deism was part of the larger strategy to save the west for civilization. And Joseph Smith was animated by the same spirit that was quickening the nation.

Lewis described the intellectual history of a nation as the exposure of dominant conflicts over ideas and the "story" that animates them. As the crucifixion and resurrection of Christ is the story behind Christian argumentation, so the American story is about an "Adamic person" without a past. Timeless. He had known God and nature, but found himself suddenly alive in a certain place and time.[27] Joseph Smith entered this debate with his own story of seeing visions, finding and translating an American scripture—the story behind all Mormon argumentation.

The Party of Hope saw America with a present and a future, but rejected the past to contact the ultimate origins. That is the wider implication of Smith's insistence upon present-day revelation, for by it he returned to revelation's source for guidance in the New World. The Old World revelation was repudiated as the ultimate authority and subjected to the revelation and scripture of the New World. John Evans concluded that Smith appeared unaware of the mass of Christian exegetical literature.[28] One could extend that observation to say that Smith shelved traditional interpretations because he claimed a right to start anew. Even when he appropriated a current approach, such as the millennial hope of Protestants or the theory of Israelite origins for the Indians, he charted his own course.

Smith's handling of temptation and sin in the vein of the Fortunate Fall is an outstanding instance of his moving within the Party of Hope. Man needed to taste the bitter to know the sweet and prize the good.[39] Temptation and sin were necessary for man so that he could experience sexuality, joy, the goodness of life, and—most important of all—exercise true freedom. The triumph of Arminianism in Smith made of sin an enabling force, freeing man to discover and make of himself a devil or god. The Party of Memory, by contrast, taught a doctrine of the Fall and original sin that left man debilitated beyond his power to extricate himself.

God willed man's freedom even at the risk of losing him. When Satan offered himself as a redemption for all mankind (predestination, Moses 4:1) according to Smith, God saw the offer as an attempt to destroy man's freedom and as a criticism of God's will for man. So man was not really beguiled, but *chose* to transgress that he might become a creator of new life through his sexuality. Further, by the proper use of his sexual and procreative powers, Smith was eventually to reveal, man could even become a god.

Smith shunned mysticism to embrace matter through his later revelations that explicate polygamy, polytheism, and a kingdom of this world. It is fair to compare him to Emerson in his effort to harmonize matter with spirit, although Emerson realized his vision in poems and essays, whereas Smith realized his in action.

If polygamy was the most sensational of Smith's revelations, the "gathering" was the most far reaching. It offered a focus for religious fervor that revivalism stirred up but let dissipate.[30] Befitting a prophet, Smith offered his converts a program: gather in America to prepare for the millennium; build a City of Refuge, the city of God. Mormon efforts were thwarted in Missouri, but on a swampy site along the Mississippi River, Smith and his converts built what was Illinois' foremost city and Smith's Mormon capital, Nauvoo. Hopeful thousands gathered there to help the America prophet build the temple into which the Lord suddenly come.

When it was clear that persecution was in the Illinois air, Smith convened a Council of Fifty[31] to lay plans for one final exodus. After his death, Apostle Lyman Wight attempted to carry out an early Council plan to establish the Kingdom of God in Texas.[32] Apostle Brigham Young, the ultimate successor to Smith in the eyes of the majority of Saints, led the church westward into Mexican territory and carved out the State of Deseret. From 1850 to 1852 Joseph Smith's followers in Deseret lived in a theocracy that exercised—and was to exercise after its dissolution at the hands of the U. S. government—tremendous influence over the settlement of the American west.

Joseph Smith was, therefore, the author, not only of an American scripture, but of the circumstances of an amazing life[33] and of a dynamic movement within American life. His biography, to paraphrase Lewis, is the story begotten by the noble but illusory myth that he was an American Adam. He set out to defend God, and in that defense died a martyr's death. Through his Book of Mormon, his revelations, and the church he restored, his converts declare, Joseph Smith is *still* "an ambassador for the religion of Jesus Christ" (DC 135:7). By virtue of his martyrdom, they believe, he still defends God.

FOOTNOTES

1. "A Mormon Conventicle," *Howitt's Journal,* reprinted in *Littell's Living Age,* (October-November, 1847), from which it is reprinted in Mulder and Mortensen, *Among the Mormons,* p. 159.

2. 1 Ne 4:13; 10:11; 12:22-23; 13:35; 15:35;   2 Ne 1:10; 26:15, 17: 19; Mos 1:5; Al 45:10, 12; 50:22; Hel 6:34; 15:11, 15; 3 Ne 21:5; 4 Ne 1:34, 38; Moro 9:20, 35; Eth 4:3.

3. "From the Covenant to the Revival," in *"Nature's Nation* (Cambridge, Mass.: Harvard University Press, c. 1967), p. 94.

4. *Ibid.,* p. 97.

5. *Ibid.,* p. 102.

6. Perseverance: 1 Ne 13:37; 2 Ne 31:15-20; Om 26; Mos 2:41; 4:6; 30; Al 5:13; 3 Ne 15:9.

7. Obedience to commandments: 1 Ne 2:20-22; 15:11; 2 Ne 1:20; 9:27; Enos 10; Mos 1:11; 2:4; 13:22, 31, 33, 36, 41; Al 7:23; 12:32; 28:1; Hel 5:6; 3 Ne 12:20.

8. Miller, "Covenant to Revival," p. 102.

9. Anti-monarchial sentiment: 2 Ne 5:18; Mos 2:14-18; 6:7; 23:6-14; 29:13-18, 23, 30, 31; Al 43:45; 46:10; 51:5, 8; 3 Ne 6:30; Eth 6:22-26.

10. Restoration of the true Church: Morm 1:13-15; 3:2-3; 8:10-11, 26, 28, 32-33, 37-41; 9:7-26; 4 Ne 1:19 (the ideal church), 20, 26-34, 38-42; 3 Ne 11:28-29, 32; 15; 16:6-7, 10-13.

11. DC 10:63; 3 Ne 11:28-29.

12. DHC, II, 182. But he grew more cautious: DC 39:21; 49:7; 133:11.

13. Namely, Lyman E. Johnson, Orson Hyde, and Smith's brother, William.

14. *Palmyra Reflector,* February 14, 1831, from a Painesville, O. correspondent. A church in the town of Mendon, Monroe County, ten miles from Palmyra, was influenced by Mormonism in 1832; WS, April 18, 1832. The preacher said

> that he shall never die, but be *translated,* after the manner of Enoch, and that in eighteen months Mormonism will be the prevailing religion; and that in five years the wicked are to be swept from the face of the earth.

16. Howe, p. 274.

17. PT, March 15, 1831.

18. In contrast to the Adventist movement set in motion by William Miller and carried on by Ellen G. White.

19. *Quest for Empire: The Political Kingdom of God and the Council of Fifty in Mormon History* (East Lansing, Mich.: Michigan State University Press, c. 1967), p. 18. Cf. William Mulder, "Mormonism's 'Gathering': An American Doctrine with a Difference," CH, XXIII (1954), pp. 248-64. The Millerites had failed to consider such an insurance clause and had to explain the Lord's failure to appear as due to their misunderstanding of certain key biblical passages.

20. PT, March 16; 1831.

21. Richard L. Evans, *A Century of 'Mormonism' in Great Britain* (Salt Lake City: Deseret News Press, c. 1937), Appendix, "British Mission Emigration by Years," p. 245.

22. That story is told by William Mulder's *Homeward to Zion: The Mormon Migration from Scandanavia* (Minneapolis: University of Minnesota Press, c. 1957).

23. Cf. Orson Hyde, *A Voice from Jerusalem, or a Sketch of the Travels and Ministry of Elder Orson Hyde* (Boston Albert Morgan, 1842).

24. DHC, I, 338.

25. *Revelation in Mormonism*, p. 182. The LDS edition of the Doctrine and Covenants lists Sec. 136 as a revelation through Brigham Young; so also the Proclamation ending polygamy through Wilford Woodruff in 1890. The RLDS maintain that the Doctrine and Covenants is still open for further revelations, whereas the LDS, ironically, have closed the canon of the Doctrine and Covenants, although they maintain that they still receive revelation for the church. Cf. Arbaugh, *ibid.*, pp. 172-82.

26. *The American Adam: Innocence, Tragedy, and Tradition in the Nineteenth Century* (Chicago: University of Chicago Press, c. 1955).

27. *Ibid.*, p. 89.

28. John Henry Evans, *Joseph Smith: An American Prophet* (New York: The Macmillan Company, c. 1933), p. 11.

29. DC 29:39; Moses 5:10-13; 6:55.

30. Cf. William Mulder's "Mormonism's 'Gathering,'" pp. 250, 260, n. 3.

31. Cf. Hansen, chap. IV, 72-89.

32. Cf. Davis Bitton, "Mormons in Texas: The Ill-Fated Lyman Wight Colony, 1844-1858," *Arizona and the West*, XI (Spring, 1969), 5-26.

33. Arbaugh, *Revelation in Mormonism*, p. 28.

The immediate strength of Smith's defense of God was personal revelation provided for each believer in the Book of Mormon, and it would also prove to be one of its weaknesses. To explain why Oliver Cowdery and Hiram Page failed to sell the copyright to the Book of Mormon after a revelation told them they would succeed, Smith said that "some revelations are of God, some revelations are of man, and some revelations are of the devil."[1] This kind of reply offered no security to one who relied on revelation coming through the Mormon priesthood, for Smith was as high as one could go.

Moreover, that security was also tied to the truth of Smith's story of the origins of the Book of Mormon and the Testimony of the Three Witnesses, which was to guarantee the existence of the plates and the validity of the translation; that Smith was, in effect, a man through whom God was working. Each convert could obtain the assurance of an angel that what the witnesses heard and saw is true; yes, could "know" that it is true. When pressed, however, the witnesses also admitted that their "seeing" the plates was more like something that they imagined, and if the believer should ever doubt that such "seeing" was valid, then he had no assurance at all of the truth of Smith's defense of God.

Not only might the believer doubt the witnesses "seeing" the plates, but what assurance has he if he knows that even the Book of Mormon witnesses doubted or no longer believed that they had seen an angel?[2] Or worse, if one of them, like David Whitmer, claimed to know by revelation from an angel that Smith had fallen into error?[3]

Ultimately, all comes down to the question of whether one can believe Joseph Smith, and this places us back with Thomas Paine in 1793: a person believes the Old Testament or the Koran (and now the Book of Mormon) only if he believes Moses or Mohammed (and now, Joseph Smith). As a result, there was no gain over the way people came to accept Christ as Lord and Savior.

Knowledge, then, cannot replace faith. Faith is a gift, is itself revelation, is a sign that God is at work. Knowledge may cease, and then faith must carry the believer. Smith himself said just that to Oliver Cowdery when Cowdery failed to translate the plates. Cowdery was told to "rely upon the things which are written." Therefore, if a person cannot believe the Bible on the basis of its apostolic witness, or cannot accept Christ on the strength of the apostolic witness in the Bible, then he can no more believe Christ on the witness of the Book of Mormon and the witness of Mormonism's living apostles.

To defend God, Smith tried to preserve the Bible as special revelation through the Book of Mormon, but he only made it more difficult to accept the Bible. Now the skeptic had to accept two books instead of one.

In his battle with the skeptics, Smith tried to refurbish the Bible to make it intellectually acceptable. He supplied portions that were supposedly lost, corrected any contradictions that he discerned, and eliminated italicized words that were "the work of man." Ironically, however, he also contradicted biblical statements,[4] although he could reply that these were the true texts correcting the corrupted texts in the Bible.

His defense strategy was vitiated, however, when the Book of Mormon manuscript itself turned out to have omissions, corrections, emendations and contradictions. If the Book of Mormon was to be a corrective for the Bible, what was one to make of it if it also needed a corrective? It could no longer assure that the Bible could be salvaged, for the corrective itself was defective. Or, if immediate revelation could supply the corrective, what was one to do if the revelator later received contradictory revelations?

Finally, Smith wanted to settle all doctrinal contention and denominational strife. But within a few years after his death there was a roster of half a dozen contending factions that claimed Smith as founder and the Book of Mormon as scripture. Again, no gain. The very thing that Smith criticized and tried to correct in Christendom had befallen his own movement. Personal revelation could not solve the problem of Mormons contending over who had the authority, succession, priesthood, and true doctrine. Each made the claim and could well have spawned a young man who, like Smith facing the contending denominations of his day, looked at the rival Mormon factions and came to the conclusion that none was right.

FOOTNOTES

1. David Whitmer, *An Address*, p. 54. Smith said that one could tell the difference when a former revelation is contradicted, DHC, IV, 581.

2. *Journal of Discourses*, VII, 164.

3. No less a person that Brigham Young said of the witnesses of the Book of Mormon:

   some of the witnesses of the Book of Mormon, who handled the plates and conversed with the angels of God, were afterwards led to doubt and to disbelieve that they had ever seen an angel.

Journal of Discourses, VII, 164.

4. For example, in Al 7:9-10 Smith has Jesus born at Jerusalem instead of Bethlehem. The Tanners have done a great deal to show the contradictions between Mormon scripture and the Bible, and also between Mormon revelations themselves.

APPENDIX I

Did Joseph Smith Consult Ethan Smith?

The first non-Mormon scholar to accept the influence of *View of the Hebrews* upon Joseph Smith was Fawn Brodie.[1]

Thomas F. O'Dea followed suit,[2] as did Larry W. Jonas and Wesley M. Jones.[3] A line of demarcation exists between George Arbaugh's 1932 study and Brodie's 1945 work. Arbaugh knew of *View of the Hebrews* as one of the many books that advanced the theory of the Hebrew origin of the Indians, but was so convinced of the Spaulding Manuscript Theory that he never again referred to it.[4]

Mormon consideration of the influence of Ethan Smith predates Brodie. In the 1920s Brigham H. Roberts saw the implication involved if books propounding the Indian-Israelite theory were available to Joseph Smith. He listed four works that might have been available to Smith, but felt that Smith might have had access only to the works of James Adair and Ethan Smith. Nevertheless, he pointed out that no evidence existed to connect the book of Ethan Smith with Joseph Smith. The prophet had not used the theory, Roberts concluded, because he was too young, he was not a student, and it would have been too difficult to have assimilated the knowledge of American antiquities necessary to dictate the Book of Mormon.[5]

In the following years Roberts studied the possible connection still further and drew up a list of parallels between the Book of Mormon and *View of the Hebrews*. He circulated it among some people in Utah, but did not publish it.[6] After Roberts's death, his son mimeographed the list and distributed it at a meeting of the Timpanogos Club in Salt Lake City in October, 1946. The list was published and later reprinted by Jerald and Sandra Tanner.[7]

According to Roberts, some features of *View of the Hebrews* are paralleled in the Book of Mormon. (1) Indians buried a book they could no longer read. (2) A Mr. Merrick found some dark yellow parchment leaves in "Indian Hill." (3) Indians had inspired prophets and charismatic gifts. (4) Indians had their own kind of Urim and Thummim and breastplate. (5) Ethan Smith produced evidence to show that the Mexican Indians of antiquity were no strangers to Egyptian hieroglyphics. (6) An overthrown civilization in America is to be seen from its ruined monuments and forts and mounds. The barbarous tribes—barbarous because they had lost the civilized arts—greeting the Europeans were the descendants of the lost civilization.

(7) Chapter One of *View of the Hebrews* is a 32 page account of the historical destruction of Jerusalem. (8) There are many references to Israel's scattering and being "gathered" in the last days. (9) Isaiah is quoted for 20 chapters to show the certain restoration of Israel. Isaiah 18 is made a request to save Israel in America. (10) The United States is asked to evangelize the Indians. (11) Ethan Smith cited Humboldt's *New Spain* to show the characteristics of Central American civilization; the same are in the Book of Mormon. (12) The legends of Quetzacoatl, the Mexican Messiah, are paralleled in the Book of Mormon by Christ's appearing in the western hemisphere.

Consciously or not, Mormon reaction to Ethan Smith's influence seems to correspond to Roberts's list of parallels. Reactions appear after his list was given to a select group and then later made public to a wider group. There are three aspects to the question: did Joseph Smith know enough about Indian antiquities to dictate the Book of Mormon; did he know about the theory of the Indian-Israelite identification; and did he actually use *View of the Hebrews?*

One line of defense has been to assert that information about Indian antiquities was unavailable to Smith. As noted, Roberts saw only four works accessible and only two possibly so. Evan Fry of the Reorganized Church contended as recently as 1962 that books describing Mexican and American Indian archeology, such as Humboldt's *New Spain*, were not available to a boy in western New York before 1839.[8] Roberts, however, began to recognize that, at least with Ethan Smith's book, such works were widely available.[9]

Roy Weldon and Edward Butterworth list seven features of *View of the Hebrews* that are not found in the Book of Mormon, and charge that they should be if Joseph was influenced by Ethan.[10] Six resemblances are cited and dismissed because Joseph treated them differently than Ethan. For example, Ethan applied "the stick of Ephraim" of Ezekiel 37 to the ten lost tribes of Israel, but Joseph applied it only to the tribe of Manasseh. They reason that one usage should duplicate the other if there were borrowing. They also cite some differences (contradictions) with the inference that these would rule out borrowing. Dependence, however, cannot be dismissed because of what Joseph Smith did *not* use from *View of the Hebrews*, nor because he altered the features of resemblance between the two books, nor because he contradicted some of the features of the earlier work.

The next step was to recognize that information about early Indian life was indeed at hand, but to assert that since Joseph Smith was young and was not a student, he could not have assimilated enough information to produce the Book of Mormon. The Book of Mormon, however, is quite vague about details of American geography and antiquities, enough so that few areas of the map can be pinpointed as those under discussion. Dr. M. Wells Jakeman and Dr. Ross Christensen, anthropologists at Brigham Young University in 1959-60, denied that real certainty was possible about the Book of Mormon's statements about America. Not enough was known about the period of time covered, about Indian origins, or about ancient America to say that the Book of Mormon had been proved either scientifically or archeologically.[11] Even Hill Cumorah as the death site of the last Nephite is uncertain.

Lucy Smith's picture of her son as a thoughtful young man filled with Indian lore indicates that he absorbed the constant flow of information about Indians. It need only be shown, as it has been, that the ideas of the Book of Mormon were in reach of Joseph Smith.

Another approach has been to acknowledge that *View of the Hebrews* was available, but to contend that Joseph Smith did not need to consult it: the ideas were in the air.[12] Hugh Nibley advanced this position to free Joseph Smith from the charge that he used Ethan Smith's book, but Nibley undermined the earlier Mormon approach to do it. If one wishes to deny the force of Roberts's parallels as Nibley did, but admits that *View of the Hebrews* was available to Joseph Smith, then the possibility of Joseph's dependence upon Ethan is not destroyed.

Nibley is right that the ideas were in the air. The Indian-Israelite identification, with its many parallels between Hebrew and Indian culture and religion, was offered by Mordecai M. Noah as the reason for his establishing a City of Refuge for world Jewry. The article about Professor Seyffarth discovering the old and new testaments in Egyptian and a Mexican manuscript in hieroglyphics, and suggesting that these were interrelated cultures, offered a great theme that appeared in the Book of Mormon. The newspapers speculated about the times and places of Indian origins and their routes of emigration. All this information was available *apart* from *View of the Hebrews*. Neither Ethan Smith's book nor information about the Indian-Israelite identification theory should have been at Joseph Smith's elbow if one is to deny them as possible sources.

Spencer Palmer and William Knecht tackled the reliance of both Ethan Smith and Joseph Smith on Isaiah.[13] They concluded that "the book of Isaiah is a primary source for anyone dealing with the subject of the dispersion and gathering of Israel." If Joseph Smith had not used Isaiah in common with Ethan Smith, they say, it would appear that he was trying "to avoid suspicion."[14] This argument acknowledges that Joseph Smith knew the work of Ethan Smith, but its main point is fallacious reasoning. Palmer and Knecht are saying the same thing as Weldon and Butterworth: one usage should duplicate the other if there were borrowing, an argument that simply discounts the way human creativity works. One can show hundreds of musical influences working upon Beethoven, but the great composer brought forth a new kind of music.

The point is that Joseph Smith did know the Bible well enough to have used it as a source, as well as Ethan Smith's ideas and Masonic lore. These Mormon attempts to downplay the Mormon prophet's sources reverse older Mormon apologetics. Orson Pratt defended the authenticity of the Book of Mormon on the basis that Joseph Smith did not know Isaiah 29 before the Harris-Anthon consultation.[15] If he did know it, as it is now conceded, then the question of his intention comes to the fore.

View of the Hebrews circulated widely in New York. It also had had a condensed presentation in Josiah Priest's *The Wonders of Nature and Providence*, one of the more widely circulated books of the Manchester Rental Library in 1827. The Rev. Anson Sha, pastor of the Manchester Baptist Church, was one of the members of the rental library. During his pastorate, one member related, Joseph Smith occasionally attended his church service. The name of Ethan Smith, or at least his views, could easily have been presented in a sermon meant to kick the corpse of deism.

Francis Kirkham published the table of contents of the books by Adair, Boudinot and Ethan Smith to show how they differ in purpose and content from the Book of Mormon. That seemed to disprove any connection, but this positon is vulnerable on two counts. First, the raw materials can be made to serve many purposes. Second, the books are not dissimilar in purpose, since both Boudinot and Ethan Smith wrote to demonstrate that the Indians have a Hebrew origin and thereby bolster the proof for biblical revelation.[17]

There are other parallels between the two works by Ethan and Joseph Smith besides those listed by Roberts. The Pittsfield Parchment story (which may already have circulated in the Palmyra area as early as 1817 or 1818) with its two sets of witnesses, the visit to consult scholars about the translation to get it verified, and the belief that it proved the presence of Hebrew religion among the Indians, are all important parallels. Many others can be found; for example, the common use of Ezekiel 37 (especially verse 16) and the millennial orientation of both books. Joseph Smith knew the theory of the Hebrew origin of the Indians and knew the Bible well enough to have used them as sources. The question is, did he use *View of the Hebrews* in producing the Book of Mormon? The possibility is there and the probability is strong that he did. Nevertheless, the case is circumstantial until evidence is found that ties *View of the Hebrews* to Joseph Smith *before* he produced the Book of Mormon. The evidence now at hand makes a strong case for an operating theory as strong as one based on faith, but, like the latter, circumstantial. If no absolute connection between Ethan and Joseph Smith is found, the data still indicate that the Israelite theory of Indian origins was there as a source for Joseph Smith to use in defending God against the forces of deism and rationalism.

FOOTNOTES

1. Brodie, pp. 46-48. I. W. Riley, p. 171, referred to the Pittsfield Parchment story as part of the milieu from which Smith came.

2. Thomas F. O'Dea, *The Mormons.*

3. Larry W. Jonas, *Mormon Claims Examined* (Grand Rapids, Mich.: Baker Book Company, c. 1961); Wesley M. Jones *A Critical Study of Book of Mormon Sources* (Detroit: Harlo Press, c. 1964).

4. Arbaugh, *Revelation in Mormonism*, p. 45.

5. Roberts, *New Witnesses*, III, 28-39. Later, pp. 49-50, Roberts cited the Pittsfield Parchment story as evidence for the Book of Mormon. In *American Antiquities* (2nd ed. rev.; Albany: Hoffman and White, 1835), pp. 65-67, Josiah Priest used the story to prove the theory of a Hebrew origin for the Indians. In 1837 Parley P. Pratt, *Voice of Warning*, pp. 103-07, used Priest's just cited work plus the Stockbridge tradition, p. 81, (which Ethan Smith had used to clinch the argument of the Pittsfield Parchment story) to show that Americana supports the Book of Mormon story of Indian civilization in early America.

6. Brodie, p. 47, n.

7. Jerald and Sandra Tanner, "Ethan Smith Parallels," *Mormonism—Shadow or Reality?*, pp. 418-31.

Since the mid-1970s the writer has heard of a large collection of study materials B. H. Roberts had prepared for possible publication, which dealt with his detailed notes of parallels between the books of Ethan Smith and Joseph Smith. Finally the materials were obtained long enough for H. Michael Marquardt of Sandy, Utah to assess the material and compile a description of their contents. It is clear that the mimeographed list Roberts's son distributed at the Timpanogos Club was prepared from 446 pages of his father's material. This material constitutes a most important source for the further study of Mormon origins. No prophet is needed to predict that this will become the source and focus of dozens of articles and books in the coming generation. Several xerox copies of the original materials were made and deposited in libraries for examination. One such library is Marriott Library, Western Americana section, University of Utah, Salt Lake City. The writer obtained his xerox copy too late to consider its detailed bearing upon chapter 5, but can say that it supports overwhelmingly the writer's conclusion about the Ethan Smith—Joseph Smith connection. Cf. "Documents of B. H. Roberts," compiled by H. Michael Marquardt, August 13, 1977, at the University of Utah.

8. Evan A. Fry, *The Restoration Faith* (Independence, Mo.: Herald Publishing Company, c. 1962), p. 222.

Alexander de Humboldt and Aime-Bonpland, *Personal Narrative of Travels to the equinoctial regions of the New Continent, During the Years 1799-1804;* translated from the French by Helen Maria Williams (Philadelphia: M. Carey, 1815) was available in the Manchester Rental Library as accession number 119.

Humboldt's *Political Essay on the Kingdom of New Spain* was first published in New York in English in 1811 in two volumes with no maps. It came out in four volumes with plates, maps, plans, and tables in London during 1811-12. A second London edition came out in three volumes in 1822. In 1813 *An Abridgement of Humboldt's Statistical Essay on New Spain;* by a citizen of Maryland (Baltimore: Wayne and O'Reilly, 1813) appeared and was likely the work advertised in the *Palmyra Register.*

His *Researches, Concerning the Institutions & Monuments of the Ancient Inhabitants of America, with Descriptions & Views of Some of the Most Striking Stones in the Cordilleras;* translated from the French by Helen Maria Williams (London: Longman, Hurst, Rees, Orme and Brown, J. Murray and H. Colburn, 1814) was also available in this country. This puts to rest Fry's argument that such works were not available.

9. Roberts, *New Witnesses*, II, 28-39.

10. Roy E. Weldon and F. Edward Butterworth, *Criticisms of the Book of Mormon Answered* (Independence, Mo.: Herald House, c. 1973), pp. 14-16. Cf. also Charles A. Davies, "'View of the Hebrews' and the Book of Mormon," SH, August 1, 1962, pp. 9-11 (537-39).

11. *Brigham Young University Archaeological Society Newsletter*, No. 57 (March 25, 1959), p. 4; and no. 64 (January 30, 1960), p. 3.

12. Hugh Nibley, "The Comparative Method," in "Mixed Voices': A Study in Book of Mormon Criticism," IE, Vol. 62. Nos. 38, 10-11 (March-August, October-November, 1959).

13. Spencer J. Palmer and William L. Knecht, "View of the Hebrews: Substitute for Inspiration?," BYUS, V, 2 (Winter, 1962), 105-13.

14. *Ibid.*, p. 108.

15. Orson Pratt said of Smith in 1855: "Mr. Smith did not know anything about this prophecy at that time, for he was unacquainted with the contents of the Bible," "The Ancient Prophecies," p. 188. This position has been abandoned.

16. It was accession number 108.

17. Kirkham, *A New Witness for Christ*, II, 392. The writer made this point in "The Lost Tribes of Israel and the Book of Mormon," *Lutheran Quarterly*, XXII, 3 (August, 1970), 319-29.

APPENDIX II

Textual Comparison of Isaiah 29

INSPIRED VERSION	BOOK OF MORMON	KING JAMES VERSION
1 Woe to Ariel, to Ariel, the city where David dwelt! add ye year to year; let them kill sacrifices. 2 Yet I will distress Ariel, and there shall be heaviness and sorrow; for thus hath the Lord said unto me, It shall be unto Ariel;		1 Woe to Ariel, to Ariel, the city where David dwelt! add ye year to year; let them kill sacrifices. 2 Yet I will distress Ariel, and there shall be heaviness and sorrow; for thus hath the Lord said unto me, It shall be unto Ariel;
	(2 Nephi 25:15) After my seed and the seed of my brethren shall have dwindled in unbelief, and shall have been smitten by the Gentiles; yea,	
3 That I the Lord will camp against her round about, and will lay siege against her with a mount, and I will raise forts against her. 4 And she shall be brought down,	after the Lord God shall have camped against them round about, and shall have laid siege against them with a mount, and raised forts against them; and after they shall have been brought down low,	3 And I will camp against thee round about, and will lay siege against thee with a mount, and I will raise forts against thee. 4 And thou shalt be brought down,

in the dust, even that they are not, yet the words of the righteous shall be written, and the prayers of the faithful shall be heard, and all those who have dwindled in unbelief shall not be forgotten. 16 For those who shall be destroyed

and shall speak out of the	shall speak unto them out of the	and shalt speak out of the

ground, and their	ground, and their	ground, and thy
speech shall be	speech shall be	speech shall be
low out of the	low out of the	low out of the
dust, and their	dust, and their	dust, and thy
voice shall be as	voice shall be as	voice shall be, as
of one that hath a	one that hath a	of one that hath a
familiar spirit,	familiar spirit,	familiar spirit,

17 For thus saith the Lord God: They shall
write the things which shall be done among them,
and they shall be written and sealed up in a
book and those who have dwindled in unbelief
shall not have them, for they seek to destroy
the things of God.

. . . .

Text of the Inspired Version
and the Book of Mormon*
Isaiah 29:11 and 2 Nephi 27:6

*The King James Version has no text here. The texts
of the Book of Mormon and the Inspired Version are identical
except for numbering, punctuation, and subsequent capitali-
zation. The text is that of the Book of Mormon.

11-6   And it shall come to pass that the Lord God shall
bring forth unto you the words of a book, and they shall be
the words of them which have slumbered. 12-7   And behold
the book shall be sealed; and in the book shall be a revelation from God, from the beginning of the world to the ending
thereof. 13-8   Wherefore, because of the things which are
sealed up, the things which are sealed shall not be delivered in the day of the wickedness and abominations of the people. Wherefore the book shall be kept from them.   14-9
But the book shall be delivered unto a man, and he shall
deliver the words of the book, which are the words of those
who have slumbered in the dust, and he shall deliver these
words unto another; ---10 But the words which are sealed he
shall not deliver, neither shall he deliver the book.
15--- For the book shall be sealed by the power of God, and
the revelation which was sealed shall be kept in the book
until the own due time of the Lord, that they may come
forth; for behold, they reveal all things from the foundation of the world unto the end thereof. 16-11 And the
day cometh that the words of the book which were sealed
shall be read upon the house tops; and they shall be read
by the power of Christ; and all things shall be revealed unto the children of men which ever have been among the children of men, and which ever will be even unto the end of the
earth. 17-12 Wherefore, at that day when the book shall
be delivered unto the man of whom I have spoken, the book
shall be hid from the eyes of the world, that the eyes of
none shall behold it save it be that three witnesses shall
behold it, by the power of God, besides him to whom the book
shall be delivered; and they shall testify to the truth of
the book and the things therein. 18-13 And there is none

other which shall view it, save it be a few according to
the will of God, to bear testimony of his word unto the
children of men; for the Lord God hath said that the words
of the faithful should speak as if it were from the dead.
19-14 Wherefore, the Lord God will proceed to bring forth
the words of the book; and in the mouth of as many witnesses
as seemeth him good will he establish his word; and wo be
unto him that rejecteth the word of God!

INSPIRED VERSION	BOOK OF MORMON	KING JAMES VERSION
20 But, behold, it shall come to pass, that the Lord God shall say unto him to whom he shall deliver the book, Take these words which are not sealed and deliver them to another, that he may show them unto the learned, saying, Read this, I pray thee.	15 But behold, it shall come to pass that the Lord God shall say unto him to whom he shall deliver the book: Take these words which are not sealed and deliver them to another, that he may show them unto the learned, saying: Read this, I pray thee.	11 And the vision of all is become unto you as the words of a book that is sealed which men deliver to one that is learned, saying, Read this, I pray thee:
21 And the learned shall say, Bring hither the book and I will read them;	16 And the learned shall say, Bring hither the book, and I will read them.	and he saith,
and now because of the world, and to get gain will they say this,	16 And now, because of the glory of the world and to get gain will they say this, and not for the glory of God.	
and the man shall say, I cannot bring the book for it is sealed. Then shall the learned say, I cannot read it.	17 And the man shall say: I cannot bring the book for it is sealed; 18 Then shall the learned say: I cannot read it.	I cannot; for it is sealed:
22 Wherefore it shall come to pass, that the Lord God will deliver again the book and the words thereof to him that is not learned and the man that is not learn- and the man that is not learn-	19 Wherefore it shall come to pass, that the Lord God will deliver again the book and the words thereof to him that is not learned; and the man that is not learn- and the man that is not learn-	12 And the book is delivered to him that is not learned, saying, Read this, I pray thee: and he

INSPIRED VERSION	BOOK OF MORMON	KING JAMES VERSION
ed shall say, I	ed shall say, I	saith, I
am not learned.	am not learned.	am not learned.

---20 Then shall the Lord God say unto him: The   learned
shall not read them, for they have rejected them, and I am
able to do mine own work; wherefore thou   shalt   read   the
words which I shall give unto thee.

BIBLIOGRAPHY

Books

Adair, James. *The History of the American Indians.* London: Edward and Charles Dilly, 1775.

Adams, Samuel Hopkins. *Canal Town.* Toronto: Random House, c. 1944.

American Antiquarian Society Transactions. Worchester, Mass.: n. p.: 1820. Vol. I.

Arbaugh: George Bartholomew. *Revelation in Mormonism: Its Character and Changing Forms.* Chicago: University of Chicago Press, c. 1932.

Austin, Emily M. *Mormonism; or Life Among the Mormons.* Madison, Wis.: M. J. Cantrell Book and Job Printer, 1882.

Backman, Milton V., Jr. *American Religions and the Rise of Mormonism.* Salt Lake City: Deseret Book Company, c. 1965.

Ballou, Hosea. *A Treatise on Atonement.* Randolph, Vt.; Serano Wright, 1805.

Barrett, Ivan J. *Joseph Smith and the Restoration: A History of the Church to 1846.* Provo, Utah: Young House: Brigham Young University Press, c. 1973.

Barruel, Abbe. *The Anti-Christian and Antisocial Conspiracy.* Lancaster, Pa.: Joseph Ehrenfried, 1812.

Beaver, R. Pierce. *Church, State, and the American Indians.* St. Louis: Concordia Publishing House, c. 1966.

Becker, John E. *A History of Freemasonry in Waterloo, New York, 1817-1942.* Waterloo, N. Y.: Seneca Lodge No. 113, F. & A. M., c. 1942.

Bernard, David. *Light on Masonry.* Utica: William Williams, 1829.

Berrett: William E. and Alma P. Burton. *Readings in L. D. S. History from Original Manuscripts.* 3 vols. Salt Lake City: Deseret Book Company, c. 1953.

Boudinot, Elias. *A Star in the West; or, A Humble Attempt to Discover the Long Lost Ten Tribes of Israel, Preparatory to the Return to Their Beloved City, Jerusalem.* Trenton, N. J. D. Fenton, S. Hutchinson, and J. Dunham, 1816.

Brodie, Fawn M. *No Man Knows My History: The Life of Joseph Smith.* 2nd ed. rev. New York: A. A. Knopf, c. 1971.

Campbell, Alexander. *Delusions: An Analysis of the Book of Mormon . . . and a Refutation of Its Pretences to Divine Authority.* Boston: n. p., 1832.

Cassara, Ernest, ed. *Universalism in America: A Documentary History.* Boston: Beacon Press, c. 1971.

Cerza, Alphonse. *Anti-Masonry.* Fulton, Mo.: The Ovid Bell Press, Inc.; Missouri Lodge of Research, c. 1962.

Cheville, Roy A. *Scriptures from Ancient America: A Study of the Book of Mormon.* Independence, Mo.: Herald Publishing House, c. 1964.

Clark, John Alonzo. *Gleanings By the Way.* Philadelphia: W. J. & J. K. Simon, 1842.

Coil, Henry Wilson. *Masonic Encyclopedia.* New York: Macoy Publishing & Supply Company, Inc., c. 1961.

Collections of the New York Historical Society, for the Year 1821. New York: Bliss & White, 1821.

Copeland, Lewis, ed. *The World's Great Speeches.* New York: Garden City Publishing Company, Inc., c. 1942.

Cross, Whitney R. *The Burned-over District: The Social and Intellectual History of Enthusiastic Religion in Western New York, 1800-1850.* Ithaca, N. Y.: Cornell University Press, c. 1950.

Dictionary of American Biography. Allen Johnson, ed. 22 vols. New York: Charles Scribner's Sons, 1928-58.

Dwight, Timothy. *Travels; in New England and New York.* 4 vols. New Haven: S. Converse, Printer, 1821-22.

Evans, John Henry. *Joseph Smith: An American Prophet.* New York: The Macmillan Company, c. 1933.

Evans, Richard L. *A Century of "Mormonism" in Great Britain.* Salt Lake City: Deseret News Press, c. 1937.

Ferguson, Thomas Stuart. *One Fold, One Shepherd.* San Francisco: Books of California, c. 1958.

Ferm, Vergilius. *Classics of Protestantism.* New York: Philosophical Library, c. 1959.

Fife, Austin and Alta. *Saints of Sage and Saddle: Folklore Among the Mormons.* Bloomington, Ind.: Indiana University Press, c. 1956.

Finney, Charles Goodison. *Lectures on Revivals of Religion.* Revised. Oberlin, O.: E. J. Goodrich, 1868.

Fry, Evan A. *The Restoration Faith.* Independence, Mo.: Herald Publishing House, c. 1962.

Glaser, Lynn. *Indians or Jews? An Introduction to a Reprint of Manasseh Ben Israel's The Hope of Israel.* Gilroy, Calif.: Roy V. Bosell, c. 1973.

Goodwin, S. H. *Additional Studies in Mormonism and Masonry*. Salt Lake City: Grand Lodge of F. & A. M. of Utah, c. 1932.

Handy, Robert T., Loetscher, Lefferts A., and Smith, H. Shelton. *American Christianity: An Historical Interpretation with Representative Documents*. Vol. I. New York: Charles Scribner's Sons, c. 1960.

Hannah, Walton. *Darkness Visible: A Revelation & Interpretation of Freemasonry*. London: Augustine Press, c. 1952.

Hardie, James. *The New Free-Mason's Monitor*. New York: George Long, 1818.

Hansen, Klaus J. *Quest for Empire: The Political Kingdom of God and the Council of Fifty in Mormon History*. East Lansing, Mich.: Michigan State University Press, c. 1967.

Horne, Thomas Hartwell. *An Introduction to the Critical Study and Knowledge of the Holy Scriptures*. New edition from the 8th London edition, corrected and enlarged. 2 vols. New York: Robert Carter & Brothers, 1856.

Hotchkin, James H. *A History of the Purchase and Settlement of Western New York, and of the Rise, Progress, and Present State of the Presbyterian Church in That Section*. New York: M. W. Dodd, 1848.

Howard, Richard P. *Restoration Scriptures: A Study of Their Textual Development*. Independence, Mo.: Herald Publishing House, c. 1969.

Howe, Eber D. *Mormonism Unvailed*. Painesville, O.: By the Author, 1834.

Hudson, Winthrop S. *Religion in America: An Historical Account of the Developments of American Religious Life*. New York: Charles Scribner's Sons, c. 1965.

Humboldt, Alexander de. *Personal Narrative of Travels to the Equinoctial Regions of the New Continent, During the Years 1799-1804*. Translated from the French by Helen Maria Williams. Philadelphia: M. Carey, 1815.

Humboldt, Alexander de, and Aime-Boupland. *Political Essay on the Kingdom of New Spain*. Translated from the French by John Black. 2 vols. New York: I. Riley, 1811.

Hyde, Orson. *A Voice from Jerusalem, or a Sketch of the Travels and Ministry of Elder Orson Hyde*. Boston: Albert Morgan, 1842.

Jonas, Larry W. *Mormon Claims Examined*. Grand Rapids Mich.: Baker Book Company, c. 1961.

Jones, Wesley M. *A Critical Study of Book of Mormon Sources*. Detroit: Harlo Press, c. 1964.

Josephus, Flavius. "Antiquities of the Jews," Book I Chapter ii, in *The Life and Works of Flavius Josephus*, translated by William Whiston. Philadelphia: The John C. Winston Company: n. d.

Journal of Discourses. G. D. Watt, et. al. 26 vols. Liverpool: F. D. Richards, et. al., 1854-86.

Kidder, Daniel P. *Mormonism and the Mormons: A Historical View of the Rise and Progress of the Sect Self-Styled Latter-day Saints*. New York: G. Lane and P. P. Sanford, 1842.

Kirkham, Francis W. *A New Witness for Christ in America: The Book of Mormon*. 2 vols. 3rd edition revised. Independence, Mo.: Zion's Printing and Publishing Company, c. 1951.

Koch, Gustav A. *Religion of the American Enlightenment*. New York: Thomas Y. Crowell Company, c. 1968.

Lee, John Doyle. *Mormonism Unveiled: or the Life and Confession of the Late Mormon Bishop John D. Lee*. Omaha: F. H. Rogers, 1891.

Lewis, R. W. B. *The American Adam: Innocence, Tragedy, and Tradition in the Nineteenth Century*. Chicago: University of Chicago Press, c. 1955.

Mackey, Albert C. *The History of Freemasonry: Its Legends and Traditions: Its Chronological History*. 7 vols. New York: The Masonic History Company, c. 1905.

Marks, David. *The Life of David Marks to the 26th Year of His Age*. Limerick, Me.: Office of the Morning Star, 1831.

Marty, Martin E. *The Infidel: Freethought and American Religion*. Cleveland: The World Publishing Company, c. 1961.

Mayer, Frederick E. *The Religious Bodies of America*. St. Louis: Concordia Publishing House, c. 1961.

McChesney, James. *An Antidote to Mormonism*. New York: By the Author, 1836.

Mead, Sidney E. *The Lively Experiment: The Shaping of Christianity in America*. New York: Harper & Row, c. 1965.

Metcalf, Anthony. *Ten Years Before the Mast*. Mildad Idaho: By the Author, 1888.

Meyer, Eduard. *Ursprung und Geschichte der Mormonen mit Exkursen über die Anfange des Islams und des Christentums*. Halle: Max Niemeyer, 1912.

Millard, David. *The True Messiah*. Canandaigua, N. Y., n. p., 1823.

Miller, Perry. *Nature's Nation*. Cambridge, Mass.: Harvard University Press, c. 1967.

Milliken, Charles F. *A History of Ontario County, New York and Its People.* 2 vols. New York: Lewis Historical Publishing Company, 1911.

Morais, Herbert M. *Deism in Eighteenth Century America.* New York: Russell & Russell, c. 1934.

Morgan, William. *Illustrations of Masonry.* Reprinted as *Morgan's Freemasonry Exposed and Explained.* New York: L. Fitzgerald, 1882.

Morris, Rob. *William Morgan: or Political Anti-Masonry its Rise, Growth and Decadence.* New York: Robert Macoy, 1883.

Mulder, William. *Homeward to Zion: The Mormon Migration from Scandanavia.* Minneapolis: University of Minnesota Press, c. 1957.

Mulder, William and Mortensen, A. Russell. *Among the Mormons: Historic Accounts by Contemporary Observers.* New York: A. A. Knopf, c. 1958.

Nibley, Hugh. *An Approach to the Book of Mormon.* Salt Lake City: Deseret News Press, c. 1964.

— — —. *Since Cumorah.* Salt Lake City: Deseret Book Company, c. 1967.

Nibley, Preston. *The Witnesses of the Book of Mormon.* Salt Lake City: Deseret Book Company, c. 1953.

O'Dea, Thomas F. *The Mormons.* Chicago: University of Chicago Press, c. 1957.

Odierne, James. *Opinions on Speculative Masonry.* Boston: Perkins & Marvin, 1830.

Paddock, Z. *Memoir of Rev. Benjamin G. Paddock, with Brief Notes of Early Ministerial Associates.* New York: Nelson & Phillips, 1875.

Paine, Thomas. *The Age of Reason: Being An Investigation of True and Fabulous Theology.* Moncure Daniel Conway, ed. New York: G. P. Putnam's Sons, c. 1898.

Post, Albert. *Popular Freethought in America, 1825-1850.* New York: Columbia University Press, c. 1943.

Pratt, Orson. *Doctrines of the Gospel.* Salt Lake City: Juvenile Instructor Office, 1884. This is a reprint of *A Series of Pamphlets* with some material omitted.

— — —. *A Series of Pamphlets.* Liverpool: R. James 1848-51.

Pratt, Parley Parker. *Key to the Science of Theology.* Liverpool: By the Author, 1855.

— — —. *A Voice of Warning and Instruction to All People, or An Introduction to the Faith and Doctrine of the Church of Jesus Christ of Latter Day Saints.* Salt Lake City: The Deseret News Steam Printing Establishment, 1874.

— — —. *Writings of Parley Parker Pratt.* Parker Pratt Robison, editor. Salt Lake City: By the editor, c. 1952.

Priest, Josiah. *The Wonders of Nature and Providence.* Albany: By the Author, 1825.

Proceedings of the United States Anti-Masonic Convention, Held at Philadelphia, September 11, 1830, The. New York: Skinner and Dewey, 1830.

Publications of the American Tract Society, The. Vol XIV. New York: American Tract Society, n. d.[1827].

Reynolds, George. *A Dictionary of the Book of Mormon.* Salt Lake City: Philip C. Reynolds, c. 1954.

Rich, Ben E. *Scrap Book of Mormon Literature.* 2 vols. Chicago: Henry C. Etten & Co., n. d.

Riley, Isaac Woodbridge. *The Founder of Mormonism: A Psychological Study of Joseph Smith, Jr.* New York: Dodd, Mead & Company, c. 1902.

Roberts, Brigham Henry. *A Comprehensive History of the Church of Jesus Christ of Latter-day Saints.* 6 vols. Salt Lake City: The Church of Jesus Christ of Latter-day Saints, c. 1930. I.

— — —. *New Witnesses for God.* 3 vols. Salt Lake City: Deseret Book Company, c. 1926.

Sacher, Abram Leon. *A History of the Jews.* 4th edition, revised and enlarged. New York: A. A. Knopf, c. 1953.

Silverberg, Robert. *Mound Builders of Ancient America: The Archaeology of A Myth.* Greenwich, Ct.: New York Graphic Society Ltd., c. 1968.

Sperry, Sidney B. *Book of Mormon Compendium.* Salt Lake City: Bookcraft, Inc., c. 1968.

— — —. *The Voice of Israel's Prophets.* Salt Lake City: Deseret Book Company, c. 1952.

Smith, Ethan. *View of the Hebrews: or the Ten Tribes of Israel in America.* 2nd edition. Poultney, Vt.: Smith & Shute, 1825.

Smith, Joseph, Jr. *A Book of Commandments, for the Government of the Church of Christ.* Zion [Independence, Mo.]: W. W. Phelps & Co., 1833.

— — —. *The Book of Mormon.* Palmyra, N. Y.: E. B. Grandin, 1830.

— — —. *The Book of Mormon.* Kirtland, O.: Oliver Cowdery & Company, 1837.

— — —. *The Book of Mormon.* Nauvoo, Ill.: Joseph Smith, 1840.

— — —. *The Book of Mormon.* Salt Lake City: The Church of Jesus Christ of Latter-day Saints, 1921.

— — —. *Doctrine & Covenants.* Kirtland, O.: F. G. Williams & Company, 1835.

— — —. *Doctrine & Covenants.* Salt Lake City: The Church of Jesus Christ of Latter-day Saints, 1921.

— — —. *History of the Church of Jesus Christ of Latter-day Saints.* 7 vols. Salt Lake City: The Deseret Book Company, 1927.

— — —. *Inspired Version of the Holy Scriptures: Inspired Revision of the Authorized Version.* A New Corrected Edition. Independence, Mo.: Herald Publishing House, c. 1944.

— — —. *Pearl of Great Price.* Salt Lake City: The Church of Jesus Christ of Latter-day Saints, 1921.

Smith, Lucy Mack. *Biographical Sketches of Joseph Smith, the Prophet, and His Progenitors for Many Generations.* Liverpool: S. W. Richards, 1853.

Sprague, William. *Annals of the Congregational Pulpit.* Vol. II of *Annals of the American Pulpit.* New York: Robert Carter & Brothers, 1869.

Stone, William L. *Letters on Masonry and Anti-Masonry, Addressed to The Hon. John Quincy Adams.* New York: O. Halstaad, 1832.

Sweet, William Warren. *The Story of Religions in America.* New York: Harper and Brothers, c. 1930.

Tanner, Jerald and Sandra. *Joseph Smith and Money Digging.* Salt Lake City: Modern Microfilm Company, 1970.

— — —. *Joseph Smith's 1826 Trial.* Salt Lake City: Modern Microfilm Company, 1971.

— — —. *Mormonism Like Watergate?* Salt Lake City: Modern Microfilm Company, 1974.

— — —. *Mormonism—Shadow or Reality?* Salt Lake City: Modern Microfilm Company, 1964. Revised, 1972.

Testimony of Christ's Second Appearing, Exemplified by the Principles and Practice of the True Church of Christ. Albany: The United Society [Shakers], 1856. 1st edition in 1811

Turner, O[rasmus]. *History of the Pioneer Settlement of Phelps and Gorham's Purchase.* Rochester: Wm. Alling, 1851.

Tucker, Pomeroy. *The Origin, Rise, and Progress of Mormonism.* New York: D. Appleton and Company, 1867.

Ward, Hanry Dana. *Free Masonry. Its Pretensions Exposed in Faithful Extracts of its Standard Authors.* New York: n. p. 1828.

Wauchope, Robert. *Lost Tribes & Sunken Continents: Myth and Method in the Study of American Indians.* Chicago: University of Chicago Press, c. 1962.

Webb, Robert C. [J. C. Homans]. *The Real Mormonism: A Candid Analysis of an Interesting but much Misunderstood Subject in History, Life and Thought.* New York: Sturgie & Walton Company, c. 1916.

Webb, Thomas S. *The Freemason's Monitor; or Illustrations of Masonry.* New York: Southwick and Crookar, 1802.

— — —. *The Freemason's Monitor.* Cincinnati: Applegate & Company, 1860.

Weldon, Roy E. and Butterworth, F. Edward. *Criticisms of the Book of Mormon Answered.* Independence, Mo.: Herald House, c. 1973.

Whitmer, David. *An Address to All Believers in Christ.* Richmond, Mo.: By the Author, 1887.

Whitmer, John. *John Whitmer's History.* Salt Lake City Modern Microfilm Company, n.d.

Articles, Speeches, Sermons and Tracts

"The Aborigines," *Wayne Sentinel,* July 24, 1829.

Adamson, J. W. "The Treasure of the Widow's Son," *Mormon Miscellaneous,* Vol. I, No. 1 (October, 1975).

Allen, James B. "The Significance of Joseph Smith's 'First Vision' in Mormon Thought," *Dialogue: A Journal of Mormon Thought,* I, 3 (Winter, 1966), 29-45.

Anderson, Richard L. "Martin Harris, the Honorable New York Farmer," *The Improvement Era,* Vol. 72 (1969), pp. 18-21.

Arbaugh, George B. "Evolution of Mormon Doctrine," *Church History,* IX (1940), 157-69.

Arrington, Leonard J. "James Gordon Bennett's 1831 Report on 'The Mormonites,'" *Brigham Young University Studies,* X, 3 (Spring, 1970).

Backman, Milton V., Jr. "Awakenings in the Burned-over District: New Light on the Historical Setting of the First Vision." *Brigham Young University Studies,* IX, 3 (Spring, 1969), 301-20.

Bitton, Davis. "Mormons in Texas: the Ill-Fated Lyman Wight Colony, 1844-1858," *Arizona and the West,* XI, 1 (Spring, 1969), 5-26.

Briggs, R. C. "Interview with William Smith," *Deseret News,* January 20, 1894.

Bronk, Mitchell. "The Baptist Church at Manchester," *The Chronicle: A Baptist Historical Quarterly,* XI, 1 (January, 1948), 17-30.

Bushman, Richard L. "The First Vision Story Revived," *Dialogue: A Journal of Mormon Thought*, IV, I (Spring, 1969), 82-93.

— — —. *Joseph Smith and Skepticism.* Young House; Brigham Young University Press, c. 1974.

Channing, William Allery. "Baltimore Sermon," in *Classics of Protestantism*, Vergilius Ferm, ed., pp. 244-77.

Chase, Abner. "Revival of Religion on Ontario District," *Methodist Magazine*, VII (1824), p. 435.

"The Converted Jew," *Western Farmer*, August 29, 1821.

Crowley, Ariel. "The Anthon Transcript," *The Improvement Era*, Vol. 45, Nos. 1, 2, 4 (Jan., Feb., April, 1942); Vol. 47, Nos. 9, 12 (Sep., Dec., 1944).

Davies, Charles A. "'View of the Hebrews' and the Book of Mormon," *The Saints' Herald*, August 1, 1962, pp. 533-39 (9-11).

Davis, David Brion. "The New England Origins of Mormonism," *The New England Quarterly*, XXVII (June, 1953), 148-63.

"Deciphering of Hieroglyphics," *Wayne Sentinel*, June 1, 1827.

De Pillis, Mario. "The Quest for Religious Authority and the Rise of Mormonism," *Dialogue: A Journal of Mormon Thought*, I, I (March, 1966, 68-88.

— — —. "The Social Sources of Mormonism," *Church History*, XXXVII, I (March, 1968), 50-79.

DeVoto, Bernard. "The Centennial of Mormonism," *American Mercury*, XIX (Januaxy, 1930), 1-13.

Durham, Reed Connell, Jr. "Is There No Help for the Widow's Son?," *Mormon Miscellaneous*, Vol. I, No. I (October, 1975), pp. 11-16.

"Elias Boudinot," *Dictionary of American Biography*, II, 477-78.

Fuller, Andrew. Three Queries to the Rejecters of Christianity," *Publications of the American Tract Society*, I Vol. XIV.

Gilbert, John H. "Joe Smith," *The Post & Tribune*, Detroit, Michigan, December 3, 1877, p. 3.

Godfrey, Kenneth W. "A Note on the Nauvoo Library and Literary Institute," *Brigham Young University Studies*, XIV, I (Spring, 1974), pp. 386-89.

"Golden Bible," *Rochester Daily Advertiser and Telegraph, August 31, 1829.*

"Golden Bible," *The Rochester Gem*, September 5, 1829.

"The Great Polemical Disputation," *Wayne Sentinel*, May 29, 1829.

Hill, Marvin S. "Secular or Sectarian History? A Critique of *No Man Knows My History*," *Church History*, XLII, I (March, 1974), 78-96.

Hogan, Mervin B. "The Founding Minutes of Nauvoo Lodge," *Further Light in Masonry*. Des Moines: Research Lodge No. 2, n. d.

Howard, Richard P. "Latter Day Saint Scripture and the Doctrine of Propositional Revelation," *Courage*, I, 4 (June: 1971), 209-25.

Hullinger, Robert N. "Joseph Smith, Defender of the Faith," *Concordia Theological Monthly*, XLII, 2 (February, 1971), 72-87.

— — —. "The Lost Tribes of Israel and the Book of Mormon," *Lutheran Quarterly*, XXII, 3 (August, 1970), 319-29.

Jarvis, Samuel Farmer. "Discourse on the Relations of the Indian Tribes of North America: Delivered Before the New-York Historical Society, December 20, 1819," *Collections of the New York Historical Society, for the Year 1821*, pp. 183ff.

Jessee, Dean C. "The Early Accounts of Joseph Smith's First Vision," *Brigham Young University Studies*, IX, 3 (Spring, 1969), 275-94.

— — —. "Joseph Knight's Recollection of Early Mormon History," *Brigham Young University Studies*, XVII, I (August, 1976), 29-39.

Kimball, Stanley B. "The Anthon Transcript: People, Primary Sources, and Problems," *Brigham Young University Studies*, X, 3 (Spring, 1970), 325-52.

Knecht, William L., and Palmer, Spencer J. "View of the Hebrews: Substitute for Inspiration?," *Brigham Young University Studies*, V, 2 (Winter, 1962), 105-13.

Lancaster, James E. "'By the Gift and Power of God': The Method of Translation of the Book of Mormon," *The Saints' Herald*, November 15, 1962, pp. 798-806, 817.

Lane, George. "Revival of Religion on Ontario Circuit," *Methodist Magazine*, VIII (1825), 158-61.

Lapham, Fayette. "The Mormons," *Historical Magazine*, (New Series), VII, 5 (May, 1870), 305-09.

Leslie, Charles. *A Short and Easy Method with Deists, wherein the Certainty of the Christian Religion is Demonstrated by Infallible Proofs from Four Rules, in a Letter to a Friend.* New American Edition. Cambridge: n. p., 1805.

"Luther Bradish," *Dictionary of American Biography*, II, 567-68.

"Martin Harris, the Mormon," *Rochester Daily Democrat,* June 23, 1841.

Mitchill, Samuel Lapham. "The Original Inhabitants of America Shown to Be of the Same Family with Those of Asia," *American Antiquarian Society Transactions,* I. (1820).

"Money Digger," *Palmyra Herald,* July 24, 1822.

"Mr. Owen and Mr. Campbell," *Wayne Sentinel,* June 19, 26, 1829.

Mulder, William. "Mormonism's 'Gathering': An American Doctrine with a Difference," *Church History,* XXIII (1954), 248-64.

Nibley, Hugh. "Censoring the Joseph Smith Story," *The Improvement Era,* Vol. 64, Nos. 7-8, 10-11 (July-August, October-November, 1961).

— - —. "The Comparative Method," in the series "Mixed Voices: A Study in Book of Mormon Criticism," *The Improvement Era,* Vol. 62, Nos. 10-11 (October-November, 1959).

— — —. "A New Look at the Pearl of Great Price: Part I. Challenge and Response," *The Improvement Era,* Vol. 71, No. 2 (February, 1968), pp. 14-21.

— — —. "The Stick of Judah," *The Improvement Era,* Vol. 56, Nos. 1-6 (January-June, 1953).

"Noah, Mordecai Manuel," *Dictionary of American Biography.* XIII. 534-35.

Noah, Mordecai Manuel. "Proclamation to the Jews," *Wayne Sentinel,* September 27, 1825.

— — —. Speech at the Consecration of the Cornerstone of the City of Ararat, Buffalo, N. Y., September 15, 1825. *Wayne Sentinel,* October 4, 11, 1825.

Owen, Robert. "Declaration of Mental Independence," *Wayne Sentinel,* August 25, 1826.

Phelps, William Wines. "Israel Will Be Gathered," *The Evening and Morning Star,* June, 1833.

Pratt, Orson. "The Ancient Prophecies," *Journal of Discourses.* II, 284-98.

— — —. "Divine Authenticity of the Book of Mormon," *Doctrines of the Gospel.* Pp. 124-314.

— — —. "Divine Authority, or the Question, Was Joseph Smith sent of God:" *Doctrines of the Gospel.* Pp. 7-40.

— — —. *An Interesting Account of Several Remarkable Visions and of the Late Discovery of Ancient American Records.* New York: By the Author, 1841. British edition published in 1840

— — —. "Review of God's Dealings with the Prophet Joseph, *Journal of Discourses.* XV. 178-91.

Prince, Walter F. "Psychological Tests for the Authorship of the Book of Mormon," *American Journal of Psychology,* XXVII (July, 1917), 373-89.

Purple, W. D. Account of Joseph Smith's 1826 Trial at Bainbridge, N. Y., Chenango Union (Norwich N. Y.): May 2, 1877. Reprinted in Mulder, William, and Mortensen, A. Russell, *Among the Mormons: Historic Accounts by Contempory Observers.* PP. 34-37.

Quinn, D. Michael. "The First Months of Mormonism: A Contemporary View by Rev. Diedrich Willers," *New York History.* LIV (July, 1973). Pp. 317-31.

Red Jacket, Chief. Speech to a White Missionary, Western New York, 1805. Copeland, Lewis, ed. *The World's Great Speeches.* New York: Garden City Publishing Co., Inc., c. 1942. Pp. 266-68.

"Revival of the Jewish Government," *Wayne Sentinel,* September 27, 1825.

Roberts, Brigham Henry. "Ethan Smith Parallels," *Rocky Mountain Mason,* January, 1956.

"Samuel Latham Mitchill," *Dictionary of American Biography.* XIII, 69-71.

Schroeder, Theodore. "Authorship of the Book of! Mormon," *American Journal of Psychology,* XXX (January, 1919), 66-72

Shipps, Jan. "The Prophet Puzzle: Suggestions Leading Toward a More Comprehensive Interpretation of Joseph Smith," *Journal of Mormon History,* I (1974), 3-20.

Squier, E. G. "Report upon the Aboriginal Monuments of Westen New York," *Proceedings of the New York Historical Society.* New York: William Van Norden, 1849. Pp. 44-62.

Tiffany, Joel. "Mormonism No. II," *Tiffany's Monthly,* V (August, 1859), 163-70.

Walters, Wesley P. "Joseph Smith Among the Egyptians," *The Journal of the Evangelical Theological Society,* XVI, 1 (Winter 1973), 25-45.

— — —. "Joseph Smith's Bainbridge, N. Y. Court Trials," *Westminster Theological Journal,* XXXVI, 2 (Winter, 1974), 123-55.

— — —. "New Light on Mormon Origins from the Palmyra Revival," *Dialogue: A Journal of Mormon Thought,* IV, 1 (Spring, 1969), 60-81.

— — —. "A Reply to Dr. Bushman," *Dialogue: A Journal of Mormon Thought,* IV, 1 (Spring, 1969), 94-100.

— — —. "From Occult to Cult with Joseph Smith, Jr.," *Journal of Pastoral Practice,* Vol. I, No. 1 (1977).

Washington, George. "Farewell Address," *The World's Great Speeches.* Lewis Copeland, ed. Pp. 248-59.

Whittier, John Greenleaf. "A Mormon Conventicle," *Howitt Journal.* Reprinted in *Littell's Living Age,*

(October-December, 1847). Reprinted in Mulder, William and Mortensen, A. Russell, *Among the Mormons: Historic Accounts by Contemporary Observers.*
Wild, Asa. *"Remarkable* VISION *and* REVELATION," *Wayne Sentinel,* October 22, 1823.

Published Letters

Anthon, Charles to Eber D. Howe, February 17, 1834. Howe, *Mormonism Unvailed,* pp. 270-272.
Anthon, Charles to T. W. Coit, April 3, 1841. *The Church Record,* (1841), pp. 231-32.
Cowdery, Oliver to W. W. Phelps, Letters I-VIII, September, 1834 to September, 1835. *Messenger and Advocate,* October, 1834-October, 1835.
Davis, Matthew L. to his Wife, February 6, 1840. Ben E. Rich, *Scrap Book of Mormon Literature.* II, p. 404.
Harris, Martin to Mr. Emerson, Smithfield, Utah, November 23, 1870. *The Saints Herald,* XXII (1875), p. 630.
Larned, Sylvester to Mr. Merrick, Pittsfield, Mass., 1815(?). Ethan Smith, *View of the Hebrews.* p. 220.
Page, Hiram to William McLellin, May 30, 1847. *The Ensign of Liberty, of The Church of Christ,* I, 3 (December, 1847-63).
Phelps, William Wines to Warren A. Cowdery. *Messenger and Advocate,* November, 1834, pp. 25-26.
Phelps, William Wines to Eber D. Howe, January 15, 1831. Howe, p. 234.
Red Jacket, Chief to Captain Parish, January 18, 1821. *Western Farmer,* April 4, 1821.
Smith, Joseph, Jr. to W. W. Phelps, November, 1832. *History of the Church of Jesus Christ of Latter-day Saints.* I. P.299.
Smith, Joseph, Jr. to James Arlington Bennett, Nauvoo, Ill., November 13, 1843. *Reply of Joseph Smith to the Letter of J. A. B.— of A—n House.* New York. Liverpool, published by R. Hedlock & T. Ward, [1844]].
Smith, Joseph, Jr. to W. W. Phelps, November, 1832. *History of the Church of Jesus Christ of Latter-day Saints.* I. P. 299.
Smith, Joseph, Jr. to Moses C. Nickerson, November 19, 1833. *History of the Church of Jesus Christ of Latter-day Saints.* I. Pp. 441-42.
Smith, Joseph III, Letter to the Editor, entitled "Last Testimony of Sister Emma." *The Saints' Herald,* XXVI (October 1, 1879), p. 220.
Smith, Simon to President Joseph Smith III, December 30, 1880. *The Saints' Herald,* XXVIII (February 1, 1881), 43.
Whitmer, David to Orson Pratt, 1878. *Millenial Star,* XL (1879), 772.
Willers, Rev. Diedrich to Rev. L. Mayer and Rev. D. Young, June 18, 1830. D. Michael Quinn, "The First Months of Mormonism: A Contemporary View by Rev. Diedrich Willers," *New York History,* LIV (July, 1973), 317-31.

Newspapers and Periodicals—Mormon

Brigham Young University Archaeological Society Newsletter. Provo, Utah. 1959-60.
Brigham Young University Studies. Provo, Utah. 1960-present.
The Contributor. Salt Lake City. Oct. 4, 1879—Oct. 1896.
Deseret News. Salt Lake City. 1850—present.
Dialogue: A Journal of Mormon Thought. San Francisco. 1966-present.
The Ensign of Liberty, of the Church of Christ. Kirtland, Ohio. 1847-49.
The Evening and Morning Star. Independence, Missouri and Kirtland, Ohio. 1832-34.
The Improvement Era. Salt Lake City. 1897-present.
Latter Day Saints' Messenger and Advocate. Kirtland, Ohio. 1834-37.
Millenial Star. Manchester and Liverpool, England. 1840-present.
The Saints' Herald. Lamoni, Iowa and Independence, Missouri. 1860-present.
Times and Seasons. Nauvoo, Illinois. 1839-46.

Newspapers and Periodicals—Other

The Church Record. Flushing, N. Y. 1840-42.
Gospel Luminary. West Bloomfield, N. Y. 1825-33.
Kansas City Daily Journal. Kansas City, Missouri. 1881.
Methodist Magazine. New York City. 1818-40.
Ontario Phoenix. Canandaigua, N. Y. 1828-31.
Painesville Telegraph. Painesville, Ohio. 1822-present.
Palmyra Reflector. Palmyra, N. Y. 1829-31.
Palmyra Register. Palmyra, N. Y. 1817-21. Successively titled:
> *Western Farmer. 1821-22.*
> *Palmyra Herald. 1822-23.*
> *Wayne Sentinel. 1823-60.*
Rochester Daily Advertiser and Telegraph. Rochester, N. Y. 1826-56.
Rochester Daily Democrat. Rochester, N. Y. 1834-57.
Rochester Gem. Rochester, N. Y. 1829.
Rocky Mountain Mason. Salt Lake City. 1956.

Unpublished Material

Bidamon, Emma to Sister Pilgrim, March 27, 1876, Nauvoo, Illinois. Reorganized LDS Archives, Independence, Missouri.

Burnett, Stephen. Stephen Burnett to Br. Johnson, April 15, 1838. Joseph Smith Letter Book, 2. Joseph Smith Papers. LDS Archives, Salt Lake City, Utah.

Cheesman, Paul R. "An Analysis of the Accounts Relating to Joseph Smith's Early Vision." Unpublished Masters thesis, Brigham Young University, Provo, Utah, 1965.

Durham, Reed Connell, Jr. "A History of Joseph Smith's Revision of the Bible." Unpublished Doctor's thesis, Brigham Young University, Provo, Utah, 1965.

Gilbert, John H., Esq. Memorandum dated September 8, 1892, Palmyra, N. Y. Typescript. P. 4. LDS Archives, Salt Lake City, Utah.

Hullinger, Robert Neil. "An Apologist for Jesus Christ: The Purpose and Function of Joseph Smith's Theology." Unpublished Masters thesis, Pacific Lutheran Theological Seminary, Berkeley, California, 1969.

Membership Record Book, Manchester Rental Library, Manchester, N.Y. Canandaigua Historical Society. Canandaigua, N. Y.

Porter, Lawrence Cardon. "A Study of the Origins of the Church of Jesus Christ of Latter-day Saints in the States of New York and Pennsylvania, 1816-1831." Unpublished Doctoral thesis, Brigham Young University, 1971.

Roberts, Brigham Henry. "Documents of B. H. Roberts," compiled by H. Michael Marquardt. Typescript. 400 plus pages. Marriott Library, University of Utah, Salt Lake City.

Shipps, Jan. Letter to Robert Hullinger, June 10, 1975.

Smith, Joseph, Jr. D MS (manuscript of the Book of Mormon dictated directly by Joseph Smith to his scribes, 1829). LDS Archives, Salt Lake City, Utah.

— — —. E MS (manuscript of the Book of Mormon which Oliver Cowdery prepared from the D MS for the printer, 1829). Reorganized LDS Archives, Independence, Missouri.

— — —. Manuscript History, Book A-1, Frontispiece. LDS Archives, Salt Lake City, Utah.

Smith, Lucy Mack. Second manuscript of *Biographical Sketehes,* in the writing of Martha Jane Coray. LDS Archives, Salt Lake City, Utah.

Walters, Wesley P. Letter to Robert Hullinger, January 8, 1975.

Warner, Ross W. "The Fulfillment of Book of Mormon Prophecies: A Study of Problems Relative to the Fulfillment of Selected Prophecies in the Book of Mormon, with Particular Reference to the Prophetic View from 1830 Onward." Unpublished Masters thesis Brigham Young University, Provo, Utah, 1961.

Willers, Rev. Diedrich. The John M. Olin Library, Cornell University, Ithaca, N. Y. Diedrich Willers Collection. Willers to L. Mayer and D. Young, June 18, 1830.

INDEX OF REFERENCES

Pearl of Great Price

INDEX OF SUBJECTS AND AUTHORS

DEMCO

CP-20X